The Complete
BEAN
Cookbook

by
Victor Bennett

Decorations by Janet Anderson

BONANZA BOOKS · NEW YORK

The Complete Bean Cookbook by Victor Bennett

© MCMLXVII by Victor Bennett

Library of Congress Catalog Card Number: 67-13117

Printed in the United States of America

This edition published by Bonanza Books,
a division of Crown Publishers, Inc.,
by arrangement with Prentice-Hall, Inc.
a b c d e f g h

To the homemakers of the world, whose romance
with the so-long-unheralded bean inspired this book

Acknowledgments

The following organizations and persons have all contributed generously of their time and experience in aiding the author in Bean Cookery and Research:

The Idaho Bean Commission, 212 Continental Life Building, Boise, Idaho, for bean research and some of the recipes.

Dr. Philip S. Chen, Ph.D., author of *Soybeans for Health, Longevity and Economy*, published by Chemical Elements Publishers, Atlantic Union College, South Lancaster, Massachusetts.

Thomas Kennedy, Michigan Bean Company, Saginaw, Michigan.

Henry O. Klein, 311 California Street, San Francisco, California.

Gordon W. Monfort, California Lima Bean Advisory Board, Los Angeles, California.

Ella Lehr Nisja, Home Economics Services, Idaho Bean Commission.

Mama Marcy Rossi, Paradise, California, for kitchen testing.

Homage to the Bean

It was many years ago that a very dignified and slightly belligerent Senator took himself to the Senators' Dining Room to order bean soup, only to discover that there was no bean soup on the menu. This dereliction on the part of Senate Dining Room cooks called for an immediate declaration of war and the Senator promptly introduced a resolution to the effect that henceforth not a day should pass when the Senate was in session and the restaurant open that there would not be bean soup on the calendar. It has, therefore, become an inviolate practice and a glorious tradition that the humble little bean should always be honored.

There is much to be said for the succulent little bean. In fact, there is much to be said for any kind of a bean, be it kidney, navy, green, wax, Kentucky, chili, baked, pinto, Mexican or any other kind. Not only is it high in nutriment, but in that particular kind of nutritious value referred to as protein—the stuff that imparts energy and drive to the bean eater and particularly the Senators who need this sustaining force when they prepare for a long speech on the Senate Floor.

I venture the belief that the marathon speakers of the Senate going back as far as the day of the celebrated "Kingfish," Senator Huey Pierce Long of Louisiana, and coming down to the modern marathoners in the forensic art such as Senator Strom Thurmond of South Carolina and Senator Wayne Morse of Oregon, both of whom have spoken well in excess of twenty hours and felt no ill effects, would agree the little bean had much to do with this sustained torrent of oratory.

In my enumeration of the bean varieties, I forgot to include one of the most celebrated of all beans, namely, the soybean. Not only has this little Oriental product sustained a civilization in China for perhaps thousands of years, but it has been broken down into so many components that, like Atlas, it fairly carries the weight of the world on its tiny little shoulders. The soybean today produces soya cake for cattle feed which is highly prized by dairymen and beef producers. Its oils are used for preparing table spreads and cooking oils. It is low in unsaturated fats and is prized by dietitians and that vast host who devote so much of a lifetime to keeping a svelte figure. Its oils are further broken down for use in house paints and the soya cake can now be compressed so hard that it makes door handles and gadgetry without number.

Some day some historical bonepicker seeking a subject for a world-shaking thesis that will live as long as Shakespeare will hit upon the lonely bean. What a welter of knowledge he will develop in his research and I am sure he will come to the conclusion that without the bean, the earth would have long since slipped into orbit and disappeared among a galaxy inhabited by bean-eaters. Hail to the bean!

Senator Everett M. Dirksen

Foreword

Shunned for centuries by certain classes of society as a poor man's meal and by many agriculturalists as a pernickety vegetable requiring infinite growing care, the bean today occupies an honored place in the world's food basket because it may have brought more comfort to the hungry than any food known to man. Beans are among the oldest (dating well back beyond recorded history) and most universally used of all the world's foods.

Beans were raised as a favorite food of ancient Egypt and Greece. It is said that the Egyptians had temples dedicated to beans, worshiping them as a symbol of life itself. The Romans, famous for their feasting, used beans extensively and even gambled with them. Beans date back to the Bronze Age in Switzerland and in Hebrew history to 1000 years before the dawn of the Christian Era. The ruins of ancient Troy reveal evidence that beans were a favorite dish of the Trojans. Most authorities agree that beans were native to South America, probably in ancient Peruvian culture.

In Africa, bean baking originated with the Jews of North Africa. They baked beans every Friday to eat on Saturday, their Sabbath, when religious observance prohibits all work, cooking included. According to some authorities, beef marrow substituted for forbidden pork.

Whether or not African Jews baked beans to avoid working on their Sabbath, American Christians certainly did so to avoid working on theirs. All through New England, the Saturday ovens were laden with beanpots to supply Saturday supper, Sunday breakfast or dinner, or any combination of the three. Most baked bean specialists agree that the early colonists of Massachusetts learned the gentle art of bean baking from the local Indians, who did the job in earthen pots and may have used maple syrup as a sweetening agent, before the advent of molasses.

Historians also tell us that warfare introduced beans to much of the world—carried by ancient armies as a main staple item in the fighting rations of soldiers on the march. Our own Teddy Roosevelt said he won the battle of San Juan Hill on beans. During World War II, our Army floated waterproof bags of beans from ships to beachheads.

Their low water content and high protein rating makes them a valuable source of food wherever transportation is a problem. They are relatively inexpensive for the food value packed in them and therefore, a valuable compact source of energy at low cost. They store easily and are relatively nonperishable.

Rich in those vitamins which make them a valuable addition to the human diet, the steaming, savory plate of beans—prepared by a variety of recipes concocted in the kitchens of the world—has developed into one of the most popular dishes in international cookery. The Pasta e Fagioli of Italy, the Cassoulet of France, the Chili Con Carne and Frijoles of Mexico and the Southwest United States, the Hopping John of the South, the Red Beans and Rice of Old New Orleans, The Boston Baked Beans and Brown Bread—these are international and regional dishes that have tickled the palates of generations.

Most of us are inclined to limit our bean cookery to baked beans and black-bean soup, and it's hard to think of anything better than baked beans with ketchup and brown bread on a Saturday night, or bean soup, black as your hat, garnished with pale lemon slices.

But there is more to bean cookery than soup or baking. There is no end to the versatility of the bean. It can run the gamut from a thrifty family meal to fancy party fare; from delicious hors d'oeuvres to soups, salads and casseroles; for formal occasions or for snacks and barbecues. The bean has no peer among foods in the hands of an imaginative cook.

—Victor Bennett

Contents

Glossary

BEAN CURD: Soft, white, custard-like paste made from soy beans. Bean curd is called *tou fu* in Chinese, *tofu* in Japanese. One cake equals two cups or three-quarters of a pound. It spoils quickly in warm climates, therefore must be used immediately.

BEAN SPROUT: Sprouts of green beans, called *tou ya ts'ai* in Chinese, *moyashi* in Japanese. Heads and tails should be removed before sprouts are used. Canned bean sprouts should be drained before using.

BLACK BEAN: Often used in a rich, thick soup—especially famous in the South. Also known as the turtle bean. Used in Oriental and Mediterranean cooking.

BLACK-EYED BEAN: Pleasant, sweet, pea-like flavor and buttery texture. Singular appearance, a black dot on a yellow background. Often cooked with ham hocks or pork jowls in the South.

BUTTER BEAN: See lima bean.

COW-PEA BEAN: A sprawling herb of the pea family, more nearly related to the bean than to the pea. The seed of this plant is used for food and is popular in the Southern States.

CRANBERRY BEAN: Sweet, strong flavor; has a plump shape almost like the cranberry fruit. Combined with cabbage in Italian cookery; a favorite bean for succotash. Also known as the Roman bean.

FAVE BEAN: Vicia Faba, when green and tender has a sweet strong flavor. When mature and dried has a tough skin and is large and rippled in appearance. When they are split and shelled, they are popular with the Portuguese, Italians and other Mediterranean people who purée the cooked fave for soup. They are also mashed and used in the main course of dinner fare as well as side dishes and accompaniments.

GARBANZO BEAN (CHICK-PEA): Nut-like flavor, keeps shape well when cooked. Commonly pickled in vinegar and oil, with chives, and served as an appetizer or tossed with a green salad. Excellent as a main or side dish.

GREAT NORTHERN WHITE BEAN: A white bean grown largely in Idaho.

HORSE BEAN: See fave bean.

ITALIAN GREEN BEAN: Broad green bean. Popular in frozen food departments, also purchased fresh in season.

KIDNEY BEAN: Kidney-shaped and red in color. Closely related with the small white, Great Northern, black, pink, red, cranberry and pinto. A favorite for Mexican dishes.

LIMA BEAN: The name embraces several flat-shaped beans which are actually different varieties. There is the Fordhook, a variety preferred for freezing, and several other large green varieties usually served fresh. In the dry form, two varieties are most popular, the standard or large dry lima, and the baby lima. Many cooks think the baby lima is the small size of the standard lima. Actually they are different beans. Only the standard lima has the distinctive nut-like flavor which sets it apart from all other beans.

MUNG BEAN: The mung bean is native to India. The pods and seeds are the smallest of any of the beans named here. Extensively grown in the Orient for food as bean sprouts and a favorite in many Chinese and Philippine dishes, they are now becoming popular in the United States.

NAVY BEAN: Known as the small white bean. Bulk of the crop is used for Boston baked beans.

PINK BEAN: Related to the kidney bean. Pink in color and popular for Mexican dishes.

PINTO BEAN: Variety of mottled field beans of the same species as the kidney bean.

RED BEAN: Related to the kidney bean, red in color and a favorite for Mexican dishes and chili.

SNAP BEAN: Variety of fresh string bean.

SOLDIER BEAN: Medium-sized white bean with reddish center, sweet. Used by many New Englanders for baking.

SOYBEAN: Seed yields oil, flour and milk. Grown in Japan, China and the United States. Crisp, nut-like flavor. Made into flour which is used in bread. Also used as a base for soy sauce. Introduced into the United States in 1804; large scale production started in 1924. There are many varieties of soybeans and many hundreds of types and strains are known. However, they may be classified into two general types with respect to their uses—the commercial field type and the edible vegetable type. The commercial field varieties are suited for the production of oil, oil meal and flour, while the edible varieties are especially adapted to home use as green vegetables, and, in matured condition, for home cooking.

STRING BEAN: Any of certain varieties of beans grown for the pods, edible when young; so called from the strings on the pods. One variety with tender golden yellow pods is called *wax bean.*

YELLOW WAX BEAN: See string bean.

YANKEE BEAN: See navy bean.

Bean-Wisdom

Water: (short cut method) for all dried beans, use 3 cups water for 1 cup beans for soaking and cooking unless a cup or more of liquid is to be added as part of the ingredients. Beans should be soaked to take up part of the water lost in drying. Always use the soaking water for cooking the beans. A quick and effective way to soak beans is to add them to the measured amount of water, bring water to boiling point, and boil 2 minutes. Remove from heat. Cover. Soak 1 hour and they are ready to cook. Even when soaking overnight, this "two minute boil" softens the skins and prevents souring.

Salt: for average taste 1 teaspoon of salt in the cooking water for each cup of beans is about right. Hold off if there is a salty meat addition.

Hard water: slows down the cooking. It helps to add baking soda to the soaking water. With most tap water, add a scant ⅛ teaspoon soda to the water allowed for 1 cup dry beans. No more. Too much soda is harmful to flavor and nutritive value.

Foam: to keep down the foam when cooking beans, add 1 tablespoon of butter, drippings (consider flavor), or vegetable salad oil, for each cup of beans.

Keep shape: cook beans gently. "Simmer" is the word. Stir seldom and easy!

Tomatoes: wait to add until beans are almost tender so softening won't be delayed.

Servings: One pound of beans will provide 8 to 9 servings of ¾-cup each.

A NINETEENTH–CENTURY DEFINITION
OF COOKERY

"Cookery means the knowledge of Medea and of Circe and of Helen and of the Queen of Sheba. It means the knowledge of all herbs and fruits and balms and spices and all that is healing and sweet in the fields and groves and savory in meats. It means carefulness and readiness of appliances. It means the economy of your grandmothers and the science of the modern chemist. It means much testing and no wasting. It means English thoroughness and French art and Arabian hospitality, and, in fine, it means that you are to be perfectly and always ladies—loaf givers."

——RUSKIN

I

Hors d'oeuvres

BEAN DIP
Makes 2 cups

Ready Tray | 1 cup refried beans, chilled*
              | 1 cup sour cream
              | 1 tablespoon Salsa Jalapeña (Chili sauce)

Thoroughly mash the beans in a bowl. Add sour cream and sauce; blend until smooth.

Serve with crisp tostados, corn chips or crackers. (Tostados: a Mexican tortilla made crisp by deep-frying and breaking into chip-size pieces.)

* See Chapter IV.

BEANS EGYPTIAN
Serves 6

Ready Tray | 2 cups dried white beans
2 teaspoons salt
2 cloves garlic, finely chopped
½ cup olive oil
¼ cup fresh lemon juice
3 scallions, finely sliced

Wash beans thoroughly and soak in cold water to cover overnight. Next day, using same water, cover tightly and cook gently for 2 hours until the skins split. Drain well and cool thoroughly.

Place beans in a large bowl. Add salt, garlic, oil, and lemon juice. Mix thoroughly and chill in the refrigerator.

Sprinkle scallions lightly over beans before serving.

PARTY BEANSPREAD
Makes 1 Cup

Ready Tray | 1 cup baked beans, chilled
2 teaspoons chives, finely chopped
1 teaspoon fresh parsley, finely chopped
2 tablespoons salad oil
1 teaspoon fresh lemon or lime juice
Salt
Dash Tabasco sauce
Crackers or squares of toast

Mash beans to a smooth paste. Add chives, parsley, oil, lemon or lime juice, season to taste with salt and Tabasco sauce. Blend until smooth.

Chill thoroughly before serving on crackers or toast.

BEAN SANDWICH SPREAD
Makes 1 cup

Ready Tray

1   cup baked beans, chilled
2   teaspoons onion, finely chopped
2   tablespoons tomato ketchup or chili sauce
1   teaspoon wine vinegar
4   strips bacon, fried crisp and broken into small pieces
    Buttered plain or toasted bread or crackers

Mash beans thoroughly. Add onion, catsup, vinegar and bacon.
Blend until smooth.

Spread on buttered bread, toasted bread or crackers.

CECI MARINARA (Garbanzo Appetizer)
Serves 6 to 8

Ready Tray

2   cans (1 lb. ea.) garbanzo beans (ceci)
½   cup oil
1   small can flat anchovy fillets, drained and
    chopped fine
½   teaspoon salt
1   teaspoon freshly ground black pepper
3   tablespoons fresh parsley, finely chopped

Drain one can of garbanzos. Combine with undrained garbanzos
and place in small kettle. Heat slowly.

Heat oil and add anchovies, salt, pepper and parsley. Stir over very
low heat for a few minutes. Pour over heated garbanzos, mix well
and simmer slowly for 15 minutes.
Serve hot or cold. Thoroughly chilled in their sauce, these garbanzos
make a superb appetizer.

GARBANZO NUTS
Makes 2 to 3 cups

Ready Tray

1	pound dried garbanzo beans
¼	pound butter
4	cloves garlic, crushed
½	teaspoon dry mustard
1	teaspoon chili powder
2	teaspoons salt
1	teaspoon onion salt
1	teaspoon powdered ginger
½	teaspoon garlic salt
3	teaspoons soy sauce

Soak washed beans in water to cover overnight. Do not drain. Cook in well-salted water until just tender, but still a bit hard, approximately 1 hour. Drain and divide into 2 equal parts.

In two skillets, melt the butter, equally divided and sauté 2 garlic cloves in each. Remove garlic and add one portion garbanzos in each skillet. Sauté very slowly, turning and stirring often, until the beans begin to sizzle and turn dark golden brown. When crunchy on the outside and tender inside, they are done.

Mix mustard, chili powder, salt and onion salt. Sprinkle over one batch of garbanzos and toss lightly until thoroughly coated. Mix ginger, garlic salt and soy sauce and sprinkle over second batch and toss lightly till coated.

Serve hot as soon as possible, in separate bowls, as "niblets" to accompany cocktails. May also be used as croutons for soup.

May be frozen and reheated on baking sheet under broiler for several minutes.

MARINATED LENTILS
Makes 4 cups

Ready Tray

2	cups dried lentils
4	cups water
1½	teaspoons salt
½	cup olive oil
3	tablespoons vinegar
⅓	cup scallions or chives, finely chopped
¾	cup fresh parsley, finely chopped
	Freshly ground black pepper to taste

Boil lentils in water with salt until tender, approximately 40 minutes. Cool thoroughly.

Add oil, vinegar, scallions or chives, parsley, ground black pepper to taste and additional salt, if needed. Marinate for several hours in refrigerator before serving.

GREEN LIMA BEAN AND HAM ROLLS
Serves 4 to 6

Ready Tray

1	cup cooked green lima beans, chilled and mashed
¼	cup mayonnaise
1	teaspoon garlic salt
¼	teaspoon monosodium glutamate*
⅛	teaspoon black pepper
2	tablespoons sour cream
1	tablespoon onion juice
8	slices boiled ham, cut medium thick

Blend until smooth, beans, mayonnaise, garlic salt, monosodium glutamate, pepper, sour cream and onion juice.

Spread mixture evenly on ham, roll up and fasten with toothpicks.

* Generally available as Accent.

LIMA BEAN SPREAD
Makes 2 cups

Ready Tray	2	cups dried lima beans
	1	cup water in which beans were soaked
	1	stalk celery
	3	sprigs fresh parsley
	1	whole onion pierced with
	2	whole cloves
	½	bay leaf
	½	teaspoon salt
		Fresh cream
		Salt and white pepper
	2	tablespoons butter
		Crackers or triangles of toast

Wash lima beans thoroughly and soak in water to cover overnight. Next day, add celery, parsley, pierced onion with cloves, bay leaf and salt. Cover and bring to a boil, reduce heat and simmer gently for 3 hours or until beans are tender, adding a little water as needed to keep from becoming too dry.

Drain the beans, reserve liquid and discard vegetables. Rub beans through a sieve, adding just a small amount of bean liquid and cream to make a thick consistency for spreading. Season to taste with salt and white pepper. Blend in butter until smooth. Cool thoroughly before spreading on crackers or toast.

STRING BEAN BUNDLES
Serves 4 to 6

Ready Tray	1	pound string beans
	½	cup garlic dressing, your choice
		Thinly sliced cold cuts, your choice

Cook whole string beans in water to cover until just tender. Drain, chill thoroughly.

Cover with dressing and let stand for several hours. Drain, wrap several whole string beans with thin sliced cold cut meats and fasten with toothpick.

TWO-BITE BEAN CROQUETTES PETITE
Makes 2 dozen

Ready Tray

2 cups cooked Idaho Red Beans, drained and mashed while hot
2 tablespoons onions, finely minced
½ teaspoon oregano
1 can (4 oz.) peeled green chiles, drained and chopped fine
¼ cup grated Parmesan cheese
¼ pound sharp-aged natural Cheddar, Provolone or Monterey Jack cheese, cut in small cubes
Fine bread crumbs for breading
1 Egg, beaten with 1 tablespoon water
Oil or shortening for deep-frying

Combine mashed beans, seasonings, Parmesan cheese, adding salt if necessary. Chill thoroughly in refrigerator before shaping into small balls. Place a small cube of cheese in the center of each. Cover cheese with bean mixture. Roll these small balls in bread crumbs, then in egg-water mixture, and again in bread crumbs. This may be done early in the day or the day before. Just before serving, fry in deep fat or oil heated to 380°F. When brown, drain on paper toweling. May be served from chafing dish or container over candle warmer so they will be hot. Provide cocktail picks.

Serve with South-of-the-Border Dip.

Excellent for Christmas and all festive occasions and get-togethers.

SALTED SOYBEANS
Makes 1 pound

Ready Tray | 1 pound dried soybeans
             | Fat
             | Salt

Soak soybeans overnight in cold water to cover, or add boiling water and let stand for 1 hour. Drain and spread on towels to remove all moisture. When the surface of the beans is dry, fry in fat heated to 350° and 1-inch deep, in a saucepan. (It is very important to observe this precaution, because after the beans have been added, the fat will "boil up" vigorously.) Add a few beans at a time and fry until golden brown, about 10 minutes. Drain beans on absorbent paper and sprinkle with salt. Cool and store the salted beans in an airtight container in a cold place.

ROASTED SOYBEANS
Serves 6

Ready Tray | 1 can soybeans (drained)
             | Salt
             | Fat

Method 1: Spread canned soybeans in a shallow pan and roast in a moderate 350° oven until browned. Sprinkle them with salt while still warm.

Method 2: Dry the surface of the canned beans and fry in deep fat heated to 350°, a few beans at a time for 5 to 8 minutes, depending upon the size of the beans. When they are slightly brown and crisp, drain, salt, and use as salted peanuts.

Roasted soybeans are somewhat like roasted peanuts in flavor. They can be used in candy or eaten salted.

MAMA ROSSI'S DILLY BEANS

Ready Tray
2	pounds fresh string beans, trimmed
¾	cup olive oil
½	cup wine vinegar
½	cup water or stock from beans
1	medium size lemon, juiced and strained
1	tablespoon dill weed
¼	teaspoon paprika
½	teaspoon dried or fresh mint, chopped fine
1	whole garlic clove, peeled
	Salt
1	medium size wooden salad bowl rubbed well with garlic

Cook string beans in salted water to cover until tender, Drain, reserving 1 cup of liquid, and cool thoroughly.

Sprinkle beans in wooden salad bowl, combine olive oil, wine vinegar, lemon juice and water and pour over beans. Taste and add more salt if necessary. Sprinkle beans with dill weed, paprika, mint. Add salt to taste and whole clove garlic. Toss and let stand 24 hours at room temperature. Place beans in mason-type jar in upright position and pour liquid over beans. The longer the marination, the better the flavor. Refrigerate.

Any dried beans of your choice may be prepared in this manner as long as the dried beans are soaked over night before cooking.

SPICED SOYBEANS
Serves 6 to 8

Ready Tray | 3 cups fresh green soybeans, unshelled
1 tablespoon salt
1 teaspoon hot red pepper, chopped
1 clove aniseed
Water for boiling beans
1 teaspoon salt

Cut off ends of soybeans.

Bring to a boil sufficient water to cover soybeans. Add salt, red pepper, aniseed and soybeans, boil rapidly for 15 minutes, drain and sprinkle with 1 teaspoon salt.

Serve chilled and discard shells when eating.

MARINATED STRING BEANS

Ready Tray | Green beans
Vinegar
Cloves

Trim and wash whatever amount of green beans you desire to use. Boil quickly in plenty of salted water to a medium cooked stage.

Drain and cool for a few minutes. Dry well in a cloth and place in jars. Cover with boiling vinegar to which some cloves have been added and let stand until vinegar has cooled and beans are thoroughly marinated, approximately 4 hours.

MARINATED LIMA BEANS
Serves 4 to 6

Ready Tray | 1½ cups large dried lima beans
Water
1½ teaspoons salt
1 clove garlic, peeled
¼ cup olive oil
¼ cup fresh parsley, finely chopped
¼ cup dry white wine
1 Teaspoon fresh dill, finely chopped
Salt and pepper mill

Soak lima beans in 4 cups water overnight. Do not drain, but cook beans in water in which they were soaked. Cover and simmer gently until tender, approximately 1 hour. Add salt the last ½ hour of cooking period. Drain and cool.

Meanwhile, dice garlic fine, add a little salt and crush with back of a large spoon. Add oil and let stand for ½ hour. Pour over beans. Sprinkle with parsley, wine, dill, salt and freshly ground black pepper to taste. Chill thoroughly before serving.

SANDWICH SPREADS

To a cup of baked beans add grated cheese, chopped pickle, chopped tomato, chopped hard-cooked egg, few grains cayenne, onion juice and salt to taste. Combine thoroughly before using.

Season baked beans with minced onion, pickle relish or ketchup. Moisten with salad dressing of your choice.

Peanut butter and cooked beans make another good sandwich combination. Moisten with mayonnaise.

STRING BEANS TEMPURA
Serves 4 to 6

Ready Tray	
2	cups fresh green string beans, cut in 3-inch pieces
1	whole fresh egg, beaten light
⅞	cup flour, sifted
1	teaspoon baking powder
½	teaspoon salt
½	cup water
2	cups oil or
1	pound fat for deep frying
1	tablespoon flaked, dried bonito fish
1	cup water
⅓	cup soy sauce
½	teaspoon sugar
1	cup grated white radish or turnip

Wash beans and dry well with towel. Put aside. Combine egg, flour, baking powder and salt and stir until smooth. Add water, a tablespoon at a time, blending to a smooth batter.

Place oil or fat in deep pan and heat to 350°F.

Dip beans in batter and fry in hot fat, holding two beans together with forks for about 5 seconds after they have been placed in hot fat.

Sauce: Boil fish in water 10 minutes. Add soy sauce and sugar and boil few minutes longer. Drain and let liquid cool, then add to grated radish and stir until smooth.

Dip beans in the sauce. An excellent hors d'oeuvre.

STRING BEANS IN COCONUT MILK
Serves 4 to 6

Ready Tray		
	½	cup onions, finely chopped
	1	clove garlic, finely chopped
	2	teaspoons grated lemon rind
	½	teaspoon dried ground chile peppers
	1	large tomato, peeled and finely chopped
	4	tablespoons olive oil
	1	pound fresh string beans, cut lengthwise
	1	teaspoon salt
	1	teaspoon sugar
	1	bay leaf
	1	cup coconut milk*

Pound to a paste the onions, garlic, lemon rind, chile peppers and tomato.

Heat oil in a heavy skillet and sauté the paste for 3 minutes, stirring constantly. Add beans, salt, sugar, bay leaf and coconut milk. Bring to boil quickly, cover and simmer gently for 20 minutes, or until the beans are tender. Cool thoroughly before serving.

* *Fresh coconut milk:* grate meat of fresh coconut. To each cup of coconut meat add 2 cups hot water. Let soak 30 minutes, then squeeze through a piece of cheesecloth to extract all the liquid.

Vacuum packed flaked coconut: For each cup of flaked coconut, add 2 cups hot milk. Let stand 30 minutes, then squeeze through cheesecloth to extract all the milk.

SOUTH-OF-THE-BORDER DIP
(to be served hot)

Ready Tray
2	cups cooked Idaho Red Beans, sieved or mashed smooth
1	cube butter or margarine
¼	pound grated or thin-sliced Provolone or Cheddar cheese
4	jalapenos (prepared green chile peppers), chopped very fine
1	teaspoon jalapenos juice
2	tablespoons onion, minced
1	clove garlic, crushed

Mix all ingredients together in top of double boiler and heat until cheese is melted and mixture is hot.

Serve hot from chafing dish or food warmer with tortillas cut in 6 pie-shaped pieces and fried in deep fat, or with corn chips to dip into the mixture.

Serve with bean croquette appetizers.

DILLED STRING BEANS
Makes 1½ pints

Ready Tray
1	pound fresh green string beans
1	cup water
¾	cup wine vinegar
2	teaspoons salt
2	teaspoons dried dill weed
1	teaspoon sugar
¼	teapoon crushed dried red pepper

Wash and trim ends from beans. Arrange in covered rectangular glass dish or stand upright in 2 glass jars that will hold the whole beans.

In a saucepan, combine the water, vinegar, salt, dill, sugar and red pepper. Bring to a boil quickly and pour over the beans.

Cool, then store in refrigerator for at least 10 days before serving. Drain and serve chilled.

STRING BEANS VINAIGRETTE
Serves 6

Ready Tray		
	1½	pounds green string beans
	2	whole canned pimientos
	¼	teaspoon salt
	¼	teaspoon dry mustard
		Pepper
	¼	teaspoon paprika
	2	tablespoons red wine vinegar
	4	tablespoons olive oil
	½	teaspoon fresh chervil, finely chopped
	½	teaspoon fresh parsley, finely chopped
	½	teaspoon chives, finely chopped

Cut off tips and string the beans. Boil them whole, and rapidly, in salted water until tender. Drain and cool thoroughly.

Slice pimientos to make 6 big rings and slip a fagot of beans (several beans together) through each one.

Mix salt, mustard, a generous sprinkle of pepper and paprika in a bowl. Dissolve seasonings in vinegar, add oil and beat briskly. Add chervil, parsley and chives and blend thoroughly. Pour over beans and marinate several hours in refrigerator before serving.

II

Soups

BAKED BEAN SOUP—PRESSURE COOKED
Serves 4 to 5

Ready Tray

2	cups baked beans
1½	cups solid-pack canned tomatoes
1	onion, thinly sliced
2	cups consommé
2	tablespoons flour
2	tablespoons butter
1	cup hot water
½	teaspoon Worcestershire sauce
	Salt and pepper
	Croutons

Combine beans, tomatoes, onion and consommé in a 6-qt. pressure cooker. Close the cooker, bring to 15 pounds pressure and process 5 minutes. Cool and open the cooker. Put the ingredients through a sieve.

Cream flour and butter, add hot water, blend thoroughly and add to soup. Heat thoroughly.

Add Worcestershire sauce and season to taste with salt and pepper.

Serve with croutons.

BLACK BEAN SOUP SPANISH
Serves 4 to 6

Ready Tray

1	cup dried black beans
1	quart fresh water, slightly salted
1	ham bone
4	bay leaves
4	whole cloves
¼	teaspoon celery seed
2	celery branches with leaves, finely chopped
1	large red Spanish onion, finely chopped
1	clove garlic, finely chopped
1	tablespoon butter or olive oil
¼	teaspoon dry mustard
1	teaspoon chili powder
2	dashes Tabasco sauce
1	hard-cooked egg, thinly sliced
1	fresh lemon or lime, thinly sliced
	Whipped cream and
	Sherry wine

Soak beans in 1 quart water to cover overnight. Add ham bone, bay leaves, cloves, celery seed and celery. Cover and simmer gently.

Sauté onion and garlic lightly in butter. Blend in until smooth the mustard, chili powder and Tabasco sauce and add to the beans. Simmer until tender.

Discard ham bone. Put all in a blender or rub through a sieve.

If thicker soup desired: blend until smooth, 1 tablespoon butter and 1 tablespoon flour, add to the soup and cook until thick and smooth.

Serve piping hot and place an egg slice and lemon slice in each bowl. Garnish with a teaspoon of whipped cream blended with Sherry.

GARBANZO BEAN AND MACARONI SOUP
Serves 6

Ready Tray

1 pound dried garbanzo beans
1 small fresh rosemary branch
3 ounces olive oil
2 garlic cloves, peeled and finely chopped
6 anchovies, cut in small pieces
1 ounce tomato sauce, diluted slightly with water
6 ounces salad macaroni, uncooked
Salt and freshly ground black pepper or
1 hot chili, finely chopped

Wash the garbanzos and soak overnight in plenty of warm water. Season to taste with salt, which tenderizes the beans sufficiently.

Next day, add rosemary, cover and cook gently until tender in water in which they were soaked. When tender, remove the rosemary branch.

Brown garlic and anchovies in oil until light brown. Add diluted tomato sauce and pepper to taste, or the hot chili pepper; simmer gently for 5 minutes. Combine with the beans. Bring to a boil, add uncooked macaroni and cook until tender.

Add a little boiling water, if needed, to keep at a thick consistency. Liquid in the soup must be at a minimum.

Serve immediately in hot soup plates with crusty French bread or hard rolls.

BLACK BEAN SOUP CUBAN
Serves 6

Ready Tray

2 cups dried black beans
2 cups celery, coarsely chopped
1 onion, medium size, finely sliced
4 whole cloves
½ pound salt pork, cut in 1-inch pieces
1 teaspoon Worcestershire sauce
2 teaspoons fresh lemon juice
2 teaspoons salt
¼ teaspoon freshly ground black pepper
¼ cup Sherry wine
6 Fresh lemon slices, thinly sliced

Cover washed beans with 2 quarts cold water and refrigerate, covered, overnight. Next day, place in a larger kettle. Add celery, onion, cloves and salt pork. Bring beans to a boil, then reduce heat and simmer, covered, for approximately 3 hours or until beans are very tender.

Press bean mixture, including liquid, through a sieve to purée. Add Worcestershire sauce, lemon juice, salt and pepper, and reheat thoroughly for several minutes.

Just before serving the soup, stir in the Sherry wine. Serve in individual hot soup plates and garnish with a lemon slice.

BUTTER BEAN-HAM CHOWDER
Serves 4 to 6

Ready Tray

1½	cups dried butter beans
	Water
1	meaty ham hock
1½	teaspoons salt
1	cup onion, finely chopped
½	cup green bell pepper, finely chopped
2	tablespoons butter
1½	cups cream-style corn
1	quart milk, scalded

Soak limas overnight in 1 quart water. Add ham hock more water if needed, and simmer gently until tender, approximately 1½ hours.

Season with salt last ½ hour. Remove bones and skin from ham and shred. Mash 1 cup limas. Sauté onion and green pepper in heated butter. Stir in corn, limas, 1 cup bean cooking liquid, ham and scalded milk. Heat thoroughly, but do not boil.

GARBANZO BEAN SOUP
Serves 6 to 8

Ready Tray

1	pound dried garbanzo beans
½	cup olive oil
1	large onion, finely chopped
3	cloves garlic, finely chopped
1½	quarts water
	Salt and pepper mill

Soak garbanzo beans overnight in water to cover. Drain.

Heat oil in heavy kettle, add onion and garlic and sauté lightly. Add garbanzos, water, season to taste with salt and freshly ground black pepper. Cover and cook very slowly until the garbanzos are very tender, adding more liquid if necessary.

FAVE BEAN SOUP
Serves 6

Ready Tray

1½	pounds dried fave beans
½	pound fresh pork rind
4	ounces prosciutto, fat and lean meat
1	handful of fresh parsley
1	teaspoon marjoram
2	onions, finely chopped
1	tablespoon tomato paste
2½	quarts water
	Salt and freshly ground black pepper
6	Slices of toast

Soak the beans in cold water for 48 hours, drain and pick out only the whole ones.

Place beans in a large kettle and cover with cold water, seasoning slightly with salt. Cover and cook gently until tender and drain.

Clean and thoroughly wash the pork rind; place in water to cover and boil for 5 minutes. Drain and wash again and cut in ½-inch pieces.

Chop finely together the prosciutto, parsley and marjoram. Place in skillet and sauté lightly. Add onion and sauté until golden brown. Add tomato paste and cook gently for 10 minutes. Add pork rinds and water, cover and bring to a boil slowly. Reduce heat and simmer until pork rinds are tender. Add to the beans. Season to taste with salt and freshly ground black pepper to taste and cook 15 minutes longer.

Serve over a slice of toast in individual soup plates.

KIDNEY BEAN PUREE SOUP
Serves 6

Ready Tray | 2 cups dried kidney beans
              | 6 cups stock or water
              | 2 tablespoons butter
              | Salt and freshly ground black pepper
              | 1 cup croutons, crisply fried in butter
              | 6 slices fresh lemon

Cook the beans in the liquid until tender, approximately 2 hours. Force through food mill or strainer.

Reheat, adding more liquid if soup is too thick. Add butter and season to taste with salt and freshly ground black pepper.

Serve in hot soup plates over croutons and garnish with lemon slice.

KIDNEY BEAN SOUP, PORTUGUESE
Serves 6 to 8

Ready Tray | 1 cup red kidney beans
              | 6 potatoes, peeled and diced
              | Salt and pepper to taste
              | 4 tablespoons bacon fat
              | 3 onions, thinly sliced
              | 2 cloves garlic, finely chopped
              | 3 bay leaves
              | 1 tablespoon allspice
              | 1 small can tomato paste

Soak washed beans overnight in water to cover. Simmer beans until tender, about 2 hours. Do not drain.

Add potatoes and a little salt and cold water to cover. Bring to a boil and cook for 15 minutes.

Sauté the onion and garlic in the bacon fat until golden brown. Add to soup kettle.

Add bay leaves, allspice, tomato paste and salt & pepper to taste. Simmer slowly for 3 hours, adding more water if necessary.

BEST-EVER LIMA BEAN SOUP
Serves 6

Ready Tray	
1	cup large dried lima beans
1	meaty ham bone
4	cups water
1	onion, quartered
4	celery tops
1	teaspoon dry mustard
1	teaspoon salt
4	whole cloves
2	slices lemon
1	cup milk
	Thin lemon slices
	Crisp croutons

Rinse and drain limas. Add ham bone, water, onion, celery, mustard, salt, cloves and 2 lemon slices. Cover and boil slowly for 2 hours, or until limas are tender. Remove lemon slices, cloves and ham bone, and cut ham in small pieces. Purée limas and onion, by putting through electric blender or sieve. Reheat with ham and milk. Serve with lemon slice and croutons in each bowl.

KIDNEY BEAN SOUP
Serves 8

Ready Tray
1	cup dried kidney beans
3	cups water
1	teaspoon salt
1	teaspoon dried oregano, crushed
1	small bay leaf
3	whole cloves
	Freshly ground black pepper
1	onion, medium size, finely chopped
2	tablespoons salad oil
	Tops of 1 bunch of celery, finely sliced
1	can (12-oz.) consommé Madrilene
	Water
1	fresh lime, thinly sliced

Wash the beans, put in a large kettle with 3 cups of water; cover, bring to a boil, and simmer 2 minutes. Let soak 1 hour. Add salt, oregano, bay leaf, cloves and pepper to taste. Simmer gently for 2 hours or until beans are tender. Remove bay leaf and cloves and press beans through a sieve.

Sauté onion in oil until golden brown; sauté celery until limp and add both to the puréed beans. Add the Madrilene and enough water to make 1½ quarts of soup. Bring to a boil and simmer gently for 15 minutes longer.

Serve in soup plates, garnish with slice of lime.

CHILLED CREAM OF FRESH LIMA BEAN SOUP
Serves 10 to 12

Ready Tray

6	large leeks
6	cups freshly shelled lima beans
3	quarts chicken stock
2	sprigs fresh parsley
1	tablespoon Sauce Diable
1	teaspoon sugar
½	teaspoon ground nutmeg
	Salt and pepper to taste
6	tablespoons heavy fresh cream
1	red onion, thinly sliced in rings

Trim the leeks and discard the green parts. Wash the whites thoroughly under running water and cut into 1-inch lengths. Place in a large soup kettle with the lima beans and chicken stock. Bring to a boil, cover kettle and simmer gently for 30 minutes. Add the parsley, Sauce Diable, sugar, nutmeg and salt and pepper to taste, blending thoroughly.

Purée the soup in a blender or force it through a sieve. Cool thoroughly. Stir in the cream and serve in chilled bowls, garnish with onion rings—a few in each bowl.

This soup may be frozen if desired. Pour into suitable freezing containers. When ready to use, remove the frozen block from container and heat in a saucepan until it is just defrosted. Cool thoroughly before serving.

JIFFY LIMA BEAN-ONION SOUP
Serves 4

Ready Tray
1 large onion, quartered and cut into thin slices
2 tablespoons butter
1 can (10½-oz.) condensed consommé
2 cups cooked large dried lima beans, with liquid

Place onion and butter in a soup kettle, cover and cook slowly until onion is transparent. Add consommé and 1 can hot water. Simmer for 20 minutes. Add beans with their cooking liquid and heat thoroughly.

GARBANZO AND SHRIMP SOUP
Serves 6 to 8

Ready Tray
1½ cups cooked garbanzo beans, drained
2 tablespoons vinegar
½ cup beer
5 cups beef broth
¼ pound raw shrimp, shelled, deveined and coarsely chopped
½ cup turnips, grated
1 cup carrots, grated
4 whole fresh eggs
2 tablespoons soy sauce
½ cup scallions, chopped

Force the cooked garbanzos through a sieve. Add vinegar and beer, mix thoroughly and let stand for 5 minutes.

Bring the broth to a boil, add shrimp, turnips and carrots. Reduce heat and cook gently for 10 minutes. Add bean mixture and stir thoroughly, cooking for 5 minutes.

Beat eggs until light, add soy sauce and scallions and stir into the soup gently until the soup is set.°

Serve immediately in hot soup plates.

° When the flavors blend.

LIMA MINESTRONE, CALIFORNIA STYLE
Serves 8

Ready Tray

1	cup large dried lima beans
1	onion, finely chopped
1	clove garlic, finely chopped
¼	pound salt pork, cut in ½ inch cubes
6	cups water
2	bouillon cubes
1½	teaspoons salt
1	carrot, diced
1	turnip, diced
2	stalks celery, sliced
1	cup spinach, chopped
2	cups cabbage, shredded
1½	cups canned tomatoes
½	bay leaf
¼	teaspoon dried basil
¼	cup uncooked rice

Rinse and drain limas. Place onions and garlic in kettle with salt pork and brown lightly. Add limas, water, bouillon cubes and salt and bring to a boil. Add carrot, turnip, celery, spinach, cabbage, tomatoes, bay leaf and basil and simmer slowly for 1½ hours. Add rice and cook ½ hour longer or until the rice is tender and blended with the other ingredients.

LIMA BEAN SOUP—CUBAN
Serves 4

Ready Tray
1	cup cooked lima beans, drained
½	cup blanched almonds, peeled
1	clove garlic, peeled
3	tablespoons cooking oil
1	quart cold water
	Salt and freshly ground black pepper
	Paprika
2	slices sour dough bread, ½ inch thick, and cut in 1½ inch squares

Remove skins from lima beans. Grind beans with almonds and garlic. Combine with oil in a 2-quart kettle, add water, salt and pepper to taste, light sprinkling of paprika, and the bread. Stir and bring to a boiling point. Cover, lower heat and cook gently 30 minutes. Serve hot.

LIMA BEAN SOUP WITH MEAT BALLS
Serves 6

Ready Tray
1	cup large dried lima beans
5	cups boiling water
1	onion, finely chopped
1	tablespoon butter
1	cup canned tomatoes
1	cup celery, finely sliced
1	cup carrots, diced
1	bay leaf
2¾	teaspoons salt
¾	pound ground lean beef
¼	cup fine dry bread crumbs
3	tablespoons milk
½	teaspoon Worcestershire sauce

Rinse limas, add water and boil 2 minutes. Cover and let stand 1 hour. Sauté onion in butter until golden brown. Add to beans with other vegetables, bay leaf and 2 teaspoons salt. Cook slowly 2 hours. Mix remaining ingredients and shape into tiny meat balls. Brown lightly in hot skillet and add to soup. Simmer gently for 15 minutes.

MINESTRA OF BEANS AND RICE
Serves 6

Ready Tray		
	½	pound dried beans, your choice
	¼	pound rice
	1	large onion, finely chopped
	3	stalks celery, finely chopped
	4	tablespoons olive oil
	2	fresh tomatoes, peeled, seeded and finely chopped
	1	hot chili pepper, finely chopped
		Salt
	6	slices toast

Wash and cook beans in plenty of water, seasoned with salt only. When tender, place aside in their own liquid.

Sauté onion and celery in oil until golden brown, then add the tomatoes and pepper. Cook together, stirring often, for 10 minutes and add to the beans. Heat the beans until the boiling point is reached, add the rice and cook until rice is tender. Keep the liquid to the desired consistency of thick soup.

Serve in hot soup plates over toast.

ROSY LIMA BEAN SOUP
Serves 5 to 6

Ready Tray	1	small onion, finely chopped
	2	tablespoons butter
	1	cup large dried lima beans
	3½	cups water
	1	teaspoon salt
	2	cups tomato juice
	⅛	teaspoon powdered thyme

Sauté onion in butter until golden brown.

Add rinsed limas and water. Cover and cook slowly until limas are very soft, about 2 hours. Then force through a sieve or place in electric blender. Add salt, tomato juice and thyme and heat thoroughly before serving.

LIMA BEAN SOUP—PRESSURE COOKED
Serves 7 to 8

Ready Tray	1	cup dried lima beans
	1	small bay leaf
	1	quart boiling water
	1	teaspoon salt
	¼	teaspoon pepper
	2	tablespoons onion, finely chopped
	2	tablespoons carrot, finely chopped
	2	tablespoons bacon fat
	¼	cup flour
	1	cup milk
	1	cup light cream
		Any desired seasoning
	2	tablespoons fresh parsley, finely chopped
		Croutons

Cover beans with boiling water, cover and let stand 1 hour. Drain.

Place beans in pressure cooker with the bay leaf, boiling water, salt, pepper, onion and carrot. Close cooker, bring to 15 pounds pressure and process 30 minutes. Cool and open the cooker, take out 1 cup of beans so they will stay whole to garnish the finished soup.

Melt bacon fat and blend in flour until smooth. Add milk and cream and stir until smooth. Add to the soup and bring to boiling point, stirring well.

Add whole beans and serve sprinkled with the parsley and croutons.

UNITED STATES SENATE RESTAURANT BEAN SOUP
Serves 8

Ready Tray		
	2	pounds small navy pea beans
	4	quarts hot water
	1½	pounds smoked ham hocks
	1	onion, chopped
		Butter
		Salt and pepper

Wash beans and run through hot water until beans are white again.

Put on the stove with four quarts of hot water.

Add the smoked ham hocks and boil slowly in a covered pot, approximately three hours.

Braise chopped onion in a little butter, and when light brown, put in bean soup.

Season with salt and pepper, then serve. Do not add salt until ready to serve.

MINESTRONE-TUSCANY
Serves 16 (Makes 6½ quarts)

Ready Tray	Basic Stock:
	1 pound dried pinto, pink or cranberry beans, washed
	4 quarts water
	1 teaspoon salt
	1 10 or 12-inch long prosciutto bone, or
	½ pound salt pork cut in thick slices
	½ cup tomato sauce
	¼ teaspoon allspice
	Salt and freshly ground black pepper
	Vegetables—1 Cup each of 6 of the following:
	carrots, cut in small pieces
	boiling potatoes, cut in small pieces
	small new potatoes, cut in small pieces
	curly cabbage, coarsely chopped
	leeks, coarsely chopped
	onions, coarsely chopped
	zucchini, cut in small pieces
	green beans, cut in small pieces
	wax beans, cut in small pieces
	peas, fresh or frozen

In a large kettle place dried beans, water, salt and prosciutto bone or salt pork. (Never use smoked ham or bacon; the smokiness alters the soup's character.) Bring to a boil, cover and simmer gently for 3 hours. Drain and save stock. Force half the beans through a sieve (or whirl in a blender with some of the stock).

Combine beans, bean purée, stock (including salt pork), tomato sauce, allspice and additional salt and pepper to taste. Add vegetables, bring to a boil, cover and simmer for 1½ hours. Serve hot.

This may be made in a large quantity and stored in freezer for future delicious eating.

HENRI CHARPENTIER'S PURÉE MONGOLE
Serves 6 to 8

Ready Tray		
	¼	pound fresh string beans
	¼	pound fresh shelled lima beans
	¼	pound fresh peas
	¼	pound dried white navy beans
	½	stalk celery, coarsely chopped
	1	Bermuda onion, medium size, coarsely chopped
	2	cups milk
	4	cups beef or chicken consommé
	5	fresh tomatoes, peeled and coarsely chopped
		Salt and freshly ground black pepper
	½	cup heavy cream
	1	tablespoon sweet butter

Cover the string beans, lima beans, peas, celery and navy beans with water. Add onion and cook over medium heat until tender. Pass through a sieve making a thick purée.

Combine the milk and consommé, boil and add to the purée.

Place tomatoes in a saucepan, season to taste with salt and freshly ground black pepper and cook to a thick purée. Add to the bean purée and boil for twenty minutes.

Place the cream and butter in the bottom of a soup tureen and pour the boiling soup over, stirring thoroughly before serving.

Add more seasoning, if necessary.

FABULOUS RED BEAN SOUP
Serves 4

Ready Tray		
	2	cups dry Idaho red beans
	2	quarts water
	1	meaty ham bone
	2	medium-sized onions, peeled and quartered
	2	carrots, cut in 2-inch pieces
	2	stalks celery, cut in 2-inch pieces
		Few sprigs fresh parsley
	3	whole cloves
	2	small bay leaves
	1	teaspoon dry mustard
	¼	teaspoon crushed dry thyme leaves
	1	dash ground mace
	2	teaspoons Worcestershire sauce
		Salt
	¼	cup Sherry or Madeira wine
	2	hard-cooked eggs, finely chopped for garnish
	1	lemon or lime, thinly sliced for garnish

Place beans in a large heavy kettle, cover with water and bring to boiling point. Boil for 2 minutes. Remove from heat. Cover and allow to stand for 1 hour.

Add all ingredients except wine and garnishes to the beans and liquid. Place over heat uncovered and bring to boiling point, reduce heat to simmering, cover and simmer gently for 3½ to 4 hours, or until beans are soft enough to mash. Stir occasionally while cooking. Remove ham bone and cut ham in small pieces to add later on. Skim off any excess fat from soup.

Press beans and vegetables through a sieve or food mill. If too thick, add some hot water and stir thoroughly. Add ham pieces. Season to taste with salt if necessary. Reheat over low heat gently to prevent scorching.

Just before serving, stir in wine. Serve in individual hot soup plates and garnish with chopped egg and lemon or lime slices.

If served from a tureen, a bit of thick sour cream swirled across the surface of soup gives an interesting marbled effect.

NAVY BEAN SOUP, S. S. McGINTY
Serves 8 to 10

Ready Tray

1½	cups dried navy beans
5½	cups water
4	ounces pork sausage, diced
3	tablespoons carrot, grated
3	tablespoons green onion, chopped
1	beef bouillon cube
½	cup canned tomato soup (undiluted)
1	tablespoon instant mashed potato
1	cup water
1	teaspoon monosodium glutamate
1½	teaspoons salt

Combine beans, 5½ cups water, sausage, carrot, onion and bouillon cube. Bring to a boil, cover and reduce heat. Simmer 2 hours. Let cool 1 hour, then drain, saving liquid.

Grind or mash bean mixture and add to bean liquid with tomato soup, salt, pepper, potato granules mixed with 1 cup water and monosodium glutamate. Cook over low heat 30 minutes, stirring now and then.

NAVY BEAN AND HAM SOUP
Serves 8

Ready Tray		
	1	cup dried navy beans
	½	pound smoked ham, cut in 1-inch cubes
	1	carrot, cut in thick slices
	2	turnips, cut in thick slices
	1½	cups onion, thinly sliced
	2	potatoes, medium size, cut in ½-inch cubes
	1	cup tomato sauce
	4½	tablespoons fresh parsley, finely chopped
	2	teaspoons salt
	6	cups water

Soak beans in water to cover overnight. Drain.

Boil the ham in 6 cups of water for 1 hour, add beans and cook
gently, covered, until beans are tender. Add the carrot, turnips,
onion, potatoes, tomato sauce, parsley and salt. Cover and cook
until all vegetables are tender. Serve very hot.

MUNG BEAN SOUP
Serves 8

Ready Tray		
	1½	cups dried mung beans
	5	cups water
	½	cup fresh shrimp, cut in ½-inch pieces
	1	clove garlic, mashed
	⅔	cup tomatoes, chopped
	½	cup onion, finely sliced
	1	tablespoon bacon fat
	2½	teaspoons salt
	½	bunch watercress, cut in 1½-inch pieces

Soak beans in 2 cups of water for 4 hours. Rub the beans between the hands and remove and discard the skins, but strain and save the liquid.

Soak the shrimp in 1 cup water for 1 hour.

Brown garlic in hot bacon fat, discard garlic. Drain shrimp, reserve liquid. Fry the shrimp and onions in fat for 2 minutes. Add tomatoes, beans and the reserved liquid from the beans and shrimp, and salt. Cover and simmer gently until beans are soft. Add remaining water during the cooking period.

Garnish with watercress and serve hot.

STRING BEAN SOUP
Serves 4

Ready Tray	1	pound small tender green string beans, cut in 1-inch pieces
	1	tablespoon olive oil
	1	clove garlic, gently crushed
	1	tablespoon tomato sauce slightly diluted with water or
	2	fresh tomatoes, peeled, seeded and finely chopped
		Salt and freshly ground black pepper
	4	slices toast

In a large kettle heat the oil, brown the garlic lightly. Remove and set aside. Add tomato sauce or if the fresh tomatoes are used, be sure to cook them slowly for 20 minutes. Add the beans, season to taste with salt and freshly ground black pepper. Cover the kettle and cook slowly over medium heat until the beans are tender, adding a little hot water occasionally to keep the consistency of thick soup.

Serve in soup plates over the toast.

NAVY BEAN, BEER AND CHEESE SOUP
Serves 4 to 6

Ready Tray | ½ cube (¼ cup) butter
¼ cup flour
4 cups chicken broth
¼ cup celery, finely chopped
¼ cup carrots, finely chopped
⅛ cup fresh green bell pepper, finely chopped
1 cup cooked navy beans, thoroughly mashed
⅛ teaspoon white pepper
Salt to taste
1 cup beer
¼ cup Parmesan cheese, grated
Garlic-flavored croutons
Paprika

Melt butter and blend in flour. Gradually stir in broth. Add vegetables and simmer slowly until vegetables are tender. Add mashed
beans and stir thoroughly. Season with pepper and salt to taste.
Add beer and cheese and heat thoroughly.

Serve with croutons and a dash of paprika.

SOYBEAN MILK SOUP
Serves 6 to 8

Ready Tray | 2 quarts soybean milk*
6 tablespoons butter
2 tablespoons onion, finely chopped
1 cup celery, finely chopped
6 tablespoons flour
1½ teaspoons salt
Watercress or parsley, finely chopped

Melt butter in a frying pan, add onion and celery and cook slowly for 5 minutes. Add flour, mix until smooth and gradually add soybean milk. Transfer to double boiler and cook, stirring constantly, until smooth and slightly thickened. Cook approximately 30 minutes. Add salt and just before serving, garnish with watercress or parsley.

* Available in health food stores.

PINTO-CHILI BEAN SOUP
Serves 4 to 6

Ready Tray		
	2	cups dried pinto beans
	2	quarts boiling water
	1	teaspoon salt
	1	teaspoon sugar
	¼	teaspoon pepper
	¼	teaspoon thyme
	¼	teaspoon sage
	1½	teaspoons chili powder
	1	tablespoon butter
	1	tablespoon flour

Wash the beans thoroughly. Add the water and salt; cover and let stand 50 minutes. Then simmer until the beans are tender, approximately 2 hours. Remove 2 cups of the beans to add to the soup when finished. Rub the remainder through a sieve together with the liquid. Measure and add an equal quantity of any kind of soup stock or use water and bouillon cubes, or the liquid left from boiling ham. Add the sugar, pepper, thyme, sage and the chili powder dissolved in 1 tablespoon of cold water. Simmer slowly for 25 minutes.

Cream the butter and flour, add ½ cup of the hot soup, stirring until blended; add to the soup and bring to a boil. Add the reserved beans and simmer 5 minutes. Serve in hot soup plates.

NAVY BEAN SOUP
Serves 6

Ready Tray
2	cups navy pea beans, soaked overnight
1	meaty ham bone
3	quarts water
½	cup cooked mashed potatoes
3	onions, finely chopped
1	Bunch celery stalks and leaves, finely chopped
1	clove garlic, finely chopped
¼	cup fresh parsley, finely chopped
	Salt and freshly ground black pepper

Place soaked beans, ham bone and water in large kettle. Cover and simmer gently for 2 hours. When the beans are half cooked add mashed potatoes and stir thoroughly.

Add onions, celery, garlic, parsley and simmer slowly for 1 hour. Remove ham bone; chop up meat and return meat to soup.

Season to taste with salt and freshly ground black pepper.

Serve hot!

STRING BEAN SOUP, JULIENNE
Serves 6 to 8

Ready Tray
1	cup fresh green string beans, sliced 1½ inches long
2	carrots, thinly sliced in strips 1½ inches long
2	turnips, thinly sliced in strips 1½ inches long
2	potatoes, thinly sliced in strips 1½ inches long
2	leeks, thinly sliced in strips 1½ inches long
3	cabbage leaves, thinly sliced in strips 1½ inches long
4	tablespoons butter
8	cups rich stock
	Salt and freshly ground black pepper

Combine all vegetables and fry in butter until nicely browned.

Place in large soup pot, add stock and cook until the vegetables are tender, approximately 30 minutes.

Season to taste with salt and freshly ground black pepper.

Serve in individual soup plates.

NAVY BEAN SOUP FOR A CROWD
Serves 50

Ready Tray

½	pound butter, melted
2½	pounds onions, thinly sliced
5	stalks celery, finely sliced
4	gallons water
3½	pounds dried navy beans
1	ham bone or hock
¼	cup olive oil
4	cloves garlic, finely chopped
2	cans (No. 2) whole pack tomatoes, chopped
½	cup Worcestershire sauce
	Salt and pepper
½	cup fresh parsley, finely chopped

Pour butter in 8 gallon soup kettle. Add onions and celery and simmer gently for a few minutes. Add water, beans and ham bone; boil slowly until beans are tender, approximately 3 hours.

Heat oil to 350°, add garlic and brown until golden. Add tomatoes and cook for 5 minutes, pour into the soup and stir thoroughly. Add sauce, salt and pepper to taste and heat thoroughly.

Add parsley when the soup is served.

NAVY BEAN SOUP, ALAMEDA
Serves 6 to 8

Ready Tray
1	cup dried navy beans
4	cups water
	Split ham bone
½	cup onion, chopped
2	medium carrots, chopped
2	stalks celery, chopped
2	tablespoons green pepper, minced
½	cup tomato purée
⅛	teaspoon prepared mustard
1	whole clove
2	whole black peppers
	Salt to taste
	Chopped parsley for garnish

Soak beans overnight in water to cover. Combine beans, water, ham bone, onion, carrots, celery, green pepper, tomato purée, mustard, clove and black peppers. Cook slowly over low heat 4 hours, stirring now and then and adding more liquid, if needed. Add salt the last half hour.

Serve topped with chopped parsley.

SIMPLE WHITE BEAN SOUP
Serves 6

Ready Tray
2	cups dried beans (any of the dried white beans are suitable)
6	cups stock or water
2	tablespoons butter
	Salt and pepper
1	cup croutons, crisply fried in butter

Cook the beans in the liquid for approximately 2 hours or until tender.

Force through a food mill or strainer.

Reheat, adding more liquid if the soup is too thick. Add the butter and season to taste with salt and pepper.

Serve in individual soup plates over croutons.

WHITE BEAN AND SPINACH SOUP
Serves 4 to 6

Ready Tray

1	cup dried white beans, your choice
2	quarts boiling water or beef stock
1	bay leaf
1	onion, finely chopped
1	clove garlic, gently crushed
2	tablespoons butter
2	cups water
2	beef bouillon cubes
3	cups cooked spinach, chopped
1	tablespoon flour, blended with
2	tablespoons cold water
	Salt and pepper mill

Cover the beans with the boiling water or beef stock. Cover and let stand 50 minutes. Add bay leaf. Sauté the onion and garlic in the butter until limp. Cover and simmer slowly for 2 hours, or until the beans are soft. Then add the water, bouillon cubes and spinach. Bring to boiling point; stir in flour mixture slowly. Season to taste with salt and freshly ground black pepper. Simmer slowly for 5 minutes. Serve in hot soup plates.

YELLOWEYE BEAN SOUP
Serves 8

Ready Tray
1	cup yelloweye beans
1	ham shank
	Salt and freshly ground black pepper
2	carrots, diced
2	onions, thinly sliced
2	potatoes, sliced
1	teaspoon salt
	Lemon slices

Cover washed beans with 2 quarts cold water and soak overnight. Add all the ingredients and cook slowly until the beans are tender, adding more liquid, if necessary.

Serve with beans whole, mashed, or rub mixture through a sieve and season. Add hot water, if too thick.

Serve topped with lemon slices.

WHITE BEAN AND HAM SOUP
Serves 4

Ready Tray
1	cup dried white beans
1	Bermuda onion, medium size, quartered
1	ham bone or end of ham, cut into small pieces
4	cups broth
	Salt and freshly ground black pepper
2	slices bacon, fried crisp and broken into small pieces

Cover washed beans with water and soak overnight. Next day, add onion and ham bone, water if needed, place over medium heat and bring to a boil, reduce heat and simmer gently until the beans are tender, approximately 1½ hours. Beans may be left whole or put through a sieve with the liquid they were cooked in. Add broth and season to taste with salt and freshly ground black pepper and bring to a boil, stirring thoroughly.

Serve in individual soup plates and garnish with bacon bits.

Left over baked beans may be used. Place beans in large kettle with onion and ham bone and water to cover and bring to a boil and proceed as above.

WHITE BEAN AND BEER SOUP
Serves 6 to 8

Ready Tray

2	cups white dried beans
3	tablespoons butter
1	cup onions, finely chopped
½	cup carrots, grated
1	cup canned tomatoes
2	teaspoons salt
½	teaspoon freshly ground black pepper
1	cup beer

Wash the beans, cover with water and bring to a boil. Then turn off heat and let the beans soak in the same water for 1 hour. Drain, add 2½ quarts water and bring to a boil; cover loosely and cook over low heat for 1 hour.

Melt the butter in a skillet and sauté the onions and carrots lightly. Add to the beans with the tomatoes, salt and pepper. Cover and simmer slowly for 2 hours. Purée 1 cup of bean mixture through a sieve or in an electric blender. Return to the soup and stir in the beer. Cook for 15 minutes, until thoroughly heated. Add more seasoning, if necessary.

BEAN-VEGETABLE SOUP
Serves 8

Ready Tray		
	1	cup fresh string beans, sliced
	1½	cups fresh green lima beans
	2	carrots, thinly sliced
	1	cup cauliflower, diced
	3	small new potatoes, peeled and quartered
	4	radishes, cut in half
	1	tablespoon salt
	1	tablespoon sugar
	1	cup fresh spinach, chopped
	3	tablespoons butter
	1	tablespoon flour
	2	quarts hot milk
	1	fresh egg yolk
	⅜	cup light fresh cream
	1	cup cooked, cleaned shrimp or crawfish, coarsely chopped
	2	tablespoons fresh parsley, finely chopped

Place string beans, lima beans, carrots, cauliflower, potatoes and radishes in a large kettle, cover with water, add salt and sugar. Cover and cook gently until tender, approximately 40 minutes. Add spinach and cook 10 minutes longer.

Melt butter in large soup kettle and blend in flour until smooth. Stir in hot milk until smooth. Beat egg yolk and cream together and stir into milk gently. Add vegetables with liquid, and shrimp or crawfish, heat thoroughly. Soup should be thick.

Serve in hot soup plates and garnish with parsley.

OLD-FASHIONED BEAN SOUP, IDAHO STYLE
Serves 10

Ready Tray		
	1	pound Idaho Great Northern large white beans
	3	quarts water
	1	large meaty ham bone
	1	large onion, finely chopped
	1	bay leaf
	2	cloves garlic, finely chopped
	1	cup mashed potatoes, leftover or cooked instant
	1	cup celery, thinly sliced
	1	cup raw carrots, diced
		Salt and pepper mill
	½	cup fresh heavy cream
		Finely chopped parsley and chives for garnish

Soak beans in water overnight. Cook beans in water in which they were soaked adding more, if needed. Add ham bone, onion, bay leaf and garlic. Bring to boil rapidly. Cover tightly, reduce heat and simmer gently until beans are almost tender, approximately 1¼ hours.

Add potatoes, celery and carrots to beans. Season to taste with salt and freshly ground black pepper. Cover and simmer 1 hour longer. Remove ham bone and cut off meat. Dice and add to soup. Reheat to just boiling, stirring carefully to avoid breaking beans.

Just before serving stir in cream gently and garnish top with parsley and chives.

Grated Parmesan or shredded Cheddar cheese may be sprinkled over the top if desired.

Old-Fashioned Bean Soup for Tree Trimming Night can easily become one of the family Christmas traditions simply on the basis of its heart-warming goodness.

SPLIT PEA SOUP
Serves 4 to 6

Ready Tray
- 1 cup dried green or yellow split peas
- 1 Bermuda onion, medium size, quartered
- 1 ham bone or end of ham, cut into small pieces
- 4 cups milk
- Salt and freshly ground black pepper

Cover washed peas with water and soak overnight. Next day, add onion and ham bone, place over medium heat and bring to a boil, reduce heat and simmer gently uncovered, until the peas are tender, approximately 1½ hours. Remove ham bone, press peas through a sieve and return to the liquid they were cooked in. Add milk and season to taste with salt and freshly ground black pepper and reheat thoroughly, stirring occasionally.

Serve hot!

WHITE BEAN SOUP AND DUMPLINGS
Serves 6

Ready Tray
- 1 cup white dried beans
- 2 quarts beef stock
- 2 carrots, sliced
- 1 parsnip, sliced
- 4 tablespoons butter
- 2 onions, finely chopped
- 1¼ cups sifted flour
- 2 teaspoons salt
- ½ teaspoon freshly ground black pepper
- 1 teaspoon paprika
- 1 egg
- 2 tablespoons water
- 3 frankfurters, sliced

Soak the beans overnight in water to cover. Drain. Place the beans in a kettle with the stock and add the carrots and parsnips. Cook over low heat for 2 hours. Remove 1 cup of the beans and force through a sieve. Return the purée to the soup.

Melt the butter in a saucepan and sauté the onions until brown, stirring often. Sprinkle 2 tablespoons of the flour over the onions and stir until smooth. Gradually add 1 cup of the soup, stirring, and put all of this in the soup kettle. Add salt, pepper and paprika. Simmer gently over low heat for 1 hour.

Meanwhile, sift the remaining flour into a bowl. Make a well or depression in the center and add the egg and water. Mix to a smooth paste. Knead until the dough does not stick to the fingers. Roll out very thin on a lightly floured surface and allow to remain there for 45 minutes. Pinch off small pieces of the dough and drop into the boiling soup. Cook until they float. Fry the frankfurters for 5 minutes, drain and add to the soup. Serve hot!

LENTIL SOUP
Serves 6

Ready Tray	2	cups dried lentils
	6	cups water or chicken stock
		Salt and freshly ground black pepper
	1	cup croutons, crisply fried in butter
	6	slices of fresh lemon

Cook lentils in water or stock until tender. Force through a strainer or food mill, reserving the water in which they were cooked. Add to strained lentils and blend until smooth.

Reheat and season to taste with salt and freshly ground black pepper.

Place a few croutons in each soup plate, pour the thickened soup and garnish with fresh lemon slice.

LENTIL CREAM SOUP
Serves 6

Ready Tray		
	1	cup dried lentils
	2½	cups water
	¼	teaspoon freshly ground black pepper
	1	teaspoons salt
	1	onion, finely chopped
	1	clove garlic, gently crushed
	4	tablespoons tomato sauce
	3	tablespoons olive oil
	4	small bay leaves
	½	cup evaporated milk

Wash the lentils; then put in a kettle with the water, pepper and salt. Add the onion, garlic, tomato sauce, oil and bay leaves. Cover and simmer gently for 1 hour and 15 minutes, or until the lentil skins have burst. Remove the bay leaves and press lentil mixture through a sieve. Stir in the milk and reheat until thoroughly blended.

LENTIL CREOLE SOUP
Serves 6 to 8

Ready Tray		
	1	cup lentils
	2	quarts boiling water
	1½	teaspoons salt
	2	ounces fat salt pork, cubed
	1	onion, finely chopped
	1	cup celery, finely diced
	1	teaspoon sugar
	1	bay leaf
	¼	teaspoon pepper
	2	tablespoons flour
	2	tablespoons ketchup or tomato juice
	1	cup sweet green and red peppers, finely chopped

Cover the lentils with the boiling water; add salt and let stand for 50 minutes, covered. Fry the salt pork until the fat runs freely. Remove the pork. To the fat add the onion, celery, sugar and bay leaf. Stir into the lentils and water. Add the pepper. Cover and boil slowly until the lentils are tender, approximately 2 hours.

Blend the flour with the ketchup or tomato juice; add a little of the hot soup, then stir into the cooking soup and heat gently until it reaches a boil again.

Garnish with the fried salt pork.

LENTIL CURRIED SOUP
Serves 6

Ready Tray
½	cup dried lentils
7	cups water
2	tablespoons butter
3	tablespoons onion, finely chopped
1	clove garlic, finely chopped
¼	teaspoon dried ground chili peppers
2	teaspoons curry powder
1	teaspoon fresh lemon or lime juice
1	teaspoon salt

Wash the lentils and discard any imperfect ones. Soak in water to cover overnight. Drain well. Boil the water in a kettle and add the lentils. Cook until soft, about 1 hour.

Melt the butter in a separate saucepan, add onions, garlic, chili peppers and curry powder. Stir well and sauté over low heat for 3 minutes, stirring constantly. Add this to the lentils. Add lemon juice and salt and mix thoroughly. Cook 15 minutes before serving.

If desired, the lentils may be forced through a sieve or puréed in an electric blender.

LENTIL HAM SOUP
Serves 4

Ready Tray

1 cup dried lentils
1 Bermuda onion, medium size, finely chopped
1 ham bone or end of ham, cut into small pieces
1 carrot, finely chopped
4 cups beef broth
2 tablespoons fresh parsley, finely chopped
Salt and freshly ground black pepper

Cover washed lentils with water and soak overnight. Next day, add onion, ham bone and carrot, place over medium heat and bring to a boil. Reduce heat and simmer gently until the lentils are tender. Remove ham bone and put lentils and liquid through a sieve. Add the broth, season to taste with salt and freshly ground black pepper and parsley and bring to a slow boil. Serve hot!

LENTIL PASTINA SOUP
Serves 6 to 8

Ready Tray

¾ cup dried lentils
2 slices bacon, cut in small squares
1 onion, thinly sliced
2 cloves garlic, finely chopped
4 large tomatoes, peeled and quartered
1 stalk of celery, coarsely chopped
Salt and freshly ground black pepper
1 pinch dried mint leaves
1 2-oz. package pastina

Soak washed lentils in cold water to cover for 2 hours. Place in a large soup kettle.

Render bacon and put aside. Sauté the onion, garlic, tomatoes and celery for 5 minutes in the bacon fat.

Add bacon and sautéed mixture to beans in the soup kettle and stir until the beans have absorbed the remaining bacon fat. Season to taste with salt and freshly ground black pepper and the mint leaves.

Add 7 cups hot water and cook over rather high flame for 1 hour. Add the pastina and cook gently for 15 minutes. The soup should be very thick, but a little more water may be added if desired. Serve very hot with Italian bread.

DRIED PEA SOUP
Serves 6

Ready Tray
- 2 cups dried green peas
- 6 cups water or chicken stock
- Salt and freshly ground black pepper
- 1 cup croutons, crisply fried in butter

Cook peas in water or stock for 1½ hours. Force through a strainer or a china cap (metal colander).

Reheat and season to taste with salt and freshly ground black pepper.

Serve in individual soup plates over croutons.

The soup should be thick, but if it is too thick add more liquid.

Rice or vermicelli may be cooked with the peas. In this case another pint of liquid should be added, and the soup should not be strained.

BEAN SPROUT AND CHICKEN SOUP
Serves 4 to 6

Ready Tray	1	chicken, 5-lbs., disjointed
	1	onion, quartered
	2½	quarts water
	1	tablespoon salt
	2	teaspoons powdered ginger
	3	tablespoons oil
	1½	cups onions, thinly sliced
	1½	cups fresh bean sprouts*
	3	hard cooked eggs, sliced
	1	lemon, thinly sliced

Combine the chicken, onion, water and salt in a kettle. Bring to a boil, cover and simmer until the chicken is tender, approximately 1½ hours. Remove chicken, strain broth and add ginger. Cut the chicken in thin strips.

Heat oil in a heavy skillet and sauté the onions until golden brown. Add bean sprouts and cook quickly for 5 minutes.

To serve, arrange the chicken, vegetables and eggs in a bowl. Pour the hot soup into cups with a slice of lemon on top. Each guest helps himself to the chicken, onions and bean sprouts.

* Canned bean sprouts may be used if fresh are not available.

PUREE OF BEANS, LENTILS OR GARBANZOS

This is an easy-to-digest soup and very nourishing. One pound of either of the above legumes will serve 5.

Boil the chosen legumes in salted water until tender. The chick peas should be soaked overnight with the right amount of salt added.

When tender, they are pressed through a china cap (sieve). The purée is now diluted to the wanted thickness with hot broth, and seasoned with butter to taste.

If an onion flavor is desired, mince an onion and brown in a spoonful of hot oil; then add a couple spoonfuls of broth or hot water and simmer for 5 minutes. Strain the juice in the purée. Heat well, then serve over a slice of toast.

QUICK TRICKS WITH BEAN SOUPS

Serve with garnishes of chopped minced raw onions, parsley or chives, which may be added by each guest. Dress up with slice of lemon or top with crisp bits of bacon.

Add cut-up wieners to pot. Drop a handful of croutons (rolled at the last minute in grated cheese) in each portion. Add sour cream or salted whipped cream for a treat.

Prepare tomato soup following instructions on can. Mix with can of baked beans. Serve piping hot with sprinkling of grated cheese.

TO FREEZE: Make enough soup to last several meals. Freeze in refrigerator ice cube trays or loaf pans, remove and wrap in foil or freezer paper, and store.

Baked beans may be kept frozen as long as 6 months. Use a favorite recipe, cool to room temperature. Pack in cartons. Freeze. Store at zero or below. When ready to use, add ½ to ¾ cup boiling water to beans, either thawed or frozen, and heat slowly, uncovered.

III

Salads

BAKED BEAN SALAD, LORENZO
Serves 4

Ready Tray

1 cup baked beans
1 cup sauerkraut, coarsely chopped and squeezed
1 tablespoon green olives, finely chopped
1 tablespoon sweet gherkins, finely chopped
½ cup olive oil
¼ cup vinegar
½ cup chili sauce
½ cup chopped watercress
Salt and freshly ground black pepper
Lettuce leaves

In a salad bowl combine the beans, sauerkraut, green olives and gherkins.

In a smaller bowl blend until smooth the oil, vinegar, chili sauce, watercress, salt and freshly ground black pepper to taste.

Add dressing to the salad and toss lightly.

Serve over crisp lettuce leaves on chilled salad plates.

BARBECUE BEAN SALAD
Serves 4 to 6

Ready Tray

1	can 1-lb. barbecue beans
½	cup celery, finely chopped
2	tablespoons green bell pepper, finely chopped
1	tablespoon onion, finely chopped
	Salt and freshly ground black pepper
1	head lettuce, medium size, torn in bite-size pieces

Combine the beans, celery, bell pepper, onion and season to taste with salt and freshly ground black pepper. Toss gently and chill thoroughly.

Serve over nested lettuce on chilled salad plates.

BEAN TUNA SALAD
Serves 4 to 6

Ready Tray

2	cups cooked beans, your choice, drained and cooled
1	can (6½ oz.) chunk-style tuna
½	cup celery, thinly sliced
½	cup dill pickles, coarsely chopped
½	teaspoon salt
⅛	teaspoon freshly ground black pepper
1	tablespoon fresh parsley, finely chopped
¼	cup mayonnaise
2	hard cooked eggs, sliced
	Crisp lettuce leaves

In a large wooden salad bowl, combine all the ingredients except the eggs and lettuce leaves, toss gently.

Serve over crisp lettuce leaves and garnish with egg slices.

THREE BEAN CAESAR SALAD
(One of the world's most renowned)

Ready Tray

1	cup Great Northern large white beans, cooked, drained and well chilled
1	cup Idaho's red beans, cooked, drained and well chilled
1	cup fresh stringless green beans cut in 2-inch lengths, cooked, drained and well chilled (marinate the beans over night in 4 tablespoons olive oil and 2 tablespoons wine vinegar, drain beans before putting in salad)
1	large head romaine, iceberg or butter lettuce, torn in bite-size pieces
3	garlic cloves, peeled
12	croutons, ¾-inch cubes of sour dough French bread, well toasted and rubbed well with garlic
16	anchovy fillets
1	whole fresh lemon, juice only
2	fresh whole eggs, coddled
1½	teaspoons freshly ground black pepper
1	teaspoon dry mustard
2	tablespoons Worchestershire sauce
2	tablespoons wine vinegar
6	tablespoons olive oil, garlic-flavored
3	dashes Tabasco Sauce
6	tablespoons grated Parmesan cheese

Use large wooden bowl that is very dry. Place garlic in bowl. Mash by pressing the garlic through the prongs of a fork and cover mashed garlic delicately with salt. Take large metal spoon and press the fibers and juice of the garlic into the wood with the bowl of the spoon. The salt will aid to scratch or force out the garlic fibers. Use a pressed rotary movement. Add croutons to bowl, moving them around delicately in a circular movement to capture the garlic flavor. Set the croutons aside for use later. Add 8 anchovies and mince. Break and pour coddled eggs into the bowl; add lemon squeezed through a napkin (the reason for the napkin is to hold back the pulp and seeds). Add dry mustard, Worchestershire Sauce, vinegar and garlic-flavored olive oil. Add Tabasco Sauce.

Sprinkle 3 tablespoons of the cheese on the surface of the dressing. Using the fork, whip the dressing into a good consistency and add torn greens. Be sure that the greens are well chilled and water shaken off. Add beans and toss well, but do not bruise the greens. Sprinkle desired amount of freshly ground black pepper. Add garlic-flavored croutons and toss again gently. (Add croutons just before serving to prevent sogginess.) Sprinkle small amount of cheese on surface of tossed salad. Toss until every green leaf glistens with its dressing.

Serve on well-chilled salad plates and add, in a criss-cross X design, 2 anchovy fillets to each portion.

BEAN AND CHEESE SALAD
Serves 4

Ready Tray	1	cup dried navy beans
	4	cups water
	1	tablespoon instant minced onion
	½	green bell pepper, finely chopped
	1	cup celery, finely sliced
	1	cup sharp Cheddar cheese, diced
	½	cup mayonnaise
	1	tablespoon vinegar
	½	teaspoon prepared mustard
		Salt and freshly ground black pepper

Cover beans with water, bring to a boil and boil 2 minutes. Cover and let stand 1 hour. Then cook until tender. Drain and cool thoroughly.

Place beans in a salad bowl and add the onion, green pepper, celery and cheese.

Blend the mayonnaise, vinegar, prepared mustard, salt and freshly ground black pepper to taste. Pour over bean mixture in the salad bowl and toss gently, but thoroughly. Chill well before serving.

KIDNEY BEAN SALAD
Serves 4

Ready Tray | 4   slices crisp cooked bacon, crumbled
⅓   cup onion, finely chopped
½   cup celery, finely chopped
1   cup apple, diced
⅓   cup American cheddar cheese, diced
1   large can kidney beans, drained
½   teaspoon salt
Dash of freshly ground black pepper
Mayonnaise
Crisp lettuce leaves

Combine the bacon, onion, celery, apple, cheese, beans and seasonings. Add just enough mayonnaise to moisten. Toss gently and serve on crisp lettuce leaves on chilled salad plates.

KIDNEY BEAN AND COTTAGE CHEESE SALAD
Serves 4

Ready Tray | 1   can (No. 2) red kidney beans, drained
⅓   cup French dressing
1   tomato, diced
1   green bell pepper, finely chopped
Crisp lettuce leaves
1   cup chived cottage cheese, formed into balls for garnish

Combine the beans, dressing, tomato and bell pepper in a salad bowl. Chill for 30 minutes.

Serve in lettuce-lined bowl and garnish with cottage cheese balls.

GARBANZO BEAN AND CHICKEN SALAD
Serves 6

Ready Tray

3 cups cold boiled chicken, diced
2 cups cooked cold garbanzo beans
6 fresh tomatoes, medium size, diced
3 green bell peppers, finely chopped
½ cup mayonnaise
  Salt and freshly ground black pepper
  Crisp green lettuce leaves
3 hard cooked eggs, quartered
6 radish roses
6 ripe olives

In a large wooden salad bowl combine the chicken, beans, tomatoes, green peppers, mayonnaise, salt and freshly ground black pepper to taste. Toss gently but thoroughly.

Serve on lettuce leaves on individual cold salad plates and garnish with eggs, radishes and olives.

GARBANZO BEAN SALAD
Serves 4

Ready Tray

2 cups cooked garbanzo beans, well drained and chilled
½ cup celery, diced
¼ cup onion, finely chopped
  Salt and pepper mill
⅓ cup French dressing
  Crisp lettuce leaves

In a salad bowl combine the barbanzo beans, celery, onion and season to taste with salt and freshly ground black pepper. Add dressing, toss lightly and serve over lettuce leaves.

CRANBERRY BEAN SALAD
Serves 6 to 8

Ready Tray

2 cups dried cranberry beans
6 cups water
2 teaspoons salt
½ cup red wine vinegar
1 cup celery, sliced
½ cup green spring onions, finely chopped
½ cup green bell pepper, finely chopped
Crisp lettuce leaves

Wash the beans, then place in a large kettle with the water; cover, bring to a boil and cook 2 minutes. Remove from fire and let soak 1 hour before cooking again.

Add the salt, bring to a boil, and cook 2 hours, or until the beans are tender. Drain and stir in the vinegar; chill thoroughly.

Add the celery, green onions and green pepper; toss gently. Serve in cups of lettuce leaves.

GARBANZO CHEESE SALAD
Serves 4

Ready Tray

1 cup dried garbanzo beans
½ pound Monterey Jack cheese, diced
2 Bermuda onions, medium size, thinly sliced
½ cup olive oil
¼ cup fresh lemon juice
1 teaspoon salt
½ teaspoon ground coriander
Crisp lettuce leaves
3 hard cooked eggs, quartered

Soak the washed garbanzo beans overnight in water to cover. Cover tightly and cook for 2 hours or until tender. Drain thoroughly and chill.

Combine the beans, cheese and onions in a salad bowl.

Blend, the oil, lemon juice, salt and coriander together. Pour over ingredients in salad bowl and toss lightly.

Serve over crisp lettuce leaves and garnish with eggs.

KIDNEY BEAN-RICE SALAD
Serves 6

Ready Tray
1	large can kidney beans, drained
1	cup celery, finely sliced
1	tablespoon onion, finely chopped
1	cup cooked rice, thoroughly blanched
1	hard cooked egg, riced
1	green bell pepper, cut fine
2	tablespoons yogurt
	Salt and pepper mill

Combine beans, celery, onion, rice, egg and green pepper in a salad bowl.

Add yogurt and season to taste with salt and freshly ground black pepper. Toss lightly. Chill thoroughly before serving.

KIDNEY BEAN SALAD—TOSSED FOR A CROWD
Serves 30 to 35 (½ cup per serving)

Ready Tray

6	cans (No. 2) kidney beans, drained
18	hard cooked eggs, chopped
3	cups sweet pickles, diced
⅓	cup onion, diced
2⅔	cup celery, diced
2	cups green bell peppers, diced
1	tablespoon salt
1	teaspoon black pepper
3½	cups mayonnaise or salad dressing

In a large salad bowl combine the beans, eggs, pickles, onion, celery and green pepper. Add salt, pepper and mayonnaise and toss lightly but thoroughly. Chill thoroughly before serving.

KIDNEY SALAD ROUGE
Serves 6

Ready Tray

1½	cups dried red kidney beans
6	cups water
3	hard cooked eggs, diced
1	small onion, finely chopped
½	cup celery, thinly sliced
½	cup mayonnaise
2	tablespoons vinegar
	Salt and freshly ground black pepper

Cover beans with water, bring to a boil and boil 2 minutes. Cover and let stand 1 hour; then cook until tender. Drain and cool. Place beans in a salad bowl. Add eggs, onion and celery.

Blend until smooth mayonnaise, vinegar, salt and freshly ground black pepper to taste. Pour over beans in salad bowl and toss gently. Chill thoroughly before serving.

KIDNEY-STRING BEAN SALAD
Serves 8

Ready Tray

2	cups cooked kidney beans, drained and cooled
2	cups cooked green string beans, drained and cooled
2	cups cooked beets, drained and cooled and diced
2	dill pickles, coarsely chopped
2	scallions, finely chopped
1	cup cooked crab meat, boned
1	cup mayonnaise
1	tablespoon prepared mustard
½	cup sour cream
	Salt and freshly ground black pepper
2	hard cooked eggs, sliced
	Strips of carrots for garnish
	Radish roses for garnish

In a large salad bowl place kidney beans, string beans, beets, dill pickles, scallions and crabmeat and toss gently.

Blend until smooth the mayonnaise, mustard and sour cream. Season to taste with salt and freshly ground black pepper. Pour over salad and toss gently but thoroughly.

Serve on individual chilled salad plates and garnish with carrot strips and radish roses.

HOT KIDNEY BEAN SALAD
Serves 4 to 6

Ready Tray	2	cups cooked kidney beans, drained
	1	cup celery, thinly sliced
	¼	pound sharp American cheese, diced
	⅓	cup sweet pickle, chopped
	¼	cup green onions, thinly sliced
	½	teaspoon salt
	½	cup mayonnaise
	⅓	cup cracker crumbs
	6	crisply fried bacon curls

Combine all ingredients except the crumbs; toss lightly, spoon into 8-ounce custard cups. Sprinkle crumbs over top. Bake in very hot oven 450° for 10 minutes, or until bubbly.

Garnish with crisp bacon curls.

LENTIL SALAD
Serves 4

Ready Tray	1	cup dried lentils
	1	teaspoon dried onion, finely chopped
	1	teaspoon chives, finely chopped
	1	teaspoon fresh parsley, finely chopped
		Salt and pepper mill
	2	tablespoons wine vinegar
	½	cup olive oil
		Lettuce leaves

Soak washed lentils overnight in water to cover. Season lightly with salt, cover and cook gently until tender, but not mushy.

Drain and cool thoroughly.

Blend onion, chives and parsley. Season to taste with salt and freshly ground black pepper. Add vinegar and set aside for 15 minutes. Add olive oil and mix thoroughly.

Pour over cooled lentils, toss gently and serve over crisp lettuce leaves on individual salad plates.

This may also be used as an hors d'oeuvre by serving the lentils in a large bowl and letting the guests help themselves.

MOLDED KIDNEY BEAN SALAD
Serves 8

Ready Tray		
	2	tablespoons fresh lemon juice
	2	tablespoons water
	1	envelope unflavored gelatin
	2	cups cooked kidney beans, drained
	2	hard cooked eggs, chopped
	½	cup celery, finely chopped
	½	cup dill pickle, finely chopped
	½	cup mayonnaise
	1	teaspoon grated onion
	¼	teaspoon salt
	1	cup evaporated milk

Combine lemon juice and water in a custard cup; sprinkle gelatin over top and let stand 5 minutes to soften. Place custard cup in a small sauce pan containing an inch of hot water. Simmer, stirring until gelatin is liquified.

Combine beans in a bowl with remaining ingredients, except the milk, and mix well.

Stir in gelatin, then blend in evaporated milk. Ladle into an oiled 5-cup ring mold. Chill thoroughly until set, for about 4 hours, before serving. When chilled turn out over lettuce-covered platter and serve.

GARBANZO BEAN-PIMIENTO SALAD
Serves 4

Ready Tray | 2 cups freshly cooked garbanzos, drained
2 tablespoons olive oil
¼ cup wine vinegar
¼ cup fresh parsley, finely chopped
3 pimientos, finely chopped
3 fresh spring green onions, finely chopped
Salt and freshly ground black pepper
Crisp lettuce leaves

Place garbanzos in a medium-sized bowl. Add olive oil, vinegar, parsley, pimientos, onions and season to taste with salt and freshly ground black pepper. Toss gently but thoroughly; cover and place in refrigerator for 3 hours.

When thoroughly chilled serve over crisp lettuce leaves.

This salad may be served on individual chilled salad plates or served in a salad bowl lined with crisp lettuce leaves for a buffet luncheon.

LENTIL AND ANCHOVY SALAD
Serves 4

Ready Tray | 2 cups cooked lentils, drained and cooled
1 tablespoon fresh parsley, finely chopped
1 tablespoon capers
1 tablespoon chives, finely chopped
1 tablespoon dill pickle, finely chopped
3 tablespoons olive oil
1 tablespoon tarragon vinegar
3 anchovy fillets, cut into small pieces
Pepper mill
Crisp lettuce leaves

In a salad bowl combine lentils with parsley, capers, chives and pickle.

Blend oil, vinegar and anchovies thoroughly.

Pour the dressing over salad and toss well.

Season to taste with freshly ground black pepper

Chill thoroughly.

Serve on lettuce leaves on chilled salad plates.

LIMA BEAN SALAD
Serves 6 to 8

Ready Tray

3	cups cooked large dried lima beans, drained and cooled
1	green bell pepper, seeded and coarsely chopped
½	cup sliced green onions and tops
1	cup celery, finely sliced
½	cup cubed American cheese, cut in ½-inch cubes
1	pimiento, finely chopped
½	cup sour cream
1½	teaspoons caraway seeds
½	cup dill pickles, finely chopped
1	teaspoon salt
1	tablespoon salad oil
1	tablespoon prepared horseradish
	Salad greens

Mix together cold cooked lima beans, green pepper, green onions, celery, cheese and pimiento. Combine sour cream, caraway seeds, dill pickle, salt, oil and horseradish. Pour dressing over lima bean mixture and toss lightly. Chill slightly. Arrange in a salad bowl lined with greens.

OLD-FASHIONED KIDNEY BEAN SALAD
Serves 6

Ready Tray | 2 cups cooked kidney beans, drained
1½ cups celery, finely chopped
½ cup sweet pickle, chopped
¼ cup salad oil
1 tablespoon onion, finely chopped
2 hard cooked eggs, coarsely chopped
2 tablespoons vinegar
1 tablespoon pickle liquid
1 teaspoon salt
1½ teaspoons prepared mustard
Egg slices for garnish

Combine all ingredients, toss lightly and chill thoroughly before serving. Garnish with egg slices and serve.

LIMA CHUCK-WAGON SALAD
Serves 4

Ready Tray | 1 clove garlic
1 quart bite-size pieces of crisp lettuce
2 stalks celery, finely sliced
½ cucumber, unpeeled and thinly sliced
2 fresh tomatoes, cut in wedges
2 hard-cooked eggs, diced
1 cup cooked large dried lima beans, drained and chilled
½ cup crumbled Blue cheese
¼ cup salad oil
2 tablespoons wine vinegar
Salt and pepper mill

Rub salad bowl with cut clove garlic and discard garlic. Add lettuce, celery, cucumber, tomatoes, eggs, lima beans and toss lightly.

Blend cheese, oil and vinegar, salt and freshly ground black pepper to taste, pour over salad and toss gently.

Serve on chilled salad plates.

FRIDAY LIMA SALAD FAVORITE
Serves 4 to 6

Ready Tray

2	cups cooked large dried lima beans, drained and cooled
⅓	cup tart French dressing
1	tablespoon grated onion
¼	teaspoon garlic salt
	Pinch of curry powder
⅛	teaspoon paprika
2	tablespoons fresh parsley, finely chopped
½	cup celery, finely chopped
1	cup cooked crab, shrimp or tuna
	Lettuce cups
	Mayonnaise

Lightly mix limas, French dressing, onions, garlic salt, curry powder and paprika. Chill for 1 hour.

Combine with parsley, celery and seafood. Serve in lettuce cups and garnish with mayonnaise.

SIMPLE LENTIL SALAD
Serves 6

Ready Tray | 2   cups cooked lentils, drained and cooled
| 1   clove garlic, finely chopped
| Salt and freshly ground black pepper
| ½   teaspoon paprika
| ¼   cup vinegar
| ¼   cup olive oil
| Crisp lettuce leaves or scooped-out head of lettuce

Place lentils in a large salad bowl.

Combine garlic, salt and freshly ground black pepper to taste, paprika, vinegar and oil. Blend until smooth, pour over lentils and toss lightly.

Serve on crisp lettuce leaves or pour into scooped-out head of lettuce.

LIMA BEAN AND JELLYFISH SALAD
Serves 6

Ready Tray | 1   cup shredded jellyfish
| ½   cup shredded turnips or giant white radish
| 1½   cups cooked green lima beans, drained and cooled
| 2   tablespoons onion, chopped
| 1   teaspoon salt
| 1   tablespoon soy sauce
| 1   teaspoon sugar
| 1   tablespoon vinegar
| 3   tablespoons sesame oil

Wash jellyfish, place in lukewarm water and soak overnight. Drain, remove red matter and shred jellyfish.

Sprinkle turnips with 1 teaspoon salt and let stand for 20 minutes. Squeeze out resulting brine.

Mix shredded jellyfish and turnips with lima beans, onions, soy sauce, sugar, vinegar and sesame oil. Chill thoroughly before serving.

NAVY BEAN SALAD, COLORADO
Serves 4

Ready Tray	
½	cup dried white navy beans
	salt and freshly ground black pepper
½	pound fresh green string beans, cooked, cooled, drained
½	clove garlic, peeled
1	cup celery, finely chopped
¼	cup fresh green bell pepper, finely chopped
4	scallions, thinly sliced
1	bunch watercress, broken into bite-size pieces
2	small beets, cooked, peeled and sliced
3	hard-cooked egg yolks
1	teaspoon tarragon mustard
5	tablespoons olive oil
2	tablespoons wine vinegar
	Salt and freshly ground black pepper

Soak washed navy beans overnight in cold water to cover. Simmer gently until tender, approximately 2 hours. Drain, season to taste with salt and freshly ground black pepper.

Rub salad bowl with garlic. Add navy beans, string beans, celery, green pepper, scallions watercress and beets. Toss gently to avoid breaking beets.

Press egg yolks through a sieve, add mustard, oil, vinegar, salt to taste, and season highly with freshly ground black pepper. Blend until smooth. Pour over salad and toss lightly, serve on chilled salad plates.

HOT NAVY BEAN SALAD
Serves 4 to 6

Ready Tray	2	strips of bacon or salt pork, cut into ½-inch pieces
	⅓	cup onion, finely chopped
	3	cups boiled or baked navy beans
	½	teaspoon prepared mustard
	¼	cup wine vinegar
	¼	cup water
		Salt and freshly ground black pepper

Place bacon in a large skillet and fry until golden brown and crisp. Add onion and brown lightly. Add beans, mustard, vinegar, water, season to taste with salt and freshly ground black pepper and stir gently. Simmer slowly until the beans absorb the liquid. Serve hot!

Double the recipe if you wish to serve hot bean salad as the main dish.

LIMA BEAN-ANCHOVY SALAD
Serves 5 to 6

Ready Tray	1	cup large dried lima beans
	2½	cups boiling water
	1½	teaspoons salt
	¼	cup salad oil
	3	tablespoons wine vinegar
		Freshly ground black pepper
	1	cup celery, thinly sliced
	¼	cup green onions, sliced
	1	small can anchavies, finely chopped
	3	tablespoons mayonnaise

Rinse limas, add boiling water and boil 2 minutes, uncovered. Cover and let stand for 1 hour. Add 1 teaspoon salt, and boil slowly until beans are tender, approximately 1 to 1½ hours.

Blend oil, vinegar, remaining ½ teaspoon salt and pepper to taste.

Drain limas and pour the dressing over them. Let stand for 1 hour or longer. Drain, add celery, onion, anchovies and mayonnaise. Toss lightly and serve.

NAVY BEAN SALAD NORDIQUE
Serves 4 to 6

Ready Tray

1 pound dried navy pea beans
1 onion, finely chopped
3 whole cloves
2 sprigs fresh parsley, finely chopped
1 bay leaf
  Salt
4 tablespoons olive oil
2 tablespoons red wine vinegar
1 onion, finely chopped
1 teaspoon fresh parsley, finely chopped
2 kippered herrings, boned and cut in small pieces
  Salt and freshly ground black pepper

Soak washed beans in water to cover about 10 hours. Add one onion, cloves, parsley, bay leaf and salt to taste. Boil until tender; then strain and cool thoroughly in the refrigerator. Place in a salad bowl.

Blend oil, vinegar, onion, parsley, herrings and season to taste with salt and freshly ground black pepper. Pour over beans and toss gently but thoroughly until well blended. Serve on chilled salad plates.

LIMA BEAN ORIENTAL SALAD
Serves 4

Ready Tray
2	cups fresh lima beans, cooked and cooled
½	cup almonds, shredded
1	cup cheddar cheese, cubed
1	tablespoon pimiento, finely chopped
¼	cup dill pickle, finely chopped
⅓	cup yogurt
½	teaspoon prepared mustard
	Salt and pepper mill
	Lettuce leaves

Combine beans, almonds, cheese, pimiento, pickle, yogurt and mustard in a salad bowl. Season to taste with salt and freshly ground black pepper. Toss gently and chill.

Serve on crisp lettuce leaves.

LIMA BEAN HAM SALAD
Serves 4

Ready Tray
1	cup fresh lima beans, cooked and cooled
1	cup cooked cold beef or ham, cut in thin strips
½	cup raw apple, unpeeled and diced
½	cup cooked carrots, cooled and diced
	Salt and pepper mill
2	tablespoons sour cream
¼	cup whipping cream, whipped stiff
½	fresh lemon (juice only) or
	Equivalent amount of sweet pickle juice

In a salad bowl combine beans, meat, apple, carrots and season to taste with salt and freshly ground black pepper.

Thoroughly blend sour cream, whipping cream and lemon juice. Add to salad and toss lightly. Serve on cold individual salad plates.

PICKLED RED BEANS, IDAHO STYLE
Serves 4 to 6

Ready Tray	2	cups Idaho dry red beans
	6	cups water
	2	teaspoons salt
	⅛	teaspoon soda
	2	tablespoons butter or oil
	1	medium size whole onion, peeled
	1	cup salad oil
	¼	cup red wine vinegar
	1	teaspoon salt
	½	teaspoon dry mustard
	½	teaspoon coarse-ground black pepper
	½	teaspoon sugar
	1	cup sweet Spanish onions, coarsely chopped
	1	clove garlic, pierced with a wooden toothpick

Add beans to water in a heavy kettle. Bring to boiling point. Boil 2 minutes, remove from heat. Cover and allow to stand 1 hour.

Place beans and liquid over high heat, adding 2 teaspoons salt, soda, butter or oil and whole onion. Bring to boil, reduce heat to simmer. Cover tightly and cook beans until tender, but not mushy, approximately 2 hours. Remove onion and drain beans.

Combine until smooth the oil, vinegar, salt, mustard, pepper and sugar. Add this dressing and the coarsely chopped onions to beans. Toss together lightly. Bury garlic clove in the beans. Cover and allow to mellow in refrigerator 2 days to a week before serving.

Beans may be warm or cold when dressing is added, but warm beans absorb more of the dressing's flavor.

LIMA BEAN REMOULADE
Serves 4 to 6

Ready Tray	1½	cups cooked dried lima beans, drained and chilled
	1	hard-cooked egg, diced
	½	cup celery, diced
	3	tablespoons dill pickle, diced
	⅓	cup mayonnaise
	2	teaspoons fresh lemon juice
	2	teaspoons prepared mustard
		Dash tabasco sauce
	2	tablespoons fresh parsley, finely chopped
		Salt
		Lettuce leaves

Combine lima beans, egg, celery and pickle in a large salad bowl.

Blend mayonnaise, lemon juice, mustard, Tabasco and parsley.
Blend with lima beans in salad bowl. Season to taste with salt and
toss lightly. Serve over crisp lettuce leaves.

CURRIED LIMA BEAN AND SPINACH SALAD
Serves 4

Ready Tray	1	cup dried lima beans
	2	tablespoons butter
	1	small onion, finely chopped
	1	clove garlic, finely chopped
	1	teaspoon curry powder
		Salt and freshly ground black pepper
	1	cup consommé
	1	cup dry white wine
	½	pound spinach, cleaned and chilled
	1	tablespoon white wine vinegar
	2	tablespoons olive oil

Soak lima beans overnight in water to cover, drain.

Sauté onion and garlic lightly in butter. Add curry powder, season to taste with salt and freshly ground black pepper and stir until smooth. Add drained beans, consommé and wine. Cover and simmer until tender for approximately 45 minutes, drain and cool. Place in large salad bowl and add spinach, wine vinegar and oil and toss gently but thoroughly. Season to taste with salt and freshly ground black pepper, if more seasoning is desired.

Serve on individual chilled salad plates.

LIMA BEAN-TUNA SALAD
Serves 4

Ready Tray

1 cup cooked fresh lima beans, drained and cooled
1 cup tuna fish, flaked
2 hard-cooked eggs, coarsely chopped
⅓ cup walnut meats, coarsely chopped
½ dill pickle, finely chopped
1 tablespoon chives, finely chopped
½ cup mayonnaise
  Salt and pepper mill
  Crisp lettuce leaves

Combine beans, tuna, eggs, nuts, pickle and chives in a salad bowl.

Add mayonnaise and toss lightly.

Season to taste with salt and freshly ground black pepper.

Serve on crisp lettuce leaves on chilled salad plates.

GREEN SOYBEAN SALAD
Serves 4 to 6

Ready Tray | 1   pound green soybeans, shelled, cooked, drained and cooled.
½   cup celery, finely chopped
1   large tomato, diced
⅓   cup French garlic dressing
Salt and pepper mill

In a large salad bowl combine soybeans, celery, tomato, dressing and season to taste with salt and freshly ground black pepper. Toss lightly and chill thoroughly before serving.

KIDNEY BEAN AND SAUSAGE SALAD
Serves 6

Ready Tray | 2   cups red kidney beans, cooked and rinsed in cold water
½   pound sausage, sautéed lightly
½   cup rice, cooked, thoroughly blanched
½   cup celery, thinly sliced
1   green bell pepper, thinly sliced
3   sweet pickles, coarsely chopped
1   fresh tomato, peeled and diced
1   Bermuda onion, medium size, finely chopped
1   hard cooked egg, coarsely chopped
2   tablespoons fresh parsley, finely chopped
¼   cup olive oil
¼   cup wine vinegar
1   clove garlic, gently crushed
Salt and pepper mill
Pinch of oregano
Crisp lettuce leaves

Combine beans, sausage, rice, celery, green pepper, pickles, tomato, onion, egg and parsley in a large salad bowl.

Blend oil with vinegar, garlic clove and salt and freshly ground black pepper to taste and the oregano. When thoroughly blended discard the garlic clove and pour dressing over salad and toss thoroughly.

Chill the salad well before serving on crisp lettuce leaves on individual chilled salad plates.

BEAN SPROUT SALAD, KOREAN
Serves 6

Ready Tray

2	cups bean sprouts
¼	cup salad oil
2	tablespoons vinegar
2	tablespoons soy sauce
½	teaspoon salt
½	teaspoon freshly ground black pepper
¼	cup scallions, finely chopped
¼	cup pimiento, thinly sliced
2	tablespoons ground sesame seeds
1	garlic clove, finely chopped

Place bean sprouts in a large wooden salad bowl.

In a small bowl blend together thoroughly oil, vinegar, soy sauce, salt, pepper, scallions, pimiento, sesame seeds and garlic.

Pour the dressing over bean sprouts and toss gently.

Chill thoroughly for approximately one hour.

Serve on individual chilled salad plates.

NAVY BEAN SALAD
Serves 4

Ready Tray

½ pound boiled navy beans
1 large onion, thinly sliced
¼ cup fresh parsley, finely chopped
3 tablespoons olive or salad oil
3 tablespoons vinegar or lemon juice
Salt and freshly ground black pepper
Crisp lettuce leaves
4 slices ripe tomato
8 black ripe olives
Sour cream mixed with chives

Mix beans, sliced onions, parsley, oil, vinegar, salt and freshly ground black pepper to taste.

Serve on crisp lettuce leaves. Garnish with tomato slice and olives, top with a generous spoonful of sour cream.

MOLDED SPROUT SALAD
Serves 8 to 10

Ready Tray

1 packaged lemon-flavored gelatin
1⅔ cups hot water
4 tablespoons lemon juice
1 teaspoon salt
2 teaspoons chives, finely chopped
1 cup cabbage, shredded
1 cup carrots, shredded
1 cup celery, chopped
1 cup cooked fresh or canned sprouted soybeans

Dissolve gelatin in hot water. Add lemon juice and salt. Chill.

When partially thickened, add vegetables and pour into a large mold. Chill thoroughly until firm.

BEAN SPROUT SALAD, CANTONESE
Serves 6

Ready Tray		
	2	cups fresh bean sprouts, thoroughly washed and dried
	6	tablespoons salad oil
	2	tablespoons vinegar
	½	teaspoon sugar
	¼	teaspoon paprika
	¼	teaspoon dry mustard
		Salt and pepper mill
	2	cups cold cooked ham, cut in ½-inch cubes
	1	cup celery, thinly sliced
	2	tablespoons pimiento, finely chopped
	1½	cups cold cooked kidney beans, drained and cooled
	¼	cup fresh green spring onions, finely chopped
	2	tablespoons green olives, finely chopped
		Dash of soy sauce
	¼	cup sour cream
		Crisp lettuce leaves

Place bean sprouts in a salad bowl.

Blend together thoroughly oil, vinegar, sugar, paprika, mustard, salt and freshly ground black pepper to taste. Pour over bean sprouts and marinate for several hours. Drain.

Add the ham, celery, pimiento, beans, onions, olives, soy sauce and sour cream.

Toss lightly until well mixed.

Serve on crisp lettuce leaves.

SOYBEAN SALAD
Serves 4 to 6

Ready Tray

2	cups cooked soybeans, drained and chilled
¼	cup sweet pickles, finely chopped
2	tablespoons onion, finely chopped
¼	cup celery, finely chopped
2	hard-cooked eggs, diced
⅛	teaspoon salt
	Mayonnaise
	Crisp lettuce leaves

In a salad bowl combine soybeans, pickles, onion, celery and egg.

Add salt and enough mayonnaise to taste. Toss lightly and serve on crisp lettuce leaves.

SOYBEAN PERFECTION SALAD
Serves 8 to 10

Ready Tray

1	cup cooked soybeans, drained and cooled
1	cup raw cabbage, shredded
1	cup raw carrot, shredded
1	cup boiling water
1	cup cold water
1	package lemon-flavored gelatin
1	tablespoon green bell pepper, finely chopped
	Crisp lettuce leaves
	Mayonnaise

In a large bowl combine beans, cabbage, carrot and mix lightly.

Dissolve gelatin in the boiling water, add cold water and cool until partially thickened. Pour over vegetables, add chopped pepper and pour into a flat casserole. Chill thoroughly.

Serve on lettuce and garnish with mayonnaise.

BEAN SPROUT SALAD, SINGAPORE
Serves 4

Ready Tray
1	quart bean sprouts
1	pint boiling water
1	avocado, peeled and thinly sliced in rings
1	pimiento, thinly sliced in strips
1	teaspoon dry mustard
1	fresh lemon, using juice only
1	tablespoon tarragon vinegar
3	tablespoons pure olive oil
	Salt and pepper mill
	Pinch of sugar

Pour boiling water over bean sprouts and discard any bruised pieces. Drain and chill thoroughly.

Place a mound of chilled bean sprouts on individual chilled salad plates. Top with a chain of thin avocado rings and garnish with a small strip of pimiento.

Blend together until smooth, mustard, lemon juice, vinegar, olive oil, salt and pepper to taste and sugar.

Delicately ladle just enough dressing over mound to insure juiciness, but not sogginess. Serve immediately.

TOSSED BEAN SPROUT SALAD
Serves 4 to 6

Ready Tray

2	cups sprouted beans, steamed and chilled
1½	teaspoons salt
⅛	teaspoon pepper
¼	cup salad oil
1	tablespoon lemon juice
1	head lettuce, torn in bite-size pieces
1	large green bell pepper, coarsely chopped
½	cup onion, finely chopped

Mix salt, pepper, oil, lemon juice and small amount of onions. Chill.

Rub salad bowl with garlic if desired. Place bean sprouts, lettuce, pepper and onion together in salad bowl and toss lightly. Just before serving, add salad dressing which has been chilling. Toss lightly and serve on chilled salad plates.

BEAN SPROUT SALAD
Serves 6

Ready Tray

1	pound fresh bean sprouts
1	teaspoon salt
2	cups boiling water
1½	tablespoons fresh green onions, finely chopped
½	teaspoon sugar
1	tablespoon sesame oil
1	tablespoon white sesame seeds, browned and pulverized
3	tablespoons soy sauce
¼	teaspoon garlic, finely chopped
⅛	teaspoon cayenne pepper

Cook bean sprouts in salted boiling water for 2 minutes, drain thoroughly and chill.

Place in salad bowl and add green onions, sugar, sesame oil, sesame seeds, soy sauce, garlic and cayenne pepper. Toss lightly. Chill thoroughly before serving.

DILLED STRING BEAN SALAD
Serves 6

Ready Tray		
	2	packages (10 oz.) frozen string beans
	⅓	cup water in which beans were cooked
	3	tablespoons salad oil
	2	tablespoons fresh lemon juice
	¾	teaspoon dill weed
	¼	teaspoon basil
	1	whole garlic clove
		Salt and freshly ground black pepper
	1	cup celery, thinly sliced
		Fresh crisp lettuce leaves
	3	Hard-cooked eggs, sliced

Cook string beans in small amount of salted water until tender. Drain and cool thoroughly.

To the reserved liquid, add salad oil, lemon juice, dill, basil, garlic and season to taste with salt and freshly ground black pepper and blend thoroughly. Pour over the string beans and chill thoroughly.

When thoroughly chilled discard garlic clove, add celery and toss gently. Serve on crisp lettuce leaves and garnish with egg slices.

Garbanzo or any dried beans of your choice may be prepared in this manner, being sure that the garbanzo and dried beans are soaked overnight before cooking them.

SWEET AND SOUR RED BEANS
Serves 6 to 8

Ready Tray
5	cups cooked red beans, drained
⅔	cup granulated sugar
1	teaspoon salt
½	teaspoon coarse-ground black pepper
½	cup salad oil
⅔	cup cider vinegar or garlic-flavored wine vinegar
⅔	cup celery, thinly sliced
⅔	cup sweet onion, coarsely chopped

Place drained beans in a large bowl.

Blend sugar, salt, pepper, oil and vinegar thoroughly.

Add celery and onions to the beans.

Pour dressing over all and mix together lightly with a wooden spoon. Cover and chill in refrigerator for 24 hours before serving.

Serve very cold.

BEAN SPROUT SEAFOOD SALAD
Serves 4 to 6

Ready Tray
1	pound fresh bean sprouts
2	fresh spring green onions, finely chopped
1	cup cooked shrimp or crab meat, cut up or flaked
1	cup yogurt
1	teaspoon curry powder
1	clove garlic, gently crushed
1	tablespoon lemon juice
2	tablespoons soy sauce
	Artificial sweetener, if desired

Prepare bean sprouts by pinching off and discarding the hair-like roots.

Combine with onions and shrimp or crab meat.

Blend yogurt, curry powder, garlic clove, lemon juice, soy sauce and artificial sweetener. When smooth, discard garlic clove and pour dressing over bean sprouts and toss lightly.

Serve immediately on chilled salad plates.

GREEN STRING BEANS IN FRENCH DRESSING
Serves 4 to 6

Ready Tray

2	pounds green string beans, sliced lengthwise
1	teaspoon onion, finely chopped
1	teaspoon chives, finely chopped
1	teaspoon fresh parsley, finely chopped
	Salt and freshly ground black pepper
2	tablespoons wine vinegar
¾	cup olive oil

Boil string beans in salted water to cover until tender and drain.

Mix onion, chives and parsley together. Season to taste with salt and freshly ground black pepper. Add vinegar and set aside for several minutes. Add olive oil and mix thoroughly.

Pour over the cooked string beans and serve either hot or cold.

STRING BEAN SALAD, NIÇOISE
Serves 4

Ready Tray
2	cups cold cooked string beans, cut in 1-inch lengths
2	cups cold cooked potatoes, diced
4	anchovy fillets, chopped fine
4	black ripe olives, pitted and thinly sliced
1	tablespoon capers
2	fresh tomatoes, medium size, quartered
1	teaspoon fresh basil, chopped fine
3	tablespoons olive oil
1	tablespoon fresh lemon juice
	Pepper mill

Combine beans and potatoes in a salad bowl.

Add anchovies, olives, capers, tomatoes and basil and toss gently.

Blend oil with lemon juice and freshly ground black pepper to taste.

Add dressing to salad and toss lightly.

Serve immediately on chilled salad plates.

STRING BEAN—PARMESAN SALAD
Serves 4 to 6

Ready Tray
1	pound fresh string beans, cut lengthwise in 2-inch pieces
¾	cup boiling water
1	onion, finely chopped
½	cup olive oil
¼	cup wine vinegar
	Salt and pepper
½	cup grated Parmesan cheese
	Romaine lettuce leaves

Cook beans in water to cover until just tender and crisp. Drain, cool.

Combine onion, oil, vinegar and season to taste with salt and pepper. Blend until well mixed, add cheese and add to beans, toss gently. Chill thoroughly before serving. Serve over crisp Romaine leaves.

MIXED SALAD, INDONESIAN
Serves 6

Ready Tray

½	pound fresh string beans, cut in 1-inch lengths
½	pound fresh cabbage, coarsely shredded
1	pound fresh bean sprouts
1	cucumber, medium size, unpeeled and sliced
1	bunch radishes, sliced
2	hard-cooked eggs, sliced for garnishing
1	teaspoon salt
2	teaspoons brown sugar
1	teaspoon fresh lemon juice
1	teaspoon soy sauce
1	Bermuda onion, thinly sliced and sautéed lightly
2	cloves garlic, chopped fine, sautéed lightly
1	small hot red pepper, chopped fine
¼	pound finely-ground peanut butter
½	cup warm water from boiled vegetables

Parboil beans, cabbage and bean sprouts. Reserve cooking water. Drain and cool thoroughly. Place in large wooden salad bowl. Add cucumber and radishes.

Prepare dressing in a bowl by crushing and mixing the salt, brown sugar, lemon juice, soy sauce, onion, garlic, red pepper and peanut butter. Add the warm vegetable water and blend thoroughly.

Pour dressing over ingredients in salad bowl and toss gently but thoroughly. Serve on individual chilled salad plates and garnish with hard-cooked sliced eggs.

STRING BEAN SALAD
Serves 4

Ready Tray
1	pound string beans
3	firm tomatoes, quartered
1	large onion, thinly sliced
	Salt and freshly ground black pepper
1	clove garlic, whole
½	teaspoon thyme
½	cup olive or salad oil
¼	cup red wine vinegar

Put beans into boiling salted water and cook 15 minutes, or until tender. Drain and cool thoroughly.

Combine beans, tomatoes, onions, garlic, clove, thyme, salt and pepper to taste.

Blend the oil and vinegar until smooth, pour over beans and mix thoroughly. Chill in refrigerator before serving.

STRING BEAN SALAD, ITALIAN
Serves 4

Ready Tray
1	pound string beans, cut in half, cooked and cooled
4	tablespoons olive oil
2	tablespoons wine vinegar
1	Bermuda onion, thinly sliced
1	clove garlic, finely chopped
1	teaspoon fresh parsley, finely chopped
	Salt and pepper mill
	Lettuce leaves
1	hard-cooked egg, chopped
	Grated Parmesan cheese

Place beans in a salad bowl.

Combine oil, vinegar, onion, garlic, parsley, salt and freshly ground black pepper to taste.

Pour over beans and mix lightly. Cover and chill thoroughly in refrigerator.

Serve on crisp lettuce leaves on individual salad plates and sprinkle with egg and cheese.

TOSSED STRING BEAN SALAD
Serves 4

Ready Tray	2	pounds fresh string beans, cut through center lengthwise and in 2-inch lengths
	1	large onion, thinly sliced
		Salt and pepper mill
		Pinch of paprika
	½	cup olive oil
	½	cup wine vinegar
	½	cup water
	3	cloves garlic, mashed
	4	fresh mint leaves, chopped fine
		Crisp lettuce leaves

Cook string beans in salted water to cover until tender. Drain and cool thoroughly.

Place beans in large bowl and add onion, salt, freshly ground black pepper to taste, paprika, olive oil, vinegar, water, garlic and mint leaves. Mix thoroughly.

Cover and chill thoroughly in refrigerator.

Serve on crisp lettuce leaves.

THREE BEAN SALAD
Serves 6

Ready Tray

1 cup Great Northern large white beans, cooked and drained
1 cup Idaho's red beans, cooked and drained
1 cup fresh stringless green beans, cooked, drained and cut in 2-inch lengths
½ cup olive oil
½ cup wine vinegar
2 cloves garlic, gently crushed
   Salt and pepper mill
¼ teaspoon crushed oregano
1 large sweet Spanish onion, thinly sliced in rings
½ cup celery, thinly sliced
½ cup nippy Cheddar cheese, cut in ½-inch cubes
   Crisp lettuce leaves

Place drained warm beans in separate bowls.

Blend together thoroughly oil, vinegar, garlic, oregano, salt and freshly ground black pepper to taste. Pour enough dressing over beans in each bowl to cover. Cover and refrigerate overnight.

To serve, combine all beans with dressing in a large chilled salad bowl. Add onion rings, celery and cheese cubes. Toss together lightly. Serve in individual lettuce-lined chilled salad bowls.

Hot garlic-buttered French bread is the perfect partner, maybe not so elegant, but mighty good for dunking in what dressing may be left in one's salad bowl!

SWEET AND SOUR BEAN SALAD
Serves 8 to 10

Ready Tray
- 1 can (15½-oz.) cut green beans, drained
- 1 can (15½-oz.) cut yellow beans, drained
- 1 can (15½-oz.) red kidney beans, drained
- 1 small green pepper, chopped
- 1 small onion, chopped
- ¾ cup sugar
- 1 teaspoon salt
- ½ teaspoon pepper
- ⅓ cup salad oil
- ⅔ cup vinegar

Place first five ingredients in bowl and cover with dressing made with the seasonings, oil and vinegar.

Marinate for several hours, 24 if possible.

DRIED BEANS SALAD
Serves 4

Ready Tray
- 2 cups cooked dried beans, (your choice) drained
- ½ onion, medium size, thinly sliced
- 6 tablespoons vinaigrette
- 1 tablespoon fresh parsley, finely chopped

Drain beans and keep lukewarm. Separate onion rings.

In a salad bowl, combine vinaigrette, beans and parsley. Toss gently but thoroughly. Decorate with onion rings.

OMA KOENIG'S WAX BEAN SALAD
Serves 6

Ready Tray
2	cans wax beans, drained
1	small onion, finely chopped
3	tablespoons oil
1	tablespoon wine vinegar
½	teaspoon crushed Summer savory (Bohnenkraut)
	Salt and pepper

Mix onions, oil, vinegar, savory, salt and pepper. Let stand for ½ hour. Add beans and serve.

WAX BEAN SALAD WITH TRUFFLES
Serves 6 to 8

Ready Tray
3	pounds fresh yellow wax beans, cut into ½-inch lengths
	Salt
2	teaspoons savory, finely chopped
1	cup mayonnaise seasoned with salt and
1	teaspoon chopped savory
3	truffles, finely chopped
	crisp lettuce leaves

Cook beans in salted water to cover with 2 teaspoons savory for 10 minutes. Beans should be crisp. Drain thoroughly.

Add seasoned mayonnaise, toss gently and serve over crisp lettuce leaves. Sprinkle finely chopped truffles over the top.

STRING BEAN SALAD, CONSTANTINOPOLIS
Serves 4

Ready Tray	½	pound fresh green string beans
	4	large red peppers
	4	fresh tomatoes, medium size
	3	anchovies, chopped fine
	2	clove garlic, chopped fine
		Pepper mill
	6	tablespoons olive oil
	3	tablespoons wine vinegar

Boil green string beans in salted water, drain and cool. Remove strings and cut in 1-inch pieces. Put in salad bowl.

Bake peppers lightly in oven to dry skin. Then peel off skin, remove seeds, slice thinly and place in bowl with beans.

Wash tomatoes, blanch, peel and remove seeds° Add to peppers and beans.

Add anchovies and garlic.

Season to taste with freshly ground black pepper.

Add oil and vinegar and toss gently.

Serve with any broiled or roasted meat.

° To remove seeds from blanched and peeled tomatoes, cut in half and use tip of teaspoon to remove seeds.

VARIATIONS OF BEAN SALAD

Serve cold baked beans with sliced raw apple. Moisten with salad dressing of your choice and serve on crisp lettuce leaves.

Mix cold baked beans with diced cucumber, tender raw turnip, radish or celery. Moisten with your favorite salad dressing, toss gently and serve on crisp lettuce leaves.

To cold baked beans add a chopped green pepper, raw onion rings, sliced tomato and finely chopped parsley. Moisten with your favorite salad dressing, toss gently and serve on crisp lettuce leaves.

Try serving cold baked beans with chopped pickle or pickle relish and chopped cooked beets. Toss gently and serve on crisp lettuce leaves. Dressing may be added if desired.

Bits of leftover meat or fish with hard-cooked egg or cheese can make a baked bean salad an appetizing main dish. Serve slices of Boston Baked Brown Bread with this.

IV

Side Dishes and
Accompaniments

BLACK BEANS IN RED WINE
Serves 6 to 8

Ready Tray

1 pound black beans
1 onion, finely chopped
¼ pound salt pork, diced and scalded
1 cup beef bouillon
1 cup red wine
Salt and pepper
½ pint sour cream

Soak the beans overnight in water to cover. Place them in an uncovered saucepan in the same water with the onion and salt pork. Simmer gently until the skins curl back when a few in a spoon are blown upon. Drain. Place the beans, onion and salt pork in a bean pot or deep casserole. Add the bouillon and wine, season to taste with salt and pepper. Cover and bake in a 350° oven for 2 hours.

Serve with a bowl of sour cream to spoon over the beans.

99

BEAN CROQUETTES
Makes 6 to 8

Ready Tray
2	cups cooked red or pink beans, well mashed
2	tablespoons onion, chopped
½	teaspoon oregano
1	can peeled green chiles, finely chopped
4	tablespoons grated Parmesan cheese
	Salt to taste
⅓	pound Monterey Jack cheese, cut in small pieces
1	whole egg, beaten light with 1 tablespoon water
	Bread crumbs
	Oil for frying

Combine mashed beans, onion, oregano, chiles, cheese and salt. Mix thoroughly and form into croquettes, placing a small piece of cheese in the center of each. Be sure the cheese is well covered with the bean mixture.

Roll in crumbs, beaten egg, again in crumbs, and fry in deep oil until brown on both sides. Serve hot with chili sauce.

BEANCOTASH WITH MUSHROOMS
Serves 4 to 6

Ready Tray
1	pound fresh string beans, cut in 2-inch lengths
1	cup fresh shelled lima beans
4	ears corn, cut from the cob, fresh uncooked
1	can cream of mushroom soup, undiluted
	Salt and pepper

Simmer the green beans and lima beans separately, uncovered, in a little water until tender. Drain.

Combine the beans and add the corn and mushroom soup. Season to taste with salt and pepper and stir thoroughly.

Pour into a shallow casserole and bake in a 350° oven uncovered for 30 minutes, or until well heated and blended.

PURÉE OF BLACK BEANS WITH SOUR CREAM
Serves 4 to 6

Ready Tray		
	2	cups dried black beans
	6	cups water
	1	large onion, finely chopped
	1	green bell pepper, finely chopped
	½	cup olive oil
	1	bay leaf
	1	teaspoon salt
	½	teaspoon black pepper, freshly ground
	3	tablespoons red wine vinegar
	2	Italian red onions, finely sliced
		Sour cream

Boil the beans in water for 2 minutes. Remove from heat, cover and let stand for several hours.

Sauté the onion, pepper and garlic in oil until wilted and add to the beans.

Add bay leaf, salt and pepper and cook, covered, until the beans are tender, about 2 hours. Add a little water from time to time to keep the beans moist.

Add vinegar and purée beans in an electric blender or press through a sieve.

Reheat and serve with sliced onions and sour cream on top.

BLACK-EYED BEAN CROQUETTES
Serves 4 to 6

Ready Tray
2	cups cooked black-eyed beans
1	cup cooked smoked ham, finely chopped
½	cup cornflakes, finely crushed
1½	teaspoons onion, grated
1½	teaspoons fresh parsley, finely chopped
1	teaspoon salt
¼	teaspoon pepper
1	egg
¾	cup flour
¼	cup milk
2	cups cornflakes, finely crushed (additional amount)
	Tomato sauce

Mash the beans until soft. Add ham, ½ cup cornflakes, onion, parsley, salt, pepper and egg yolk. Mix thoroughly. Using generous table-spoon of mixture form into balls. Coat with flour. Beat egg white slightly with the milk. Roll the croquettes in this, then in the remaining cornflakes. Fry in deep fat and brown both sides. Drain on absorbent paper.

Serve with tomato sauce.

BLACK-EYED GREEN BEANS AND TOMATOES
Serves 4

Ready Tray
1	pound green black-eyed beans
2	cloves of garlic, unpeeled
2	fresh ripe tomatoes, peeled, seeded, minced and pressed through a sieve
1	ounce olive oil, more if desired
	Salt and black pepper, freshly ground

Place all ingredients in a kettle, cover with cold water, and cook over a slow fire. When water has partly evaporated, stir and cover the pot. There should be very little juice left when the beans are tender and ready to serve.

CRANBERRY BEAN SUCCOTASH
Serves 12

Ready Tray

1	pound dried cranberry beans
1	large can (46-oz.) tomato juice
2	teaspoons salt
2	tablespoons butter
1	package (10-oz.) frozen green beans, parboiled
1	green bell pepper, seeded and finely chopped
2	fresh tomatoes, medium size, coarsely chopped
1	can (12-oz.) whole kernel corn
2	tablespoons fresh parsley, finely chopped
1	onion, finely chopped
1	clove garlic, finely chopped
	Salt and freshly ground black pepper
½	cup grated Parmesan cheese

Wash the beans, then put in a large kettle with the tomato juice; bring to a boil, and simmer 2 minutes. Remove from heat and let soak 1 hour. Add salt and butter and simmer gently for 2½ or 3 hours, or until the beans are tender.

In a greased 3-quart casserole, mix together the cooked beans, green beans, green pepper, tomatoes, corn, parsley, onion, garlic, salt and pepper to taste. Sprinkle the top with grated cheese.

Bake in a moderate 350° oven, uncovered, for 30 minutes or until the cheese is delicately browned.

BRAISED BEAN CURD
Serves 4 to 6

Ready Tray
2	cakes bean curd
2	tablespoons dried shrimp, soaked and finely chopped
4	tablespoons flour
2	eggs
½	teaspoon salt
9	tablespoons oil for frying
2	tablespoons leek, finely chopped
1½	cups beef broth
2	teaspoons soy sauce
1	teaspoon salt
1½	tablespoons rice wine, or cognac brandy
1½	teaspoons cornstarch mixed with
3	tablespoons water

Wrap bean curd in cheesecloth and press gently to drain off excess liquid. Cut each cake into 8 square pieces.

Mix flour, eggs and salt to form batter.

Heat 6 tablespoons oil.

Coat bean curd squares with batter and fry on both sides until golden brown. Remove to a plate.

Heat 3 tablespoons oil and brown leek and shrimp. Add bean curd, broth and seasonings. Thicken with cornstarch mixture and serve hot.

GARBANZO BEANS, WESTERN STYLE
Serves 4 to 6

Ready Tray

1 can (1-lb.) garbanzo beans, drained
½ cup ripe olives, coarsely chopped
½ cup celery, finely chopped
½ cup ketchup
1 tablespoon Bermuda onion, finely chopped
1 tablespoon wine vinegar
1 teaspoon Worcestershire sauce
Salt and freshly ground black pepper

Place garbanzo beans in a casserole and add olives, celery, ketchup, onion, wine vinegar, Worcestershire sauce and season to taste with salt and freshly ground black pepper. Stir gently to combine the ingredients thoroughly.

Place in hot oven and bake for 20 minutes, until bubbly.

BROWN BEANS, SWEDISH STYLE
Serves 8 to 10

Ready Tray

2 cups dried brown beans
¼ cup corn syrup or molasses
4 tablespoons vinegar
Salt and freshly ground black pepper

Cook beans in 5 cups salted water for about 3 hours, or until tender.

Season with syrup or molasses, vinegar, and season to taste with salt and freshly ground black pepper. Cook for a few more minutes to blend the flavors.

BUTTERED GREEN BEANS
Serves 4 to 6

Ready Tray		
	1	pound fresh young green beans, cleaned and snipped
	1	teaspoon baking soda
	2	tablespoons butter
	¼	teaspoon salt

Cover beans with water in a saucepan, add baking soda and bring to a boil. Cook for 5 to 10 minutes. Drain, rinse with cold water and drain again.

Melt butter in a heavy saucepan. Add beans and salt. Cover and simmer slowly until beans are slightly browned.

GARBANZO BEANS IN TOMATO SAUCE
Serves 4

Ready Tray		
	1	pound dried garbanzo beans, soaked overnight
	1½	quarts water
	2	cloves garlic, finely chopped
	1	large onion, finely chopped
	⅓	cup olive oil
	2	cups canned tomatoes
	1	can pimientos, cut in large strips
		Salt and pepper mill

Drain garbanzos and add water, garlic, onion and oil; cover and cook gently for one hour. Add tomatoes and continue cooking until garbanzos are tender and tomatoes have cooked down. During the last 15 minutes of cooking add pimientos and season to taste with salt and freshly ground black pepper. Serve hot.

PRESSURE COOKER METHOD OF COOKING BEANS
Serves 4

Ready Tray

2	cups dried beans, your choice
½	teaspoon baking soda
¼	pound salt pork or bacon, cut in small pieces
1	onion, finely chopped
2	celery branches, finely chopped
1	green bell pepper, finely chopped
1	teaspoon salt
1	teaspoon prepared mustard
1	small red chili pepper, finely chopped

Soak beans overnight, covered with boiling water and baking soda. Next morning, drain and wash well with cold water.

Render salt pork or bacon in open pressure cooker over medium heat. Add onions, celery and green pepper and fry slowly until everything is cooked through. Add 5 cups of boiling water, beans, salt, mustard and chili pepper. Tighten cover and cook under pressure for 40 minutes. Let stand until pressure indicator goes down.

TENDER YOUNG GREEN BEANS
Serves 4 to 6

Ready Tray

1	pound fresh young green beans, cleaned and sliced French style
2	tablespoons butter
¼	teaspoon salt
½	cup water

Cook all ingredients together in a covered pan until water is diminished.

BEANS IN ROUX
Serves 4

Ready Tray | 1   can (1-lb.) cut green beans, drained
              | 2   tablespoons butter
              | 2   tablespoons flour
              | Salt and pepper

Melt butter in a heavy skillet. Add flour, stirring constantly. Add beans and season to taste.

GREEN BEANS, AU GRATIN
Serves 4

Ready Tray | 1   pound fresh tender Italian green beans
              | 3   ounces butter
              | 2   heaping tablespoons flour
              | 6   ounces milk
              | Salt
              | Grating of fresh nutmeg
              | 2   whole fresh eggs, beaten slightly
              | 2   tablespoons grated Parmesan cheese
              | 1   cup bread crumbs
              | Additional butter

Clean beans and cook in water to cover until tender. Drain and cut in 2-inch long pieces. Set aside and keep warm. Add 1 ounce of butter.

Make a smooth cream sauce with the 2 ounces butter, flour and milk. Season to taste with salt and add the nutmeg. Add beaten eggs and cheese, stir until smooth. Combine all with the beans.

Butter the inside of a large, round baking pan. Add bread crumbs and roll around so that they adhere to the sides of the baking pan.

Save the loose crumbs. Transfer the mixed beans and sauce to the baking pan, shaking this well for everything to settle, sprinkle with balance of bread crumbs and dot top with small pieces of butter. Bake in 400° oven for 45 minutes, cool for a few minutes before serving.

Good as side dish or may be used as a main entree.

GREEN BEANS WITH TOMATO
Serves 4

Ready Tray

2	pounds fresh semi-mature green beans, shelled
2	ounces prosciutto fat
1	small onion
1	celery branch
1	handful fresh parsley
1	heaping tablespoon lard
4	tomatoes, peeled, seeded and passed through a sieve
	Salt and freshly ground black pepper

Wash and place the shelled beans in cold water to boil. When near done, take the pot off the fire and set aside until the following sauce is ready.

Mince the prosciutto with the onion, celery and parsley, reducing all to a paste, and sauté over slow fire in the lard. When it reaches a golden color add the tomato juice and cook slowly until slightly thickened. Add the drained beans, season to taste with salt and freshly ground black pepper, continue cooking until the beans are thoroughly cooked and the sauce is fairly absorbed.

CARAMEL LIMA BEANS
Serves 4 to 6

Ready Tray | 1   cup large dried lima beans
½   cup sugar
1   teaspoon salt
4   strips bacon

Rinse lima beans, add 2½ cups water and soak for several hours. Then bring to a boil and simmer gently while preparing caramel.

Melt sugar in saucepan over moderate heat, stirring until light brown. Pour into boiling beans, add salt. Turn into casserole and cover. Bake in 300° slow oven for 2½ hours. An hour before serving, uncover, top with strips of bacon and bake until the beans are tender and bacon delicately browned.

Excellent with hot dogs or hamburgers for outdoor eating.

LENTILS AND FRUIT
Serves 6 to 8

Ready Tray | 3   slices bacon, diced
1   onion, finely chopped
1   pound dried lentils
2   quarts water
½   cup tomato sauce
    Salt and pepper mill
    Sliced bananas or
    Pineapple chunks

Fry bacon and onion, until bacon crisp and onion lightly browned. Add lentils, water, tomato sauce and season to taste with salt and freshly ground black pepper. Cover tightly and simmer gently until lentils are tender and liquid is thick, approximately 1½ hours. Serve with sliced bananas or pineapple chunks.

FRIED LIMA BEANS
Serves 4

Ready Tray
1	pound fresh shelled lima beans
5	tablespoons oil
½	cup water
3	tablespoons sugar
1	teaspoon salt
¼	teaspoon monosodium glutamate

Heat oil and fry lima beans until color becomes greener.

Add water and seasonings and boil for 5 minutes over high flame.

These may be served hot or cold.

ITALIAN GREEN BEANS
Serves 6

Ready Tray
2	packages (9-oz. ea.) frozen Italian green beans
3	tablespoons slivered blanched almonds
3	tablespoons butter
	Salt and freshly ground black pepper

Cook beans in small amount of boiling salted water until tender, drain and place beans in warmed serving dish.

In skillet, over low heat, brown almonds lightly in butter, stirring occasionally. Pour over beans and serve immediately.

BEAN SAUCE, HAWAIIAN
Makes 2 Cups

Ready Tray	1	can red kidney beans
	⅓	cup water
	1	clove garlic, finely chopped
	1	cup apricot jam
	1	teaspoon Kitchen Bouquet
	1	tablespoon chili powder
	½	teaspoon cinnamon
	½	teaspoon ground cloves
	⅛	teaspoon pepper
	½	teaspoon salt
		Pinch ground anise or fennel

Rub beans through a sieve or run in electric blender until smooth.

Combine remaining ingredients in saucepan, bring to a boil. Cook, stirring constantly, 5 minutes.

Add beans and simmer gently for 10 more minutes.

Excellent when served over rice or varied meats.

LIMA BEANS JAPANESE
Serves 6

Ready Tray	3½	cups fresh shelled lima beans
	½	cup sugar
	1	teaspoon salt
	1½	cups boiling water

Wash the beans, add boiling water and salt. Cook covered for 20 minutes, or until beans are soft.

Add sugar and cook for 5 minutes longer.

Serve hot or cold as a side dish.

Black beans or dried lima beans may be prepared in the same manner, but must be soaked overnight before cooking.

KIDNEY BEANS AND RICE
Serves 6 to 8

Ready Tray

1½	cups dried red kidney beans
2	teaspoons salt
1	cup uncooked rice
3	tablespoons soy sauce
2	tablespoons Sherry wine

Cover beans with water and bring to a boil. Remove from heat and let stand 1 hour, covered. Drain and add fresh water to cover and 1 teaspoon salt. Bring to a boil, cover and cook slowly over low heat for 1 hour, or until the beans are tender.

Wash the rice in several changes of water. Add 1 cup water and 1 teaspoon salt. Cover, bring to a boil and reduce heat, cook gently for 20 minutes, or until the rice is tender. Drain. Add to the beans. Add soy sauce and wine. Mix lightly, cover and cook over low heat until dry, about 8 minutes.

FARMER'S LIMA BEANS
Serves 4 to 6

Ready Tray	4	slices lean bacon, finely chopped
	1	tablespoon flour
	1	cup chicken broth
	2	pounds freshly shelled lima beans
	1	teaspoon grated orange rind
	⅛	teaspoon white pepper
	¼	cup heavy fresh cream
	1	tablespoon fresh parsley, finely chopped
		Salt to taste

Sauté bacon until transparent. Pour off all but 1½ tablespoons of the fat in the skillet, blend in flour until smooth and gradually add chicken broth. Cook, stirring constantly, until slightly thickened. Add the beans, orange rind and pepper. Cover pan and simmer gently over a low heat for 30 minutes or until beans are tender, stirring occasionally. Add the cream, parsley and salt to taste and serve hot when thoroughly blended.

BEANS, MAÎTRE D'
Serves 4 to 6

Ready Tray	2	cups dried white pea beans
	3	tablespoons butter
	2	tablespoons fresh parsley, finely chopped
		Salt and freshly ground black pepper

Soak washed beans in cool water overnight. Add a little salt and place over medium heat. Simmer approximately 2 hours or until tender. Drain.

Reheat in melted butter, add parsley and season to taste with salt and freshly ground black pepper.

GREEN LIMA BEANS
1 pound shelled beans makes 6 servings

Wash pods, drain and shell. Boil limas in small amount of water, 20 to 30 minutes. Add salt and pepper to taste when they are finished cooking. Serve like green beans with melted butter.

Or serve with Cheese Sauce, Hollandaise, or White Sauce.

Or combine with stewed tomatoes and onions and serve hot.

Or chill and serve in salads.

As purchased, 1 pound shelled beans equals 3 to 4 pounds in pods.

FRESH LIMA BEAN SOUFFLÉ
Serves 4

Ready Tray
1	cup fresh shelled lima beans
1	can condensed dried lima bean soup, undiluted
4	tablespoons flour
1	jigger rum
¼	cup sour cream
3	eggs, separated
	Salt and pepper

Put lima beans through the meat grinder, using the coarsest blade or purée them in the blender with the rum. Add soup, flour, sour cream, rum and yolks of the eggs.

Beat the egg whites until stiff and fold into bean mixture gently. Turn into greased casserole. Bake uncovered in 350° medium oven for 1 hour, or until the top springs back when lightly touched.

DHAL
An East Indian Lentil Gravy Sauce Served With Boiled Rice
Serves 4 to 6

Ready Tray
1	cup lentils
4	cups soup stock
2	tablespoons butter or margarine
1	tablespoon curry powder
3	green spring onions, minced
	Boiled rice

Wash the lentils, add to soup stock, cover and simmer gently until tender, 1½ to 2 hours. Then put the lentils through a sieve. The pulp should be the consistency of thin gravy.

Meanwhile, heat the butter, add the curry powder and onions and fry slowly for 1 minute. Add the lentils and simmer for 20 more minutes.

Serve with boiled rice.

Dhal made with split peas: use prepared split peas in place of lentils and proceed as for making Dhal.

REFRIED BEANS
Serves 6

Ready Tray
1	pound pink or red beans
2	quarts water
	Salt
7	ounces bacon drippings

Soak washed beans overnight in water to cover. Season to taste with salt. Cover and cook slowly until tender. Drain and mash beans until smooth.

Place 4 ounces bacon drippings in large skillet and heat until very hot. Add beans, cook until they are dry and have absorbed the fat. Cool.

To refry the beans: heat them in the balance of the bacon drippings. Mix, turn and stir frequently to avoid burning or sticking to the pan. Season to taste and serve very hot with a topping of sour cream, grated cheese, melted cheese or Mexican sausages which have been fried crisp.

MUNG BEANS AND RICE
Serves 6

Ready Tray	¾	cup dried mung beans
	1	teaspoon salt
	¾	cup uncooked rice
	¾	cup onion, thinly sliced
	3	tablespoons bacon fat
	1¼	cups stewed tomatoes
	⅛	teaspoon pepper

Cover beans with water and soak for 2 hours. Add ½ teaspoon salt and boil until tender. Drain.

Wash rice, add 1 cup water and ½ teaspoon salt, cover and bring to boiling point; reduce heat and continue cooking until water has evaporated and rice is dry.

Fry onion in hot bacon fat until tender, but not browned. Add rice, beans and tomatoes, cover and simmer until thoroughly heated. Season with pepper and additional salt, if desired. Serve hot!

CANDIED NAVY BEANS
Serves 4 to 6

Ready Tray | 1½   cups dried navy pea beans
2   canned pimientos, finely chopped
2   apples, medium size, unpeeled, cored and diced
Salt and pepper
2   tablespoons nutmeats, chopped
1   tablespoon brown sugar or honey
1   tablespoon butter or bacon drippings

Cook beans and drain. Add pimientos, apples, salt and pepper to taste and mix well. Place in well-greased baking dish, sprinkle with sugar and nutmeats. Dot with fat and bake uncovered in a hot oven for 10 minutes, or until thoroughly heated.

PEA BEANS BRETONNE
Serves 4 to 6

Ready Tray | 2   cups dried pea beans
1   large onion, thinly sliced
2   tablespoons butter
1   tablespoon flour
Salt and freshly ground black pepper

Soak washed beans in cool water to cover, overnight. Place over medium heat, cover and simmer gently, approximately 2 hours, or until tender. Drain. Reserve the liquid.

Sauté onion lightly in butter until golden brown. Add flour and brown. Add beans and ½ cup water in which the beans were cooked. Season to taste with salt and freshly ground black pepper, cover and simmer slowly 20 minutes.

SCALLOPED SOYBEANS
Serves 6 to 8

Ready Tray

3	cups cooked soybeans, drained
1	onion, finely chopped
1	cup celery, diced
½	green bell pepper, diced
½	cup tomato sauce
½	teaspoon salt
¼	cup boiling water
½	cup dry bread crumbs sautéed with
3	tablespoons butter

Place soybeans and seasonings alternately in a baking dish. Cover with buttered crumbs and bake slowly for 1½ hours at 350°

Serve from casserole.

REFRIED BEANS—MEXICAN
Serves 6

Ready Tray

6	tablespoons butter
2	cans, (1-lb. ea.) red kidney beans, thoroughly drained
1	teaspoon salt
¼	teaspoon chili powder
⅛	teaspoon ground cumin

Melt butter in large, heavy skillet. Add beans and mash thoroughly with a potato masher.

Add salt, chili powder and cumin. Place over low heat and cook until thick and bubbling, stirring often, to prevent sticking to bottom of pan.

PEA BEAN PURÉE
Serves 4 to 6

Ready Tray | 1 pound dried white pea beans
              | 3 tablespoons butter
              | Salt and freshly ground black pepper

Soak washed beans in cool water overnight. Add a little salt and place over medium heat. Simmer approximately 2 hours or until tender. Drain, but save some liquid.

Force through a sieve or food mill. Moisten with a little of the water in which the beans have cooked. The purée should be thicker than soup, but not as thick as mashed potatoes.

Reheat with butter and season to taste with salt and freshly ground black pepper.

Serve very hot.

REFRIED BEANS AND CHEESE—MEXICAN
Serves 8

Ready Tray | 1   pound dried pinto beans
              | 5   cups water
              | 1   pound medium-aged Monterey Jack cheese, cut in
              | small pieces
              | Crushed dried red chiles
              | Salt
              | ¼   pound butter
              | ¼   pound lard

Combine beans and water in a kettle. Cover and simmer until beans are tender, approximately 3 hours. Drain.

Put beans and cheese through the medium blade of a food chopper, or mash together thoroughly. Add chiles and salt to taste.

Heat butter and lard in a large frying pan, add bean mixture and cook over medium heat for 30 minutes, stirring often.

Good as a side dish or as filler in tortillas!

SCALLOPED GREEN SOYBEANS
Serves 6 to 8

Ready Tray
3	cups cooked green soybeans
3	cups milk
6	tablespoons fat
6	tablespoons flour
1	teaspoon salt
1	cup fine dried bread crumbs

Heat butter and lard in a large frying pan, add bean mixture and the bread crumbs. Put into baking dish, cover with crumbs and bake until brown at 350°.

BEAN SPROUTS AND FRIED CELERY
Serves 4 to 6

Ready Tray
6	stalks celery, cut in 1½ inch pieces
2	tablespoons peanut oil
2	cups bean sprouts
1½	teaspoons salt

Sauté the celery lightly in the oil for 2 minutes over a high flame. Add bean sprouts and salt and cook 2 minutes longer. Serve immediately.

BEAN SPROUTS AND GINGER
Serves 4

Ready Tray	3	tablespoons peanut oil
	1	pound fresh bean sprouts
	2	tablespoons soy sauce
	2	teaspoons sliced fresh ginger root
	½	teaspoon salt
	3	scallions, thinly sliced

Heat oil in a heavy skillet. Sauté the bean sprouts over a high flame for 1 minute, constantly stirring.

Add ginger, salt and cover, cooking for 3 minutes.

Add soy sauce and scallions and cook 2 minutes longer.

Serve immediately.

FRIED BEAN SPROUTS WITH GREEN PEPPERS
Serves 4

Ready Tray	1	pound fresh bean sprouts
	3	green peppers, seeded and thinly sliced
	5	tablespoons oil
	2	tablespoons rice wine or brandy
	1	teaspoon salt
	¼	teaspoon monosodium glutamate

Remove heads and tails of bean sprouts and soak sprouts in water until ready to use. Drain thoroughly before using.

Heat oil and fry bean sprouts and green peppers lightly. Add wine or brandy, salt and monosodium glutamate. Heat thoroughly and serve hot.

STRING BEANS OR WAX BEANS
1 pound serves 4

Wash thoroughly, remove tips and string running along outer edge. Cook in boiling water to cover, 15 to 20 minutes. Drain, season and serve with melted butter.

Or sauté with chopped bacon and sliced onions.

Or serve with Cheese Sauce, Hollandaise or White Sauce.

Or chill and use in salads.

STRING BEANS WITH ARTICHOKE HEARTS, AUSTRALIAN
Serves 4

Ready Tray

1 pound fresh green string beans, left whole
1 tablespoon butter
8 artichoke hearts, fresh or canned and drained
   Salt and pepper mill

Cook beans in boiling water until tender. Leave the beans whole. Drain, add butter and shake vigorously. Add artichoke hearts and place over low fire and heat thoroughly. Season to taste with salt and freshly ground black pepper.

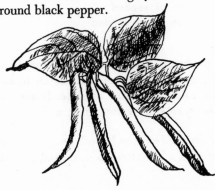

SOYBEAN CROQUETTES
Serves 4 to 6

Ready Tray		
	3	cups cooked soybeans, thoroughly mashed
	3	cups cooked soybean grits
	1	cup milk
	¼	cup flour
	¼	cup butter
	1½	cups celery, finely chopped
	2	tablespoons fresh parsley, finely chopped
	2	tablespoons onion, finely chopped
	1	tablespoon salt
		Eggs and crumbs for coating

Make a thick white sauce of the butter, flour and milk. Combine with other ingredients and shape into croquettes. Dip in beaten egg and roll in crumbs. Place on a greased baking sheet and bake in a hot 410° oven for 20 to 30 minutes.

Serve sour cream on the side.

FRIED STRING BEANS
Serves 4

Ready Tray		
	1	pound fresh tender string beans
		Salt
		Flour as needed
		Olive oil as needed

Trim and string the beans, if necessary. Wash and drain thoroughly. Place in a kettle, cover with water and season to taste with salt. Boil over fast fire to a point short of *done*. Drain and rinse them for a few seconds under cold water. Drain well.

Flour lightly and fry the beans in hot oil. Drain and serve hot. They can be decorated with a little tomato sauce and parsley.

SAVORY STRING BEANS
Serves 4

Ready Tray

1	pound fresh green string beans
¾	teaspoon salt
2	slices bacon, diced
⅓	cup onion, finely chopped
2	teaspoons fresh savory, finely chopped or
1	teaspoon dried savory leaves

Wash beans and drain. Trim ends and cut beans in 2-inch lengths. Place beans and salt in medium saucepan, in ½-inch boiling water and cook covered, 15 to 20 minutes or until tender.

Meanwhile, in a small skillet, sauté bacon, onion and savory until bacon is crisp and onion is tender.

Drain beans; toss lightly with bacon mixture until well combined.

Serve hot.

STRING BEANS, MAÎTRE D'HÔTEL
Serves 4 to 6

Ready Tray

2	pounds fresh green string beans, sliced lengthwise
3	tablespoons butter
1	tablespoon fresh parsley, finely chopped
	Salt and freshly ground black pepper

Boil string beans in salted water until tender and brain.

Add butter, parsley and season to taste with salt and freshly ground black pepper.

Serve hot.

PINTO BEANS WITH CHEESE
Serves 6

Ready Tray
1	cup dried pinto beans
3	cups water
1	teaspoon salt
2	slices bacon, cut in small pieces
1	onion, finely sliced
½	green bell pepper, seeded and finely chopped
½	pound sharp Cheddar cheese, cut in 1-inch cubes
1	fresh tomato, finely chopped
1	tablespoon chili powder
¼	cup dry white table wine
	Freshly ground black pepper

Wash the beans. Place beans and water in a large kettle, cover, bring to a boil and simmer for 2 minutes. Remove from heat and let soak 1 hour. Add salt to the beans, cover, and simmer for 2 hours, or until the beans are tender.

Fry bacon until crisp; remove from pan and sauté onion and green pepper in the remaining bacon drippings until limp. Stir in bacon, beans, cheese, tomato, chili powder, wine and pepper. Cook slowly, stirring constantly for 5 minutes, or until the cheese is melted.

SNAP BEANS SUPREME
Serves 4

Ready Tray
2	pounds fresh snap beans
2	egg yolks, beaten light
½	cup light cream
⅛	teaspoon fresh dill, finely chopped
⅛	teaspoon fresh savory, finely chopped
	Salt and freshly ground black pepper
	Pinch of freshly grated nutmeg

Cook beans in lightly salted water until just tender, or approximately 12 minutes. Drain and place in a saucepan over medium heat.

Blend egg yolks and cream together and pour over the beans. Add dill and savory and heat gently, but do not boil, until slightly thickened.

Season to taste with salt and freshly ground black pepper. Garnish with nutmeg.

STRING BEAN CUSTARD
Serves 4 to 6

Ready Tray	½	pound finely shredded string beans
	3	eggs, beaten light
	1¾	cups heated milk
	1	cup soft white bread crumbs
	¾	teaspoon salt
	⅛	teaspoon pepper
		Dash of nutmeg
	1	tablespoon butter
	1	cup hot water
		Paprika
		Buttered toast

Place string beans in a bowl. Add eggs, heated milk, bread crumbs, salt, pepper, nutmeg and butter. Mix thoroughly.

Fill custard cups ¾ full with the mixture; tie waxed paper over the tops. Put the rack in the cooker and set in the custard cups. If necessary make 2 layers by putting a wire rack or perforated aluminum inset over the first layer of cups. Pour in the hot water.

Close the cooker, bring to 15 pounds pressure and process 6 minutes.

Open cooker and unmold custard cups on buttered toast. Sprinkle with a little paprika.

BEAN STUFFED PEPPERS
Serves 8 or 9

Ready Tray
9	green bell peppers
1	teaspoon salt
2	cups soybean pulp*
½	cup diced celery, cooked in ¼ cup water
½	cup canned tomatoes
1	teaspoon onion, finely chopped
	Buttered bread crumbs

Remove seeds and inner partitions from peppers. Parboil peppers for 3 minutes in salted water. Sprinkle inside with salt.

Fill with mixture of bean pulp, celery, tomatoes and onion.

Cover tops with buttered crumbs. Place in greased pan and bake in a hot 410° oven for 30 minutes, or until the peppers are tender.

* The soybean pulp is prepared by pressing cooked soybeans through a coarse sieve or putting through food grinder.

STRING BEANS AND CELERY
Serves 4

Ready Tray
1	pound fresh string green beans, julienne
1	cup celery, finely sliced
2	tablespoons butter
	Salt
	Paprika

Cook beans in a little water until just tender. Drain.

Sauté celery in butter for 10 minutes, or until celery is soft.

Add celery to the beans and season to taste with salt. Sprinkle with paprika when serving.

STRING BEANS POULETTE
Serves 4 to 6

Ready Tray	2 pounds fresh green string beans, sliced lengthwise
	2 tablespoons butter
	2 tablespoons flour
	1 cup scalded water
	1 teaspoon fresh parsley, finely chopped
	1 teaspoon scallion or onion, finely chopped
	Salt and white pepper
	1 whole fresh egg yolk

Boil string beans in salted water until tender and drain.

Melt butter, stir in flour and blend until smooth. Add water and stir over low heat until thickened and smooth. Add parsley and scallion and season to taste with salt and white pepper.

Separate the egg yolk from the white. Beat the yolk lightly, adding 1 tablespoon of water and stir in a little of the hot sauce and blend well. Pour into the remaining sauce and blend thoroughly. Place over low flame but do not boil, and stir until the desired thickness is reached.

Pour the sauce over the green string beans and serve hot.

BRAISED STRING BEANS AND BAMBOO SHOOTS
Serves 4 to 6

Ready Tray |
1	pound fresh string beans, cut in 2-inch lengths
3	tablespoons peanut oil
1	cup bamboo shoots, thinly sliced
1	teaspoon salt
½	teaspoon sugar
¾	cup water

Wash beans and drain thoroughly.

Heat oil in a saucepan. Add beans and cook over low heat for 3 minutes, stirring often. Add bamboo shoots, salt, sugar, and water and cook over low heat for 10 minutes, or until the vegetables are tender. Drain if any liquid remains.

BEAN STUFFED TOMATOES
Serves 8 or 9

Ready Tray |
9	large tomatoes
1	teaspoon salt
2	cups soybean pulp*
½	cup celery diced, cooked in ¼ cup water
1	teaspoon onion, finely chopped
½	teaspoon green bell pepper, finely chopped
	Buttered bread crumbs

Remove pulp from center of tomatoes. Sprinkle inside with salt. Fill with mixture of pulp, celery, onion and green pepper.

Cover tops with buttered crumbs. Place in greased pan and bake in a hot 410° oven for 30 minutes, or until tomatoes are soft.

* The soybean pulp is prepared by pressing cooked soybeans through a coarse sieve or putting through a food grinder.

SCALLOPED EGGPLANT
Serves 4 to 6

Ready Tray

1	medium size eggplant
2	cups cooked tomatoes
1	small onion, finely chopped
½	green bell pepper, finely chopped
2	tablespoons bacon fat
2	teaspoons salt
¾	cup soft bread crumbs
¼	cup soy grits mixed with
¼	cup water

Pare the eggplant, cut into small pieces and cook with tomatoes for 15 minutes. Sauté lightly the onion and green pepper in ½ tablespoon of bacon fat, add to tomato and eggplant, with seasonings. Mix lightly. Melt remaining fat, stir in bread crumbs and add moistened soy grits. Place alternate layers of vegetables and soy grits-crumb mixture in a greased baking dish saving enough crumbs for the top. Bake for 45 minutes at 350°.

STRING BEANS WITH PARSLEY
Serves 8

Ready Tray

2	pounds fresh green string beans, cut in 2-inch lengths
	Chicken broth
⅓	cup melted butter
3	tablespoons fresh lemon juice
⅓	cup fresh parsley, finely chopped
	Salt and freshly ground black pepper

Place beans in a covered saucepan in chicken broth, enough to barely cover and cook until tender.

Drain the beans thoroughly, add butter, lemon juice, parsley and salt and pepper to taste and toss well. Serve immediately.

STRING BEANS A LA NIÇOISE
Serves 4 to 6

Ready Tray
1	pound fresh string beans, cut diagonallly
¼	cup olive oil
1	onion, thinly sliced
2	fresh tomatoes, peeled and quartered
½	green bell pepper, diced
1	stalk celery with tops, finely chopped
¼	cup water
	Salt and pepper to taste
1	bouquet garni, consisting of
	2 cloves, 1 bay leaf, 6 sprigs parsley and
	½ teaspoon chervil tied together in muslin
	or cheesecloth

In a skillet heat the oil and add onion, tomatoes, green pepper, celery, water, salt and pepper to taste and the bouquet garni. Cook until vegetables are tender and sauce has reduced a little, approximately 15 minutes. Remove the bouquet garni and stir in the beans. Cook until just tender and the beans are heated through. Serve at once while steaming hot.

STRING BEANS, VIENNESE STYLE
Serves 10

Ready Tray
3	pounds fresh green string beans
3	tablespoons fat
3	tablespoons flour
1	onion, finely chopped
1	tablespoon fresh dill, finely chopped
1	teaspoon fresh parsley, finely chopped
½	cup soup stock or vegetable stock
1	tablespoon vinegar
	Salt and pepper to taste
1	cup sour cream

Clean beans, cut off ends, wash and cut into 2-inch lengths. Cook in salted water about 20 minutes and drain.

Melt fat, blend in flour, add onion and brown. Add dill, parsley and soup stock, bring to a boil.

Add beans, vinegar, salt, pepper and sour cream. Bring to a boil again, stirring constantly and serve immediately.

STRINGLESS BEANS WITH EGG SAUCE
Serves 4

Ready Tray
1	can (1-lb.) blue lake or Kentucky Wonder stringless beans
½	cup beef broth*
2	tablespoons butter
2	tablespoons flour
	Salt
¾	cup milk
¼	teaspoon prepared mustard
¼	teaspoon Worcestershire sauce
½	teaspoon fresh lemon juice or vinegar
2	hard-cooked eggs, diced

Drain beans and add beef broth and heat thoroughly.

In a saucepan, melt the butter, blend in flour and season to taste with salt. Stir in milk and cook until mixture comes to a boil or is thickened, stirring frequently. Add mustard, Worcestershire sauce, lemon juice or vinegar and blend until smooth. Add the eggs.

Drain beans well, pour hot sauce over them and serve immediately.

* Substitute beef broth, consommé, or any meat or fowl stock for bean liquid to enhance flavor.

STRING BEANS PIMIENTO
Serves 4

Ready Tray | 1 package (10-oz.) frozen French-style green beans
2 tablespoons Bermuda onion, finely chopped
2 tablespoons olive oil
3 pimientos, cut in thin strips
1 tablespoon fresh parsley, finely chopped
Salt and freshly ground black pepper
1 can (4-oz.) sliced mushrooms

Cook beans in a small amount of water until tender, then drain thoroughly.

In a large skillet, sauté onion in hot oil until transparent. Add beans, pimientos, parsley, season to taste with salt and freshly ground black pepper. Add the mushrooms and the liquid. Heat thoroughly and serve hot.

STRING BEANS WITH PROSCIUTTO
Serves 4

Ready Tray | 1 pound fresh tender string beans, cut in
2-inch lengths
Salt
4 tablespoons butter
¼ pound prosciutto, thinly sliced, cut in
½-inch strips

Clean, wash and boil beans in plenty of salted water over hot fire. When tender, drain and rinse under cold water.

Melt butter in a pot, add the drained beans, stir well so that the beans absorb the full flavor, then add the prosciutto, toss gently and when thoroughly heated, serve hot.

A good side dish.

STRING BEAN SOUFFLE'
Serves 4 to 6

Ready Tray	1	pound fresh tender string beans
		Salt and pepper
	2	ounces butter
	1	heaping tablespoon flour
	½	cup milk
	4	egg whites
	1	handful grated Parmesan cheese

Trim and wash beans. Place in boiling salted water and cook over fast fire until tender. Drain and rinse under cold water for a few seconds. Mash beans in a bowl and pass through a sieve, making a thick purée.

Prepare the cream sauce: Melt the butter and blend in the flour until smooth. Add milk and cook gently until thickened. Pour over bean purée and mix thoroughly.

Beat the egg whites stiff and fold into the purée gently. Blend in the cheese.

Pour into a buttered casserole and place in a moderate oven, 350°F. and bake for 20 minutes, or until it raises full and becomes firm.

STRING BEANS, HUNGARIAN
Serves 4

Ready Tray
1½	pounds fresh string beans, cut in 2-inch lengths
1	tablspoon butter
½	teaspoon salt
	Pepper to taste
½	cup heavy sweet cream
¼	teaspoon nutmeg
¼	cup bread crumbs

Simmer the beans in a little water until just tender. Drain.

Place in an uncovered baking dish. Dot with butter, add salt, pepper to taste, nutmeg and cream. Cover with bread crumbs and bake in a 350° oven for 20 minutes, or until the top is lightly browned.

STRING BEANS STROGANOFF
Serves 6

Ready Tray
1½	pounds fresh string beans, cut in 3-inch lengths
1	ounce bacon fat
1	ounce flour
1	onion, finely sliced
	Salt
1½	cups broth
1	cup sour cream
1	tablespoon red wine vinegar
2	ounces bacon, diced and fried crisp

Boil the beans in salted water until just tender. Drain.

Fry onion in fat, blend in flour and gradually add broth, stirring smooth. Season to taste with salt. Add beans, bacon and simmer for a few minutes. Add vinegar and stir well. Just before serving, add sour cream and heat through, but do not boil. Serve with boiled potatoes.

STRING BEANS WITH MUSHROOMS
Serves 4 to 6

Ready Tray	1	pound fresh string beans, sliced lengthwise
	2	cups water
	½	teaspoon salt
	2	tablespoons butter
	½	pound button mushroom caps
		Salt and pepper to taste
		Fresh parsley, finely chopped

Simmer beans in the water and salt for 20 minutes or until tender, drain thoroughly and set aside.

Melt butter, season the mushroom caps to taste with salt and freshly ground black pepper and sauté until golden brown. Add beans and cook until they are coated with butter. Sprinkle with parsley and toss gently before serving. Serve hot.

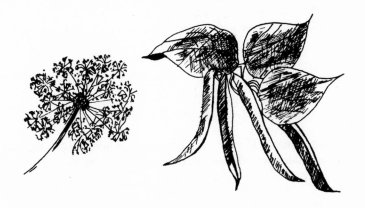

STRING BEANS WITH CREAM SAUCE
Serves 4 to 6

Ready Tray
- 1 pound fresh srting beans
- 3 ounces butter
- 1 tablespoon flour
- 6 ounces milk
- Pinch of nutmeg
- Salt and pepper

Prepare the beans for cooking, and boil them quickly in salted water until tender. Drain thoroughly and add 2 ounces butter.

Melt remaining butter and blend in flour until smooth. Add milk, nutmeg and season to taste with salt and pepper. Cook gently until a thick smooth sauce is obtained, than pour over the beans and stir gently. Serve hot.

STRING BEANS WITH OLIVE OIL
Serves 6

Ready Tray
- ½ cup olive oil
- 4 onions, finely chopped
- 2 pounds fresh string beans, cut in 2-inch lengths
- 1 cup tomato juice
- Salt and freshly ground black pepper

Heat the oil in a saucepan. Add onion and cook gently over low heat for 15 minutes, stirring often. Do not allow onions to brown.

Add beans, cover and cook over low heat for another 15 minutes, stirring occasionally. Add tomato juice and season to taste with salt and freshly ground black pepper. Cover and cook 15 minutes longer.

These may be served hot or cold, as desired.

V

Entrées and Casseroles

BAKED BEANS—SOUTH PACIFIC STYLE
Serves 6 to 8

Ready Tray
2	large cans pork and beans
½	pound ham or bacon, diced
1	large onion, finely chopped
1	can (9-oz.) crushed pineapple
1	teaspoon saté seasoning
¼	cup ketchup or chili sauce
1	teaspoon monosodium glutamate
	Salt and pepper to taste

Place beans in a casserole.

Cook bacon or ham until crisp. Drain off fat, reserving just enough to sauté the onion lightly. Add to the beans.

Add pineapple, saté, ketchup, monosodium glutamate and season to taste with salt and pepper. Stir gently and place casserole in a very slow 250° oven. Bake uncovered for 2 hours, or until thoroughly heated and blended and the top forms a nice brown crust.

Serve from the casserole.

BAKED BEANS, AUSTRALIAN STYLE
Serves 8 to 10

Ready Tray	1	pound dried green lima beans
	1	pound brown kidney beans
	1	can (No. 2) Boston baked beans
	¼	pound thinly sliced bacon, cut in 3-inch lengths
	1	tablespoon vinegar
	1	heaping tablespoon brown sugar
	2	teaspoons dry mustard
	1	tablespoon tomato sauce

Soak the lima and kidney beans for 24 hours in water to cover. Drain. Combine lima, kidney and baked beans and turn into a large casserole.

Lace the beans with bacon.

Blend vinegar, sugar, mustard and tomato sauce until smooth. Pour over the beans. Cover the casserole, place in 350° oven and bake 30 minutes; then reduce the heat to 250° and bake until the beans are tender. If too dry, add a small amount of liquid from time to time.

BAKED BEANS
Serves 4

Ready Tray	1	can (2-lb.) of baked beans
	1	small Bermuda onion, finely chopped
	1	tablespoon butter
	1	teaspoon dry mustard
	¼	cup ketchup
	¼	cup dry white wine
	8	strips of bacon

Place beans in a large casserole.

Brown onion in butter. Add mustard, ketchup and wine and blend until smooth. Pour over beans and stir gently.

Make a lattice work of the bacon over the top of the beans. Place casserole in a 350° oven and bake until the bacon is brown, approximately 40 minutes.

The bottle of chilled white wine used for the preparation of the above recipe will be a fine accompaniment for this entrée.

BAKED BEANS AND PINEAPPLE
Serves 6

Ready Tray

2	cans (1-lb. 4-oz.) pork and beans
½	pound bacon, finely chopped and fried crisp
2	onions, finely chopped
1½	teaspoons dry mustard
1	can (9-oz.) crushed pineapple
¼	cup chili sauce
	Salt and pepper mill

Combine beans, bacon, onions, mustard, pineapple and chili sauce. Season to taste with salt and freshly ground black pepper. Turn into a large casserole, place in a slow 275° oven and bake 1½ to 2 hours, uncovered.

Serve from casserole.

BAKED BEAN GLORY
Serves 6

Ready Tray

1 can (No. 2) baked beans
1 onion, finely chopped and lightly sautéed in olive oil
1 small can tomato sauce, Spanish style
1 cup unsweetened prunes, cooked, pitted and cut
1 cup ripe olives, pitted and sliced
½ cup grated Cheddar cheese

Mix all ingredients together lightly.

Place in a casserole or bean pot and bake for 45 minutes in a 350° oven, uncovered.

Serve directly from baking pot.

BAKED BEANS BARBECUE
Serves 6 to 8

Ready Tray

4 cups canned or home baked beans
¾ cup cooked pork, coarsely chopped
1 cup ketchup
2 tablespoons pickle relish
1 teaspoon Worcestershire sauce
1 dash Tabasco sauce
½ cup onions, finely chopped and lightly browned

In a large heavy skillet combine the beans, pork, ketchup, relish, Worcestershire sauce, Tabasco sauce and onions. Heat thoroughly over low heat.

VARIATIONS FOR BAKED BEANS

WITH MOLASSES: If you like the dish sweeter, add additional molasses or brown sugar.

MAPLE-FLAVORED: Substitute maple sugar or maple syrup for the molasses and brown sugar.

WITH TOMATO: Add ½ cup ketchup or chile sauce to the beans.

BEAN CURD WITH FISH
Serves 4

Ready Tray	1	pound fish, your choice, cut into bite-size pieces
	5	tablespoons peanut oil
	1	tablespoon rice wine
	2	tablespoons soy sauce
	1	stalk leek, diced
	3	slices fresh ginger root
	2	cakes bean curd, cut into 1-inch squares*
	4	tablespoons soy sauce
	1	tablespoon sugar
	2	tablespoons rice wine
	½	teaspoon salt
		Dash monosodium glutamate
	5	small red peppers, finely crushed

Sauté fish in oil until golden on both sides. Add 1 tablespoon rice wine, 2 tablespoons soy sauce, leek and ginger root. Cover and simmer slowly for 10 minutes.

Add bean curd and the balance of the ingredients, cover and simmer for 15 minutes. Serve hot.

* Bean curd: soft, white, custard-like paste made from soy beans. One cake equals 2 cups or ¼ of a pound. It spoils quickly in warm climates. May be purchased in any Chinese food store.

BEAN AND BEEF BAKE
Serves 4

Ready Tray | 3 slices bacon
2 cups onion, thinly sliced
½ pound ground beef
1⅔ cups canned pork and beans with tomato sauce
1 teaspoon salt
Freshly ground black pepper to taste
½ cup ketchup
2 tablespoons molasses

Cut each bacon strip in 3 pieces and fry slowly until crisp. Remove bacon; brown onion and ground beef in bacon drippings. Combine with remaining ingredients and mix well. Pour in 1½ quart casserole; bake in moderate 350° oven for 1 hour, uncovered.

Serve from casserole.

BLACK BEANS AND RUM
Serves 6

Ready Tray | 1 pound dried black beans
1 onion, medium size, thinly sliced
1 bay leaf
¼ teaspoon dried thyme leaves
1 celery branch, finely chopped
1 tablespoon fresh parsley, finely chopped
¼ pound salt pork, cut in ½-in. cubes
1 tablespoon butter
1 tablespoon flour
Salt to taste
¼ teaspoon Tabasco sauce
¼ cup dark rum
Commercial sour cream

Cover washed beans with cold water and soak overnight, covered, in the refrigerator. Next day, place in large kettle with soaking liquid. Add onion, bay leaf, thyme, celery, parsley, salt pork and enough cold water to make 2 quarts. Bring to boiling point, reduce heat and simmer gently until beans are tender, or approximately 2½ hours. Stir the beans several times while cooking. Drain beans and reserve the liquid. Place beans in a 2-quart casserole.

Preheat oven to 350°. Melt butter in a small saucepan, remove from heat. Stir in flour, salt, Tabasco and 2 cups of the reserved bean liquid. Reheat over low heat until mixture bubbles, add rum and pour over beans. Bake uncovered for 40 minutes.

Serve topped with sour cream.

BEAN CURD WITH GROUND BEEF
Serves 4

Ready Tray		
	2	cakes bean curd, cut into small triangles
	¼	pound ground beef
	3	tablespoons sesame oil
	1	clove garlic, finely chopped
	5	chili peppers, finely chopped
	1	tablespoon leek, finely chopped
	2	tablespoons soy sauce
	1	teaspoon sugar
	2	teaspoons cornstarch, mixed with
	½	cup beef broth
		Sesame oil

Heat oil and fry garlic, red peppers and leek until golden. Add meat and cook until meat changes color. Add bean curd, soy sauce and sugar. Cover and cook for 10 minutes. Then add cornstarch mixture, and stir until slightly thickened.

Turn out into serving dish, sprinkle with seasame oil and serve hot.

BEAN AND CHICKEN CASSOULET
Serves 8

Ready Tray		
	½	pound sweet Italian sausages
		Flour
	1	fat hen (4½-5 lbs.) cut in serving pieces
	3	tablespoons bacon fat
	3	cans (No. 2) baked beans with molasses
	12	small whole white onions, peeled
		Salt and pepper

Sauté the sausages quickly to remove excess fat.

Flour the chicken and sauté in bacon fat on both sides until brown. Place in a large casserole. Add beans, sausage, onions and season to taste with salt and freshly ground black pepper.

Cover and bake in medium 350° oven for 1½ hours, or until the chicken is tender.

BEAN CROQUETTES
Serves 4

Ready Tray		
	4	ounces dried beans, your choice
	1	ounce butter
	1	heaping tablespoon flour
	3	ounces milk
		Salt
	1	pinch nutmeg
	1	whole fresh egg, beaten
		Bread crumbs
		Oil

Boil beans until tender, drain and press through a fine sieve into a bowl.

Place butter and flour in saucepan over low heat, mix well and add milk, stirring until mixture thickens. Add bean purée. Season to taste with salt and nutmeg and stir gently until it thickens again.

Pour in a dish to cool and set firm. When cooled, turn onto a well-floured bread board and roll to ¾-inch thickness. Cut in pieces about 2 inches long and shape in a conical form. Dip in beaten egg and then in bread crumbs. Fry in hot deep oil to a golden brown. Serve hot.

BLACK BEANS CUBAN
Serves 6 to 8

Ready Tray
2	cups (1-pound) dried large black beans
5	cups cold water
1	teaspoon salt
4	cloves garlic, peeled
2	tablespoons oil
¼	teaspoon powdered sage
1	bay leaf
1	green bell pepper, seeded and finely chopped
1	Bermuda onion, peeled and finely chopped
1	tablespoon cidar vinegar
	Salt and freshly ground black pepper

Wash beans, drain, soak overnight in refrigerator with enough water to cover. Pour into 2-quart kettle, using soaking water, and adding water, if necessary, to stand over beans 2 inches deep. Add salt and 1 large clove garlic, cut in half. Cover kettle, let cook slowly until beans are tender, about 2½ hours. Drain.

Sauce: Heat oil in saucepan and add remaining 3 cloves garlic, (which have been mashed), sage, bay leaf, green pepper and onion. Place over low heat and simmer slowly; add vinegar and season to taste with salt, stirring occasionally and simmer until sauce has thickened. Pour sauce over beans and sprinkle with freshly ground black pepper to taste.

QUICK BEANS
Serves 8

Ready Tray | 2 | cans (16-oz. ea.) small baked beans
| 1 | small onion, diced
| ⅓ | cup brown sugar, firmly packed
| ⅛ | teaspoon nutmeg
| ⅛ | teaspoon cinnamon
| ⅛ | teaspoon liquid smoke
| ¾ | cup ketchup
| 2 | slices bacon, diced, fried out
| 1 | cup corn flakes

Drain about half the juice from the beans. Add onion, sugar, spices, liquid smoke and ketchup to beans. Mix well. Turn into a 2-quart casserole. Sprinkle top with bacon and corn flakes. Bake at 350° for 30 minutes, or until bubbly.

If you like beans served cold, mix and bake this casserole the day before because time improves the blend of spices and seasonings.

BEANS NEC NATAMA
Serves 4 to 6

Ready Tray | 2 | cans (No. 2) pork and beans
| ½ | large onion, finely sliced
| 2 | slices bacon, diced
| ½ | cup beer
| 1 | teaspoon prepared mustard
| ½ | teaspoon Worcestershire sauce
| 1 | tablespoon Sherry
| | Pepper mill

Sauté onions with bacon. When onions begin to turn brown, add the beer, mustard, Worcestershire sauce and wine. Simmer gently for 2 minutes, then add the beans and let them cook down. If more liquid is needed, add a little more beer. Add freshly ground black pepper to taste.

BEAN CURD WITH SHRIMP
Serves 4

Ready Tray	1	pound fresh shrimp
	1	teaspoon ginger juice
	½	teaspoon salt
	1	teaspoon cornstarch
	6	tablespoons peanut oil
	5	tablespoons leek, finely chopped
	2	cakes bean curd, cut into small squares
	1	tablespoon rice wine or cognac
	2	teaspoons salt
	½	tablespoon sugar
	2	teaspoons cornstarch, mixed with 2 teaspoons water

Wash and shell shrimp. Remove black vein from each. Dredge shrimp with ginger juice, salt and cornstarch.

Heat 3 tablespoons oil, sauté shrimp until golden brown on both sides and remove to a plate. Heat the balance of the oil and brown the leek. Add bean curd, sautéed shrimp and seasonings. Cover and boil gently for 10 minutes. Add cornstarch mixture to thicken and serve hot.

One cup sliced cucumbers may be added to this dish to add a little more zest!

MIXED BEAN POT
Serves 8

Ready Tray | 3 cans (1-lb.) beans (your choice) vegetarian baked beans, limas, pintos, kidney beans, garbanzos, etc.
2 tablespoons instant minced onions, soaked in 2 tablespoons water
2 tablespoons olive oil
¼ cup chili sauce
2 tablespoons molasses
¼ teaspoon hot mustard
2 teaspoons Hickory smoked salt

Empty beans into 2-quart casserole. Sauté onions in oil until tender, but not brown. Stir into beans along with chili sauce, molasses, mustard and smoked salt.
Bake in a 350° oven for 40 to 50 minutes, uncovered, until top is well browned. Serve from casserole.

BEAN ROAST
Serves 8

Ready Tray | 2 tablespoons green pepper, minced
2 tablespoons onion, minced
4 tablespoons bacon fat
4 cups leftover mashed baked beans
2 eggs, slightly beaten
2 cups bread crumbs
1 cup whole pack tomatoes
Salt and freshly ground black pepper
Paprika

Brown green pepper and onion in fat. Add beans, eggs, bread crumbs and tomatoes. Season to taste with salt and freshly ground black pepper and paprika. Stir gently and pack into greased baking dish. Bake uncovered for 30 minutes at 350° or until thoroughly heated.

Serve from casserole with gravy or tomato sauce.

BLACK BEANS, PORK AND RICE
Serves 4

Ready Tray

1½	cups dried black beans
¼	cup olive or salad oil
1	clove garlic, chopped fine
1	large onion, chopped fine
1	green bell pepper, choppd fine
	Salt and freshly ground black pepper
1	pound pork, lean, cut in ½-in. cubes
½	pound pork sausages, cut in ½-in. pieces
½	cup orange juice
½	cup dry red wine
2	cups cooked rice
6	slices orange with rind

Soak beans overnight in water to cover.

Heat olive oil in large skillet, add garlic, onion, bell pepper and brown lightly. Stir in 1 teaspoon salt, ¼ teaspoon freshly ground black pepper, beans and enough water to cover. Cover and simmer until tender or approximately 45 minutes, adding water, if necessary. Purée one cup of beans with a little liquid, and set aside.

Sauté the pork and sausages until golden brown. Stir in the orange juice and wine and season to taste with salt and freshly ground black pepper; simmer gently for 5 minutes. Remove meat from the sauce, add the puréed beans and simmer for 5 minutes.

Arrange rice around rim of your most attractive casserole, then place the beans, meat and sauce in the center. Garnish surface of rice rim with orange slices.

CHILLED BEAN CURD WITH SHRIMP
Serves 2

Ready Tray		
	2	cakes bean curd
	½	cup dried shrimp, soaked in lukewarm water for 10 minutes
	2	tablespoons leek, finely chopped
	2	tablespoons soy sauce
	¼	teaspoon monosodium glutamate
	1	tablespoon sesame oil

Place bean curd on plate and cover with shrimp. Sprinkle with leek, soy sauce, monosodium glutamate and sesame oil.

Chill thoroughly before serving.

BUTTER BEANS AND CHEESE
Serves 4

Ready Tray		
	3	tablespoons butter
	3	tablespoons flour
	1	teaspoon salt
	1½	cups milk
	1	teaspoon prepared mustard
	1½	cups grated American cheese
	½	teaspoon Worcestershire sauce
	2½	cups cooked dried butter beans
	1	large tomato, sliced in four slices

Melt butter and blend in flour and salt. Gradually add milk; cook and stir over low heat until sauce is thickened.Add mustard, cheese and Worcestershire sauce and stir until cheese melts.

Divide beans into 4 shallow individual baking dishes. Top with ¾ of the sauce. Place one tomato slice on top of each. Cover with remaining sauce and bake in 375° oven for 20 minutes, or until top is lightly browned and bubbly.

BUTTER BEANS AND LAMB
Serves 6

Ready Tray

1½	cups dried butter beans
1	shoulder of lamb, 3 to 4 pounds
1	onion
½	lemon
1	cup white table wine
1	teaspoon dried mint leaves
6	peppercorns
2	teaspoons salt
2	tablespoons flour

Rinse limas, cover with water and let stand.

Place lamb in large bowl. Slice onion and lemon over it. Add wine, mint and peppercorns. Cover and let stand several hours, turning occasionally. Drain lamb, reserving marinade; brown meat well in hot Dutch oven. Add marinade, drained lima beans and 1 cup bean liquid to meat. Sprinkle with salt. Cover tightly and cook slowly 2 hours, until meat and limas are tender, adding liquid if needed.

Mix flour to smooth paste with a little cold water and stir into kettle to thicken liquid. Boil thoroughly.

Slice lamb and serve with beans around the meat.

BLACK BEAN SAUCE AND SHRIMP
Serves 4

Ready Tray		
	1	tablespoon Chinese black beans, dried
	2	tablespoons cooking oil
	1	pound raw shrimp, shelled and deveined
	1	clove garlic, finely chopped
	1	tablespoon cornstarch
	½	cup water
	3	scallions, thinly sliced
		Salt and pepper

Wash the beans, drain and crush.

Heat oil in a heavy skillet and sauté shrimp and garlic for 5 minutes.

Mix cornstarch, beans and water together, add to shrimp, stirring constantly until thickened. Add scallions, season to taste with salt and pepper. Cover, reduce heat and cook gently for 5 minutes, or until all ingredients are thoroughly blended and the shrimp is tender.

BUTTER BEANS AND HAM
Serves 6 to 8

Ready Tray		
	1	meaty ham hock
	1	large onion, peeled and pierced with
	4	whole cloves
	3	cups large dried lima beans
	2	teaspoons salt
	1	teaspoon dry mustard
	1	tablespoon Worcestershire sauce
	¼	cup brown sugar, firmly packed

Cover ham hock with water and add the onion pierced with cloves. Simmer gently for 1 hour, covered.

Add rinsed lima beans and remaining ingredients and simmer until ham and lima beans are tender, approximately 2 hours.

Remove onion and ham rind before serving.

CRANBERRY BEANS AND HAM SHANK
Serves 4 to 6

Ready Tray		
	1	pound dried cranberry beans
		Salt to taste
	1	bay leaf
	1	small onion, pierced with
	2	whole cloves
	1	ham shank, cracked
	2	tablespoons butter
	1	teaspoon freshly ground black pepper
	2	cloves garlic, finely chopped
	2	beef bouillon cubes dissolved in
	1	cup boiling water
	1	tablespoon soy sauce
	4	tablespoons onion, grated

Cover washed beans with 6 cups cold water and soak overnight, covered, in the refrigerator. Next day place in a large kettle, and season to taste with salt. Add bay leaf, onion pierced with cloves and ham shank. Bring to boiling point; reduce heat and simmer gently until beans are tender, approximately 1½ hours. Drain thoroughly and reserve the liquid.

Trim meat from ham shank and cut into bite-size pieces. Sauté ham in butter in a skillet until well browned. Add pepper and garlic, dissolved bouillon cubes and soy sauce and blend well.

Preheat oven to 375°. Place beans in a large casserole. Stir in 1½ cups of bean liquid, ham mixture and grated onion. Bake, uncovered, approximately 40 minutes or until the top is brown and crusty.

OLD SOUTHERN HOPPING JOHN
Serves 4 to 6

Ready Tray
2	cups fresh cow-pea beans
2	quarts water
4	slices smoked "side meat," bacon or home smoked country bacon, ¼-inch thick and cut in half
1	cup uncooked brown or white rice
	Salt and freshly ground black pepper

Cover beans with 2 quarts water, slightly salted, add meat or bacon and simmer slowly until the peas are not quite done. Pour off all but 3 cups of cooking water. Add rice. Put all in top of double boiler, or cook over low heat in pan; remove from heat when rice is well steamed and tender. Season to taste with salt and freshly ground black pepper. Place bacon around rice and bean mixture while cooking. Rice may be cooked separately and blended with beans.

This may be served as entrée or side dish.

BUTTER BEAN LOAF
Serves 6

Ready Tray
2	(1 lb.) cans butter beans, drained
2	tablespoons melted butter
1	tablespoon cream
½	teaspoon salt
1	cup mild Cheddar cheese, grated
1	cup tomato juice
1	tablespoon flour

Put first five ingredients into blender and blend until smooth. Bake in a buttered 1-qt. casserole in a 350° oven for 20 to 30 minutes.

Sauce: Heat tomato juice and thicken with flour dissolved in water. Turn bean loaf out on a platter and pour sauce over it.

BUTTER BEANS AND PORK CHOPS
Serves 4

Ready Tray
4	pork chops
	Salt and freshly ground black pepper
1	tablespoon oil
3	cups cooked large dried lima beans
1	large onion, thinly sliced
1	large green sweet pepper, thinly sliced
⅓	cup hot water
⅓	cup ketchup

Sprinkle pork chops with salt and pepper to taste and brown in hot oil on both sides. Put lima beans, onions and green pepper in layers in a casserole. Sprinkle each layer with salt and pepper to taste. Top with pork chops.

Add hot water to frying pan, stir in ketchup and pour over pork chops. Bake in moderate 350° oven for 1 to 1½ hours, uncovered.

Serve from casserole.

BLACK-EYED BEANS AND BACON*
Serves 4 to 6

Ready Tray
1	pound black-eyed beans
½	pound bacon, finely chopped
3	onions, finely chopped
	Salt to taste
4	small red chili peppers, finely chopped or
5	peppercorns, crushed
1	clove garlic, finely chopped
½	cup white wine

Soak beans overnight in water to cover. Next day, add bacon, onions, salt, peppers and garlic. Cover and simmer gently until beans are just tender. Add wine and simmer until beans are very tender, adding more liquid if necessary to keep from being too dry.

* Sometimes called Black-Eyed Peas.

BLACK-EYED BEAN CASSOULET
Serves 6

Ready Tray
1	pound dried black-eyed Beans
1	very small fresh pork shoulder
12	small white onions
2	cloves garlic, finely chopped
1	cup beef bouillon
1	cup white wine
2	tablespoons soy sauce
1	bay leaf
½	teaspoon thyme
	Pepper to taste

Soak beans overnight in water to cover. Next day simmer 30 minutes. Drain.

Bake shoulder of fresh pork 30 minutes in a hot 450° oven. Place in bottom of a large casserole. Add peas, onions, garlic, bouillon, wine, soy sauce, bay leaf, thyme and pepper. Cover and bake in 350° oven for 3 hours, or until everything is tender.

FRESH CRANBERRY BEANS AND PASTA
Serves 6 to 8

Ready Tray

2	pounds fresh cranberry or Roman beans, shelled
6	fresh tomatoes, peeled and finely chopped or
2	cups canned tomatoes
2	tablespoons olive oil
4	ounces prosciutto fat, minced
1	handful fresh parsley, finely minced
½	teaspoon fresh basil, finely chopped or dried basil
	Salt to taste
1	pound pasta

Cook shelled beans in tap water with a little salt, until well done.

Pass the tomatoes through a sieve, saving the juice.

Place oil in a pan, adding the minced prosciutto fat and place over medium heat, stirring until fat is partly rendered. Add tomato juice, parsley and basil. Season to taste with salt and cook slowly until sauce begins to thicken.

Drain beans and add to the sauce, replace on the stove and simmer gently until sauce and beans are well blended, stirring often.

Cook the pasta in boiling water until tender. Strain and add to the beans and simmer for 10 minutes, stirring well.

If the sauce is absorbed, add a little boiling water in which the pasta was cooked. Serve hot.

BLACK BEAN-MEAT DINNER
Serves 6

Ready Tray		
	3	cups dried black beans
	7½	cups water
	½	pound dried beef
	3	scallions, finely chopped
	1	Bermuda onion, medium size, finely chopped
	¼	cup butter
	2	tablespoons olive or salad oil
	½	clove garlic, finely chopped
		Dash of cayenne
	½	pound smoked sausage links
	½	pound smoked ham
	¼	pound smoked tongue
	¼	pound sliced bacon, cut into 1-inch pieces
		Salt
		Hot cooked rice

Soak beans overnight in water, or boil in water for 2 minutes; remove from heat and let stand 1 hour.

Add dried beef. Simmer, covered, for 2 hours.

Sauté scallions, and onion in butter and salad oil until soft. Add garlic and cayenne, sauté a few minutes longer and set aside.

At the end of 2 hours, remove 3½ cups of the cooked beans. Add sausage, ham, tongue and bacon to the remaining bean mixture. Continue to simmer, covered, for 15 minutes. Mash the 3½ cups beans, combine with reserved sautéed mixture, add to meat mixture, and blend. Cook, stirring, until thickened. Season to taste with salt. Remove sausage, ham and tongue to serving platter. Slice or cut into serving pieces; top with some of the hot mixture. Serve remaining bean mixture in deep vegetable dish or tureen accompanied by hot cooked rice.

BROWN BEANS WITH TOMATO SAUCE
Serves 6

Ready Tray
1½	cups dried Mexican brown beans
3	cups water
2	teaspoons salt
½	cup fresh parsley, finely chopped
1¾	cups onions, peeled and sliced
1	tablespoon bacon or ham fat
1	cup tomato sauce

Wash beans, drain, cover with 3 cups water and refrigerate overnight. Next day add salt and bring to boiling point. Reduce heat, cook slowly until tender or approximately 2 hours.

Add parsley, onions, fat and tomato sauce and simmer gently until excess liquid has evaporated, approximately 45 minutes. Serve hot.

CRANBERRY BEAN SURPRISE
Serves 6 to 8

Ready Tray
3	onions, thinly sliced
1	tablespoon bacon fat
1½	pounds hamburger meat
3	cups tomato juice
3	cups cooked cranberry beans
½	teaspoon chili powder
	Salt and freshly ground black pepper to taste

Fry onions in bacon fat until golden brown. Add hamburger, breaking it up as it cooks for a few minutes, then add the tomato juice, beans, chili powder and season to taste with salt and freshly ground black pepper. Simmer gently for 30 minutes, until all ingredients are thoroughly blended and heated.

MOORS AND CHRISTIANS—CUBAN STYLE*
Serves 4 to 6

Ready Tray | 1½ | cups black beans, soaked overnight
4 | slices lean bacon, chopped fine and fried out
½ | clove garlic, gently crushed
1 | onion, finely chopped
1 | teaspoon chili powder
| Salt and cayenne pepper
| Meat stock or broth
2 | tablespoons mango chutney
2 | cups boiled rice

Boil beans in salted water until just tender. Drain. Add bacon, garlic and onion. Season with chili powder, salt and cayenne to taste. Add enough meat stock or broth to cover beans, add chutney and simmer slowly until the beans fall apart a little and make a thick, rich sauce. Pour over the pale, warm Christians. Seasoning is typically hot.

*Christians: Mound of boiled rice
Moors: Black beans

SPICY CRANBERRY BEANS
Serves 6

Ready Tray | 1 | pound dried cranberry beans
1 | onion, medium size, thinly sliced
¼ | pound salt pork, cut into small pieces
2 | teaspoons salt
1 | teaspoon whole cloves, tied in a piece of cheesecloth
1 | can (8 oz.) tomato sauce
1 | tablespoon Worcestershire sauce
2 | tablespoons molasses

Cover beans with water and soak overnight in the refrigerator. Next day place in large kettle, adding enough water to make 6 cups, onion, salt pork, salt and cloves. Bring to boil, then reduce heat, cover and simmer until tender or approximately 2 hours, stirring occasionally. Remove cloves and add tomato sauce, Worcestershire sauce and molasses and stir gently, simmering 30 minutes longer before serving.

FRESH FAVE BEAN BOURGUIGNON
Serves 6 to 8

Ready Tray

3	tablespoons butter
3	pounds of beef bottom, top round or rump of beef, cubed
½	pound salt pork, thinly sliced and finely chopped
	Flour
	Salt and freshly ground black pepper
2'	onions, thinly sliced
2	cloves garlic, cut in half
2	cups red wine
1	cup beef broth
1	bay leaf
1	sprig of fresh thyme
6	sprigs of fresh parsley
12	small white onions, peeled
6	carrots, peeled and sliced in large pieces
2	cups fresh shelled fave beans
½	pound fresh mushrooms, cut in half
1	additional tablespoon butter

Melt butter in a heavy skillet or Dutch oven. Sprinkle the cubed beef with flour, salt and pepper. Brown well on all sides in the butter. Add onions, garlic and salt pork and cook gently until onions are golden brown. Remove the garlic. Add the wine, broth, bay leaf, thyme and parsley. Cover tightly and simmer slowly for 2 hours, adding more red wine, if necessary.

Add the carrots, whole onions, cover and cook 30 minutes longer.

In another pan sauté the mushrooms with the fresh fave beans in butter until tender; then add to the meat, stirring gently. Serve hot.

CHILI CON CARNE BEANS
Serves 4

Ready Tray
1½	pounds cube steaks, (fat free—low calorie count)
1	teaspoon olive oil
2	teaspoons chili powder
½	teaspoon creole seasoning
1	can (8-oz.) tomato sauce
2	cups water
2	cups cooked red kidney beans, drained and cooled
2	teaspoons onion juice
⅛	teaspoon garlic powder
	Salt to taste

Cut cube steaks into 1-inch squares.

Brush an electric skillet with oil. Set at 350°. Add meat and sauté, stirring frenqueptly, until browned. Add chili powder and creole seasoning. Add tomato sauce, water, beans, onion juice and garlic powder. Bring to a boil. Reduce skillet heat to 300°. Continue to cook, stirring frequently until meat is tender and flavors are well blended, approximately 20 minutes. Season to taste with salt.

DEVILLED KIDNEY BEANS
Serves 6

Ready Tray
1	onion, medium size, thinly sliced
4	slices bacon, finely chopped
3	cups cooked kidney beans
2	cans (3-oz.) devilled ham
4	small carrots, thinly sliced
1	pimiento, finely chopped
1	tablespoon molasses
2	teaspoons salt
1	teaspoon dry mustard

Sauté onion and bacon in a large soup kettle. Add other ingredients and cook uncovered, stirring occasionally, for ½ hour or until all are thoroughly heated and the flavors have blended through.

BAKED KIDNEY BEANS AND HERBS
Serves 6

Ready Tray		
	2	cups cooked kidney beans
	1	large Bermuda onion, finely chopped
	2	cloves garlic, finely chopped
	1	green bell pepper, finely chopped
	4	tablespoons olive oil
	5	fresh ripe tomatoes, medium size, peeled, seeded and chopped
		Salt and freshly ground black pepper
	1	bay leaf
	½	teaspoon thyme
	2	tablespoons fresh parsley, finely chopped
	2½	tablespoons fresh chives, finely chopped
	4	tablespoons Parmesan chees, freshly grated

Place beans in a large casserole.

Sauté onion, garlic and green pepper in olive oil until just tender. Add tomatoes and simmer gently for a few minutes.

Season to taste with salt and freshly ground black pepper. Add bay leaf and thyme and cover. Simmer slowly for 30 minutes.

Pour sauce over beans and add the parsley and chives. Place in a 350° oven and bake until sauce is well blended with the beans and liquid has cooked down, for approximately 40 minutes.

Sprinkle with cheese and return to oven to brown lightly before serving.

GARBANZO BEANS AND CHICKEN
Serves 4

Ready Tray

1	3-pound fryer, disjointed
1½	teaspoons salt
¼	teaspoon powdered ginger
6	tablespoons butter
2	cups onions, finely chopped
2½	cups cooked garbanzo beans, drained
1	teaspoon ground cumin
1	tablespoon ground coriander
¾	teaspoon freshly ground black pepper
1½	cups chicken broth

Rub chicken with the salt and ginger.

Melt butter in a heavy skillet and brown chicken and onions. Add garbanzos, cumin, coriander and pepper. Cover and cook over low heat for 15 minutes, shaking the pan frequently. Stir in the broth, cover and cook 30 minutes, removing the cover the last 10 minutes. There should be very little gravy left when serving.

FAVE WITH PROSCIUTTO RINDS
Serves 4

Ready Tray

1	pound dry fave beans, split, shelled and washed
½	pound prosciutto rind, cut in 1-inch strips
	Salt
	Butter

No soaking of the beans is required. Place beans and prosciutto rinds in kettle, cover with cold water. Place over medium heat, cover and cook gently until tender. Drain whatever little water remains. Season to taste with salt and butter. Mash the beans thoroughly and serve with meat of your choice.

In the days when vicia faba was the only bean known in the lands bordering on the Mediterranean, the above recipe was the main dish of the people, as it still is today.

This dish may also be used as a side dish.

FAVE FAGIOLI MARTINESE
Serves 4

Prepare previous recipe of Fave Beans with Prosciutto Rinds

Ready Tray | 1 **pound of leaf chicory, radicchi, radiccheti or swiss chard, your choice**
Salt

Clean greens thoroughly. Approximately 40 minutes before fave beans and prosciutto rinds are cooked, place greens in a kettle with water to cover. Season to taste with salt, cover and cook gently until greens are tender. Drain thoroughly and cut greens in 1½ inch lengths. Add to the prepared mashed fave beans and mix lightly before serving.

Serve with meat of your choice, preferably a good, rich sausage.

This is a superb dish to an epicurean's delight. Although the greens are slightly bitter, they enhance the flavor of the combination.

HORSE BEANS, SPANISH STYLE
Serves 8

Ready Tray
⅓	cup butter
1	onion, finely chopped
½	cup flour
⅛	teaspoon ground nutmeg
	Salt and pepper mill
2½	cups chicken broth
3	egg yolks, beaten light
2	tablespoons fresh lemon juice, strained
¼	cup fresh parsley, finely chopped
2	pimientos, finely chopped
4	cups hot cooked horse beans

Melt ¼ cup of butter and sauté the onion lightly. Blend in the flour and nutmeg until smooth and season to taste with salt and freshly ground black pepper. Stir in broth slowly and cook until thick and smooth, stirring constantly. Reduce heat and add egg yolks, remaining butter and lemon juice, blending thoroughly. Remove from heat and add parsley, pimientos and beans. Stir thoroughly before serving.

CHILI CON CARNE FOR A CROWD
Serves 50

Ready Tray
1½	pounds onions, finely sliced
¼	pound fat
5	pounds ground beef
4	quarts tomatoes, chopped
½	pound celery, finely chopped
¼	pound green bell pepper, chopped
¼	cup A.1. Sauce
3	tablespoons salt
1	teaspoon ground cloves
5	teaspoons chili powder
3	quarts drained, cooked or canned kidney beans

Brown onions in fat and remove from 'skillet. Add meat to fat and brown. Combine with tomatoes, celery, green pepper and browned onions. When hot, add A.1. sauce, salt, cloves and chili powder. When thoroughly mixed, add beans and turn into one large or several smaller casseroles and bake at 300° uncovered for 45 minutes to 1 hour. This may be simmered on top of the stove, covered, for 1 hour.

KIDNEY BEAN CASSOULET
Serves 4 to 6

Ready Tray		
	1	pound dried kidney beans
	1	onion, coarsely chopped
	4	slices bacon
	½	pound sausage meat
	1	pound boneless veal, cut in small pieces
	2	cloves garlic, crushed
	1	teaspoon minced parsley
	½	teaspoon crushed rosemary
	1	cup dry red wine
		Salt and freshly ground black pepper to taste

Rinse beans and soak overnight in water to cover. Remove floaters, but do not drain. Add onion, bacon and more water, if needed to cover. Simmer gently, covered, 1½ to 2 hours, or until beans are tender, but not broken. Stir occasionally, adding water as needed in small amounts.

Meanwhie, form sausage into marble-sized balls and brown lightly on all sides in skillet. Remove sausage and all but 2 tablespoons of the fat from the pan. Turn veal into skillet. Add salt and pepper to taste, garlic, parsley, rosemary and wine. Cook slowly, covered, for 1 hour. Remove from heat and add sausage balls. Place beans and meat with sauce in beanpot or large casserole in layers, using 3 of beans and 2 of meat. Cover and bake in moderate 350° oven 1½ hours, removing cover the last ½ hour to form brown top crust. Serve from casserole.

BLACK-EYED BEANS—SOUTHERN STYLE
Serves 4

Ready Tray	2	cups dried black-eyed Beans
	1	onion, finely chopped
	6	slices bacon, diced
	1	teaspoon salt
		Pepper to taste
	1	teaspoon dry mustard
	¼	cup preserved ginger, chopped
	¾	cup honey

Soak beans overnight in water to cover. Next day cover and simmer gently until tender, approximately 1½ hours.

Sauté onion with bacon until onion is golden brown and bacon crisp. Mix with the beans, add salt and season to taste with pepper, mustard and ginger. Place in a deep casserole with a cover and pour honey over all. Cover and bake 1½ hours at 325°. Remove cover the last ½ hour of baking so the top will brown nicely.

HORSE BEANS AND WINE
Serves 4

Ready Tray	4	tablespoons olive oil
	1	onion, finely chopped
	1	clove garlic, finely chopped
	¾	cup smoked ham, cubed
	2	tablespoons fresh parsley, finely chopped
	2	cups fresh horse beans, shelled and washed
	1	cup white table wine
		Salt and pepper mill

Heat oil in heavy skillet, add onion, garlic, ham and parsley and sauté until onions are transparent. Add beans, wine and season to taste with salt and freshly ground black pepper. Cover and simmer gently until beans are tender, approximately 30 minutes.

GARBANZO BEANS WITH COCONUT
Serves 4 to 6

Ready Tray

1	pound dried garbanzo beans
3	tablespoons olive oil
3	cloves garlic, whole
½	pound ham, diced
⅛	pound bacon, diced
3	tablespoons onion, finely chopped
2	tablespoons green bell pepper, finely chopped
1	Spanish garlic sausage, cubed
½	cup tomatoes, peeled and seeded
2	sweet red peppers, sliced
½	teaspoon saffron
½	teaspoon paprika
2	small cans tomato sauce
½	cup coconut cream
2	tablespoons coconut pulp
½	cup plumped seedless raisins

Soak washed garbanzo beans in water to cover overnight. Next day season lightly with salt. Bring to a boil and simmer gently until tender. Drain and reserve the liquid.

In a deep pot heat the oil and brown the garlic lightly; discard garlic and add the ham and bacon and sauté lightly. Add onions, green pepper and cook until onion is transparent. Add sausage, tomatoes, sweet pepper, saffron and paprika and cook gently together for 3 minutes. Add tomato sauce, coconut cream, coconut pulp, raisins and the drained beans. Add a little of the bean liquid, just enough to make a smooth sauce. Simmer gently for 20 minutes, adding more bean liquid if necessary.

Serve hot with white boiled rice.

KIDNEY BEANS CARIBBEAN
Serves 6 to 8

Ready Tray		
	1	cup dried kidney beans
	3	cups water
	¼	pound salt pork
	2	tablespoons oil
	1	Bermuda onion, medium size, finely chopped
	1	clove garlic, finely chopped
	1	green bell pepper, seeded and finely chopped
	1	teaspoon salt
	½	teaspoon freshly ground black pepper
	½	teaspoon dried thyme
	1	cup rice
	4	plantains (or 4 underripe bananas)
	4	tablespoons butter
	½	teaspoon curry powder

Soak washed beans in water overnight. Next day, add salt pork and bring to a boil, reduce heat and simmer gently for 45 minutes or until beans are tender.

Heat oil, add onion, garlic and green pepper and sauté lightly until golden brown. Add salt, pepper and thyme and blend thoroughly. Add sautéed mixture and rice to beans and simmer gently until rice is tender, approximately 25 minutes.

Brown the bananas quickly in the butter and sprinkle with the curry powder.

Serve the beans and rice with the bananas as a garnish.

MEXICAN KIDNEY BEAN STEW
Serves 6

Ready Tray
3	large onions, peeled and sliced
3	cups cooked large kidney beans or Mexican frijoles
1	cup sweet green or red peppers, chopped
1	teaspoon salt
2	cups drained canned tomatoes
2	tablespoons butter or savory drippings
2	tablespoons chives, minced

Boil the onions in very little water until tender.

Add the cooked beans, peppers, salt and tomatoes. Cover and simmer until peppers are tender, about 25 minutes. Add the butter and serve sprinkled with the chives. Serve with chili sauce.

KIDNEY BEANS IN SOUR CREAM
Serves 4

Ready Tray
1	pound dried red kidney beans
3	large onions, thickly sliced
3	tablespoons butter
1	cup sour cream
	Salt and pepper mill

Soak beans overnight in water to cover. Simmer in the same water until the skins curl back when blown upon. Drain and place in a casserole with a cover.

Sauté onions in butter until golden brown. Add sour cream, season to taste with salt and freshly ground black pepper, stir thoroughly and pour over beans. Cover and bake in 350° oven for 2 hours, or until beans are tender.

KIDNEY BEANS BAKED WITH
SALT PORK AND TOMATO SAUCE
Serves 6

Ready Tray

3	cups cooked kidney beans
1	pound salt pork, cut in ½-inch pieces
1	large onion, thinly sliced
½	cup beef broth
½	cup concentrated tomato purée
½	teaspoon fresh basil, finely chopped
1	teaspoon dry mustard
	Salt and freshly ground black pepper

Place a layer of beans in a casserole. Place salt pork and onion slices over the beans.

Blend thoroughly the beef broth, tomato purée, basil, dry mustard and season to taste with salt and freshly ground black pepper. Pour over beans, just enough to cover. Place another layer of beans, pork and onion slices, repeat with last layer of beans. Cover with sauce. Cover the casserole, place in 250° oven and bake slowly for 3 to 4 hours. Remove cover the last ½ hour to allow the surface to brown gently before serving.

KIDNEY BEAN CASSEROLE
Serves 6

Ready Tray

2	Bermuda onions, medium size, finely chopped
4	tablespoons butter
4	cups cooked kidney beans, drained
¼	pound prosciutto Italian ham, thinly sliced
	Salt and freshly ground black pepper
1	tablespoon fresh parsley, finely chopped
½	teaspoon fresh oregano, finely chopped
	Broth or red wine
	Grated Parmesan cheese

Sauté onions in butter until golden brown. Add beans and mix gently.

Line a glass casserole with the prosciutto. Add a layer of beans with onions and season to taste with salt and freshly ground black pepper. Add parsley and oregano, another layer of prosciutto and cover with a layer of beans. Add a little broth or wine if it seems too dry. Place in a moderate 350° oven and bake 40 minutes.

Sprinkle with freshly grated Parmesan cheese before serving.

KIDNEY BEANS CHILI
Serves 4

Ready Tray	4	green bell peppers
	2	packages (3-oz.) cream cheese
	6	slices bacon, finely chopped
	2	onions, small, finely chopped
	2	teaspoons chili powder
	2	cans red kidney beans, large size

Cut tops off green peppers, remove seeds; parboil 5 minutes. Drain and cool thoroughly.

Cut cheese into halves, lengthwise, and place half inside each pepper. Replace tops and fasten with toothpicks.

Sauté bacon and onion until bacon is crisp and onions are lightly browned. Place peppers in the skillet and turn over on their sides. Cover and simmer gently for 15 minutes. Brown both sides.

Add chili powder to beans and pour beans over peppers, cover and simmer gently for 20 minutes, until heated thoroughly.

KIDNEY BEANS AND HAM IN RED WINE
Serves 4 to 6

Ready Tray		
	3	fresh spring green onions, finely chopped
	½	green bell pepper, seeded and finely chopped
	1	cup cooked ham, diced
	3	tablespoons butter
	1	small can tomato paste
	1	cup red wine
		Salt and pepper mill
	3	cups cooked kidney beans, drained
	6	bacon strips

Sauté onions, pepper and ham in butter until vegetables are limp. Add tomato paste to wine and blend until smooth. Add to onions and season to taste with salt and freshly ground black pepper. Cook gently for 8 minutes.

Place beans in a buttered casserole and cover with the sauce and lace bacon strips over the top.

Bake uncovered in 350° oven for 30 minutes or until bacon is crisp.

KIDNEY BEANS AND CHILI ITALIAN
Serves 6

Ready Tray		
	2	cups dried kidney beans
	¼	pound salt pork, cut into small pieces
	2	cloves garlic, finely chopped
	½	cup onion, finely chopped
	½	teaspoon dried oregano leaves
	1	pinch cumin
	2	cans (10½ oz. ea.) tomato purée
	2	tablespoons chili powder
		Salt and freshly ground black pepper
	6	slices fresh sour dough bread, ½-inch thick
		Parmesan cheese, grated

Cover beans with cold water; refrigerate covered, overnight. Next day, place beans and liquid in a large kettle adding more water, if needed, to make 5 cups. Bring to boiling point; reduce heat and simmer slowly, covered, approximately 1 hour or until tender. Drain thoroughly.

Sauté salt pork until crisp on all sides. Add garlic and onion and sauté until golden brown. Add oregano leaves, cumin, tomato purée, chili powder and season to taste with salt and freshly ground black pepper and add beans. Stir gently, cover and simmer over low heat until all ingredients are well flavored and blended, approximately 1½ hours. Stir occasionally during cooking time.

Serve over sour dough bread and let each guest sprinkle the freshly ground Parmesan cheese to his own taste.

KIDNEY BEANS AND HOCKS
Serves 4 to 6

Ready Tray
1	pound red kidney beans
1	large ham hock
3	large onions, coarsely chopped
4	small dried red peppers, finely chopped
¾	teaspoon salt
½	teaspoon garlic powder
¼	teaspoon cuminseeds

Soak washed beans overnight in water to cover.

Next day, add ham hock, onions, peppers, salt, garlic powder and cuminseeds and simmer slowly until beans are tender, approximately 2 hours.

Excellent entrée for a cold winter day, served with crunchy pieces of French bread and a salad.

SAUTÉED LENTILS
Serves 4

Ready Tray   2   cups quick-cooking lentils
                   Salt
               8   strips bacon, coarsely chopped
               8   fresh spring green onions, finely chopped
               1   tablespoon fresh parsley, finely chopped
                   Paprika

Place lentils in kettle and cover with cold water. Season to taste with salt, place over medium heat and bring to a boil; reduce heat and simmer gently until the lentils are tender, but not mushy. Drain thoroughly.

Place bacon in frying pan and sauté lightly; then add the onions and sauté until golden brown. Add lentils, parsley and a dash of paprika, blend well, cover and place over low heat and let cook for 20 minutes.

LENTIL AND EGG CURRY
Serves 6

Ready Tray   1   cup dried lentils
               3   tablespoons butter
               2   onions, thinly sliced
               1   tablespoon curry powder
               ¾   cup water
               1   teaspoon salt
               6   hard-cooked eggs, sliced

Soak the lentils overnight in water to cover. Drain well.

Melt the butter in a saucepan. Add onion and curry powder and sauté for 10 minutes, stirring often. Add the water and lentils. Cover and cook over low heat for 45 minutes or until lentils are tender. Add the salt and eggs and mix gently, cook for few minutes longer until eggs are heated through. Serve hot!

LENTIL CASSEROLE
Serves 6

Ready Tray | 2½ cups quick-cooking lentils
1 onion pierced with
3 whole cloves
1 bay leaf
1 teaspoon salt
6 thick loin pork chops
Salt and freshly ground black pepper
6 bacon strips

Place lentils in a kettle with onion, bay leaf and salt. Cover with cold water and place over medium heat and bring to a boil. Reduce heat and allow lentils to simmer gently until tender, being careful that they do not burst or become mushy.

Meanwhile, brown pork chops on both sides and season to taste with salt and freshly ground black pepper.

When lentils are tender, remove onion and bay leaf. Drain the lentils, reserving liquid.

Spread a layer of lentils on the bottom of an earthenware casserole. Place pork chops over the lentils, and cover the chops with another layer of lentils. Pour lentil liquid over the lentils and pork chops, place in a moderate 350° oven, and bake for 1 hour. Add additional boiling water, if necessary, to keep the contents moist.

Make a lattice of the bacon strips and place over the lentils during the last 20 minutes of baking to brown crisply.

Serve from casserole.

LENTILS WITH LAMB CURRY
Serves 6 to 8

Ready Tray
2	cups onions, finely chopped
2	cloves garlic, finely chopped
2	tablespoons curry powder
1½	teaspoons salt
½	cup yogurt
2	pounds lamb, cut in 1-inch cubes
2	cups cooked lentils, drained
¼	pound butter
4	cups boiling water

Pound together the onions, garlic, curry powder and salt. Gradually blend in the yogurt. Add lamb, tossing until well coated. Let stand for 1 hour.

Melt butter in a Dutch oven, add the undrained meat and cook over low heat for 15 minutes, stirring frequently. Stir in lentils and boiling water. Cover and cook over low heat for 35 minutes, or until the meat and lentils are tender and dry.

CURRIED LENTILS WITH ONIONS
Serves 4 to 6

Ready Tray
2	cups dried lentils
	Salt
½	cup butter
3	cups onion, finely chopped
1	teaspoon curry powder
2	tablespoons fresh parsley, finely chopped
1	hard-cooked egg, finely chopped

Cover lentils with cold water and soak overnight, covered, in the refrigerator. Next day, drain. Place in a large kettle, cover again with fresh cold water and season to taste with salt. Bring to boiling point; reduce heat, and simmer, covered, until lentils are tender or approximately 2 hours, stirring several times while cooking. Drain well.

Melt butter in a large skillet and sauté onion until golden brown. Add curry powder and lentils and cook over low heat, stirring continuously, until the lentils appear to be dry.

Sprinkle parsley and egg over lentils before serving.

LENTILS CREOLE
Serves 4

Ready Tray
1	cup dried lentils
2	teaspoons salt
2	tablespoons butter or margarine
2	sweet peppers, minced
1	onion, chopped
2	cups canned tomatoes
¼	teaspoon freshly ground black pepper
1	teaspoon sugar
	Cooked rice or noodles

Cover the lentils with boiling water and soak for 50 minutes. Then boil in salted water about 1½ hours, and drain.

Melt the butter in a saucepan: add green peppers and onions and cook slowly until the butter browns.

Add the tomatoes, pepper and sugar, then the lentils and simmer 30 to 40 minutes.

Serve over rice or noodles.

VARIATIONS FOR LENTIL CASSEROLE
Serves 6

DUCK: Combine lentils with 6 pieces or slices of cold roast duck. Add ¼ cup finely chopped onions, lightly sautéed in 3 tablespoons butter, 2 tablespoons chopped parsley and ¼ teaspoon dried thyme. Blend lentil liquid with 1 cup red wine and add to casserole. Bake as in Lentil Casserole.

HAM: Use 6 thin slices of baked Virginia ham with the lentils. Add 1 teaspoon dry mustard to the lentil liquid before pouring over lentils and ham.

WITH HAM: Combine cooked lentils with 1½ cups diced cooked ham, ½ cup finely chopped onion, and 1 finely chopped clove of garlic, all of which have been sautéed lightly in butter. Add 2 tablespoons finely chopped fresh parsley and ½ teaspoon dried thyme and blend well. Add ½ cup red wine to the liquid in which the lentils were cooked and pour over lentil and ham mixture. Place in a moderate 350° oven and bake as in Lentil Casserole. When the liquid in the casserole cooks down, add additional red wine.

WITH SALAMI: Place a layer of cooked lentils in the bottom of a buttered casserole, then add a layer of thinly sliced salami, another layer of lentils, and another of salami, finishing with a layer of lentils. Top with bacon strips. Bake in 350° oven 30 minutes.

WITH HOT SAUSAGE: Combine lentils with slightly cooked Italian (6) or Spanish hot sausages and bake as in Lentil Casserole. Sprinkle top of casserole with grated Parmesan cheese 20 minutes before removing from oven.

WITH PORK SAUSAGE: Combine lentils with 12 pork sausages which have been parboiled for 10 minutes. A layer of salami in the center of the casserole is a good addition. Proceed as in Lentil Casserole.

KIDNEY BEANS IN RED WINE
Serves 4

Ready Tray
1 pound dried kidney beans
1 large Bermuda onion, sliced in thin rings
6 slices bacon, cut in 1-inch squares
1 teaspoon salt
¾ teaspoon crushed pepper corns
2 cups Burgundy wine

Soak beans overnight in water to cover. Next day, drain and cover beans with boiling water.

Add onion and salt and cook until tender and water has boiled down about ½ the original amount, or approximately 1 hour.

Fry bacon to light brown, drain on paper and then add to the beans with the crushed pepper corns and wine. Cook for 20 minutes over medium heat.

Remove 1 cup beans, mash thoroughly and return to beans in kettle to thicken liquid. Serve very hot.

CORNED BEEF AND LIMA BEAN PIE
Serves 6

Ready Tray
1 can (1-lb.) corned beef
⅓ cup ketchup
1 whole egg
4 cups large dried lima beans, cooked and seasoned
  Cheese sauce

Mix together corned beef, ketchup and beaten egg. Line 8-inch pie pan with mixture and bake in moderate 350° oven for 25 minutes. Fill with hot lima beans and serve with cheese sauce.

LIMA BEANS AND BEEF, JEWISH STYLE
Serves 8

Ready Tray
1	cup dried lima beans
2	quarts water
2	pounds lean short ribs
½	cup coarse barley
1	tablespoon salt
1	teaspoon ground ginger
¼	teaspoon black pepper
½	clove garlic, finely chopped

Soak lima beans in water for 6 hours.

Meanwhile, place short ribs in a heavy kettle, add the beans and liquid, barley, salt, ginger, pepper and garlic. Bring to a boil quickly, cover, reduce heat and simmer gently for 30 minutes. Cut meat into serving pieces and return to kettle to blend all ingredients. Turn into a large casserole and bake in a slow 250° oven for 5 hours, covered.

BAKED LIMA BEANS FOR A CROWD
Serves 25

Ready Tray
5	pounds large dried lima beans
6	quarts water
3	large onions, peeled and each pierced with
4	Whole cloves
1	pound bacon
2	tablespoons salt
3	cans (8 oz. ea.) tomato sauce
1	cup molasses
½	cup vinegar
2	tablespoons dry mustard

Rinse lima beans, add water and soak overnight.

Cut bacon in chunks. Add onions, bacon and all seasonings to beans, bring to boil. Turn into large casseroles and bake, uncovered, in moderately slow 325° oven for 2 hours or until tender.

LIMA BEAN CASSEROLE ESPAÑOLE
Serves 6

Ready Tray
1	pound large, dried lima beans
½	cup fresh carrot, finely chopped
1	cup onion, finely chopped
1	cup celery, finely chopped
2	cups fresh tomato, finely chopped
	Salt and freshly ground black pepper
2	tablespoons butter
2	tablespoons olive oil
1	clove garlic, finely chopped
1	pinch dried thyme leaves
1	teaspoon dry mustard
1	teaspoon paprika
2	tablespoons dry white wine

Cover washed beans with cold water and refrigerate, covered, overnight. Next day place beans and liquid in a large kettle. Add carrot, onion, celery, tomatoes, season to taste with salt and freshly ground black pepper and cold water, if needed, to cover. Bring to a boiling point, reduce heat and simmer, covered, until the beans are tender, stirring often. Drain beans and put into large casserole.

Preheat oven to 300°. Add butter, oil, garlic, thyme, mustard and paprika to beans. Stir gently, cover and bake until beans are tender or approximately 2 hours, stirring several times during baking so that beans cook evenly. Just before serving, stir in the wine.

LIMA BEANS AND BEEF FLANK
Serves 4

Ready Tray
1	pound large dried lima beans
1	beef flank, cut in 1½ inch squares
2	tablespoons bacon fat
1	onion, thinly sliced
1	clove garlic, finely chopped
½	cup red Burgundy wine
1	teaspoon Worcestershire sauce
	Salt and pepper

Soak beans overnight in water to cover. Simmer gently in the same water until tender.

Sauté meat in bacon fat until browned on both sides. Place in a deep casserole.

Add beans with liquid, onion, garlic, wine, Worcestershire sauce and season to taste with salt and pepper. Cover and bake in 350° oven for 2 hours. Serve from casserole.

LIMA BEANS AND CHIPPED BEEF
Serves 4

Ready Tray
1	jar (2½ oz.) dried beef
2	tablespoons butter
1	tablespoon flour
1	cup commercial sour cream
2	cups cooked dried butter beans
¼	teaspoon Worcestershire sauce
1	tablespoon grated Parmesan cheese

Soften dried beef in hot water, drain well.

Melt butter, add beef and stir in flour. Add sour cream gradually and heat to boiling. Add remaining ingredients. Heat thoroughly before serving.

LIMA BEANS AND CHICKEN
Serves 6

Ready Tray

1	cup sliced chicken fillet
1	teaspoon rice wine or brandy
1	teaspoon cornstarch
¼	teaspoon salt
3	tablespoons oil
5	cups chicken broth
2	cups shelled lima beans, skins removed
1	cup bamboo shoots, cut into squares
1	cup canned champignon mushrooms, halved
2	teaspoons salt
½	teaspoon sugar
1	tablespoon rice wine or brandy
2½	tablespoons cornstarch, mixed with
2½	tablespoons water

Dredge chicken with 1 teaspoon wine or brandy, cornstarch and salt. Heat oil and sauté chicken fillet until golden brown. Remove to a plate.

Heat broth and add lima beans, bamboo shoots and mushrooms and bring to a boil. Add 2 teaspoons salt, ½ teaspoon sugar, 1 tablespoon wine or brandy, monosodium glutamate and the chicken fillet.

Thicken with cornstarch mixture and heat thoroughly. Serve hot.

BAKED LIMA BEANS SUPERB
Serves 8

Ready Tray
1	pound dried baby lima beans
2	teaspoons salt
1	cube (½ cup) butter
½	cup brown sugar, firmly packed
1	tablespoon prepared mustard
2	tablespoons molasses
1	cup commercial sour cream

Soak washed lima beans overnight in water to cover. Add 1 teaspoon salt and more water, if needed to cover, and simmer until tender. Drain.

Cut butter in chunks and add to hot beans. Stir in sugar, molasses, mustard and remaining 1 teaspoon salt. Fold sour cream into mixture carefully. Turn into 2-quart casserole and bake 45 minutes at 350° uncovered.

LIMA BEANS CON CARNE FOR A CROWD
Serves 25

Ready Tray
4	cups large dried lima beans
8	teaspoons salt
4	large onions, finely chopped
2	pounds bulk sausage
4	pounds ground beef
1	can (No. 10) tomatoes
4	tablespoons chili powder
1	pound grated American cheese
4	packages (3½ oz.) corn chips

Cook beans in 2½ quarts water with 4 teaspoons salt until tender, about 2 hours.

Cook onions in skillet with sausage and beef until meat is lightly browned. Stir in tomatoes, chili powder, remaining 4 teaspoons salt and undrained beans. Simmer slowly, covered, for 45 minutes. Top each serving with cheese and chips.

LIMA BEANS FERMIÈRE
Serves 6 to 8

Ready Tray

1	pound dried lima beans
3	cups water
2	teaspoons salt
¼	teaspoon pepper
¼	teaspoon savory
¼	teaspoon nutmeg
⅛	teaspoon fennel
⅛	teaspoon marjoram
⅛	teaspoon oregano
⅓	pound salt pork, ham or bacon, or a combination of any of these, cut into ¼-inch cubes, browned and drained
2	onions, peeled and sliced
4	carrots, sliced thin
¼	cup parsley, chopped

Cover washed beans with water and soak overnight. In the morning, put in a large kettle (add water, if needed), salt, pepper, savory, nutmeg, fennel, marjoram and oregano and simmer until semi-soft, 20 to 30 minutes.

Brown the onions and carrots in some of the bacon fat. Mix all ingredients together. Bake, uncovered, in a 3-qt. casserole in a 350° oven for about 1 hour, or until all vegetables are tender.

Stir in the chopped parsley.

LIMA BEANS, MEDITERRANEAN
Serves 6 to 8

Ready Tray

2 large onions, thinly sliced
2 tablespoons bacon fat
2 cups cooked dried lima beans, drained
½ pound salt pork, cut in 1-inch cubes and scalded
1 large can tomatoes
¾ cup green bell pepper, finely chopped
¾ cup celery, finely chopped
2 cups uncooked rice
   Salt and pepper

Sauté onion in fat until golden brown. Place in the bottom of a large casserole. Add beans, pork, tomatoes, green pepper, celery, rice and season to taste with salt and freshly ground black pepper, and 3 cups water. Cover and bake in 350° oven 2 to 3 hours, adding more liquid if too dry during baking period.

LIMA BEANS AND BRAISED LAMB
Serves 5

Ready Tray

1 pound dried baby lima beans
1 pound lamb stew meat, cut in 1-inch cubes
1 can (8-oz.) tomato sauce
1 teaspoon Bouquet Garni, crushed*
½ teaspoon salt
½ teaspoon smoked salt
   Toasted French bread slices

Soak beans in water to cover overnight. Do not drain.

Trim excess fat from meat and render a piece of the fat in a heavy kettle. Brown lamb well in fat on all sides. Add tomato sauce and undrained beans. Add bouquet garni and salt to the beans and lamb. Cover and simmer slowly until the beans and lamb are tender, approximately 1½ to 2 hours.

Serve in soup plates with toasted French bread.

° Can be purchased commercially.

LIMA BEANS AND MUSHROOMS
Serves 6 to 8

Ready Tray

1	pound large dried lima beans
	Water
3	tablespoons butter
¼	cup green bell pepper, finely chopped
1	can (4-oz.) sliced mushrooms
1	can tomato soup
1	tablespoon onion, finely chopped
1½	teaspoons salt
¼	teaspoon dried basil, crushed
	Grated Parmesan cheese
2	tablespoons dried, fine bread crumbs

Soak beans overnight in water to cover. Next morning add fresh water if needed to cover, and simmer 2 hours, or until tender. Drain.

Melt butter in skillet and sauté pepper until tender. Drain liquid from mushrooms; add water to total 1¾ cups; pour into skillet. Add soup, onion, salt and basil. Cook, stirring for 4 minutes after mixture comes to boil.

Pour over beans and add mushrooms and ¼ cup of the cheese. Toss lightly and turn into 2-quart casserole; sprinkle with bread crumbs mixed with 2 tablespoons cheese. Bake, uncovered, at 350° for 30 minutes, or until the top is delicately browned.

Serve from casserole.

LIMA BEANS AND PORK SHOULDER
Serves 4 to 6

Ready Tray

1	pound large dried lima beans
4½	teaspoons salt
2	tablespoons shortening
2	pounds pork shoulder, cut into 1-inch cubes
2	onions, medium size, finely chopped
2	bay leaves
¼	cup light brown sugar, firmly packed
½	teaspoon freshly ground black pepper

Cover beans with cold water and soak overnight covered in the refrigerator. Next day, add fresh water to make 6 cups liquid, and place in a large kettle with 2 teaspoons salt. Bring to boiling point; reduce heat and simmer, covered, 1 hour.

Place shortening in large skillet and sauté pork cubes until browned on all sides. Add to beans with the onion, bay leaves, sugar, pepper and remaining salt. Simmer gently, covered, until the beans are tender, stirring several times so that the beans are evenly cooked.

LIMA BEANS SAGEBRUSH
Serves 4 to 6

Ready Tray

4	cups large dried lima beans, cooked
1½	teaspoons salt
½	teaspoon freshly ground black pepper
1½	teaspoons sage
4	small onions, thinly sliced
1	cup grated American cheese
½	cup light cream
6	slices bacon

Put half of undrained beans in greased casserole. Sprinkle with salt, pepper and sage. Place onions in a layer over the beans. Add remaining beans and sprinkle with cheese. Pour in cream and top with bacon slices. Bake in moderate 350° oven uncovered for 30 minutes, or until bacon is crisp.

LIMA BEANS—NEAPOLITAN
Serves 6

Ready Tray

1	cup large dried lima beans
2½	cups boiling water
½	pound bulk pork sausage
½	pound ground lean beef
1	onion, finely chopped
1	clove garlic, finely chopped
2	cups canned tomatoes
1½	teaspoons salt
¼	teaspoon basil
⅛	teaspoon thyme
½	bay leaf
½	cup grated Parmesan cheese

Rinse limas, add boiling water and boil 2 minutes, uncovered. Cover and let stand while preparing remaining ingredients.

Brown sausage and beef together. Drain off excess fat. Add onion and garlic and cook until transparent, stirring often. Add tomatoes, salt, basil, thyme, bay leaf and soaked limas. Simmer gently for 2 hours or until beans are tender and sauce is thick. Stir in cheese before serving.

LIMA BEAN CASSEROLE
Serves 8

Ready Tray

2½	cups dried lima beans
2	tablespoons butter
1	large onion, finely chopped
1	green bell pepper, finely chopped
1	clove garlic, finely chopped
2	cups tomato purée
1	teaspoon Worchestershire sauce
	Salt and pepper mill
	Grated Parmesan cheese

Cook the beans in salted water to cover until tender. Drain.

Melt butter and sauté lightly the onion, green pepper and garlic. Add tomato purée, Worcestershire sauce and season to taste with salt and freshly ground black pepper. Simmer slowly for 20 minutes. Pour over the beans and stir thoroughly but gently.

Turn into casserole with alternate layers of beans and cheese. Bake in a moderate 350° oven for 25 minutes, uncovered, or until the top is delicately browned. Serve from casserole.

HERBED LIMA BEANS
Serves 4 to 6

Ready Tray

1½	cups dried butter beans
1	can (10½ oz.) consommé
½	cup tomato juice
1	clove garlic, finely chopped
1	carrot, finely chopped
1	onion, finely chopped
1	stalk celery, finely chopped
½	teaspoon oregano
¼	pound salt pork, thinly sliced

Rinse beans, cover generously with boiling water and boil 2 minutes. Cover and let stand for 1 hour. Drain and add undiluted consommé, tomato juice, vegetables, oregano and salt pork. Boil gently until tender for 1 hour.

Turn into casserole, arranging salt pork on top. Bake in 350° moderate oven, uncovered, for 1 hour.

Serve from casserole.

LIMA BEAN CASSOULET, AUSTRALIAN
Serves 8 to 10

Ready Tray		
	2	pounds dried lima beans
	1	pound lean pork, cut into one-inch pieces
	2	Hungarian sausages with paprika, cut into one-inch pieces
	4	pork sausages, cut into one-inch pieces
	½	pound bacon, cut in thick slices, and in one-inch pieces
	2	cloves garlic, finely chopped
	2	onions, finely chopped
	1	tomato, finely chopped
	1	cup white dry wine
		Salt and pepper to taste

Soak washed beans in water to cover overnight. Next day, add fresh water if needed, and boil slowly, uncovered, for 1 hour.

Sauté lightly until golden brown the pork, sausages and bacon. Add garlic, onions and tomato and sauté until onions are limp.

Remove beans from water, leaving a small amount of liquid. Mix with the meat mixture and turn into a large casserole. Add the wine, cover and bake in slow 275° oven for 2 hours, or until beans are tender and the meat flavor has blended thoroughly.

LIMA BEANS IN SAUCE LUISA
Serves 8

Ready Tray	1	small onion, finely chopped
	⅓	cup butter
	½	cup sifted flour
	⅛	teaspoon nutmeg
		Salt and pepper
	2½	cups chicken broth
	3	egg yolks, beaten
	2	tablespoons fresh lemon juice
	¼	cup fresh parsley, finely chopped
	2	pimientos, finely chopped
	4	cups large dried lima beans, cooked and drained

Cook onion in ¼ cup butter until soft. Blend in flour, nutmeg, salt and pepper to taste. Stir in broth and cook until thick, stirring often, approximately 10 minutes. Turn heat low and beat in egg yolks, remaining butter and lemon juice. Cook 3 minutes longer. Remove from heat and stir to a smooth sauce. Add parsley, pimiento and lima beans, cook until heated.

Makes 1 pint of sauce, which may be used for other vegetables.

LIMA BEANS AND FRANKS
Serves 6

Ready Tray	⅓	cup onion, finely chopped
	1	can (8-oz.) tomato sauce
	2	tablespoons syrup
	2	tablespoons vinegar
	1	teaspoon Worcestershire sauce
	1	teaspoon prepared mustard
	¼	cup ketchup
	4	cups cooked large dried lima beans
	6 or 8	frankfurters
		American cheese

Combine onion, tomato sauce, syrup, vinegar, Worcestershire sauce, mustard and ketchup and simmer gently for 5 to 10 minutes.

Pour over lima beans and turn into a casserole.

Slit frankfurters lengthwise, making a pocket, but do not cut completely through. Fill pockets with strips of cheese. Arrange over top of limas and bake in moderately hot 375° oven for 25 minutes or until hot and bubbly.

LIMA BEANS AND ORANGE MARMALADE
Serves 8

Ready Tray

2	cups large dried lima beans
1	large onion, peeled and pierced with
12	whole cloves
1	bay leaf
1	teaspoon salt
1	can (8-oz.) tomato sauce
⅔	cup orange marmalade
2	teaspoons vinegar
1	teaspoon dry mustard
	Generous dash of Tabasco sauce
8	strips of bacon
8	slices of orange

Rinse limas, add 5 cups boiling water and boil, covered, for 2 minutes. Cover and let stand for 1 hour. Add onion pierced with cloves to the beans with the bay leaf and salt. Cover and simmer gently for 1 to 1½ hours, until lima beans are tender. Drain.

Blend tomato sauce, orange marmalade, vinegar, mustard and Tabasco sauce. Pour over beans and mix gently. Turn into buttered casserole and top with bacon slices. Bake in moderately slow 325° oven approximately 1 hour, uncovered.

Serve from casserole and garnish with orange slices.

LIMA BEANS PILAF
Serves 30

Ready Tray	4	cups large dried lima beans
	4	pounds round steak
	2	cloves garlic
	6	teaspoons salt
	1	teaspoon pepper
	4	tablespoons chili powder
	4	tablespoons prepared mustard
	4	tablespoons salad oil
	4	large onions, finely chopped
	2	cups long grain rice
	1	can (No. 10) tomatoes
	1	cup sliced ripe olives
	4	cans (10½-oz. ea.) bouillon

Add rinsed limas to 2½ quarts water. Boil 2 minutes, remove from heat; let soak while preparing remaining ingredients.

Rub steak with garlic, 2 teaspoons of the salt, pepper and chili powder. Spread top side with mustard; cut in 1-inch squares. Heat salad oil, add onions and rice. Cook, turning occasionally with pancake turner, until golden brown.

In 2 large casseroles put a layer of meat squares; then rice (go easy on rice, it triples in bulk when cooked); tomatoes, and beans. Sprinkle with some of remaining salt, pepper and chili powder; repeat layers, ending with ripe olives. Casserole should be only ⅔ full to let beans and rice expand as they cook. Pour in as much beef bouillon as casserole will hold; cover, bake in moderate 350° oven about 3 hours, or until beans are tender. Add more bouillon, or water, from time to time.

LIMA BEANS WITH SOUR CREAM
Serves 4

Ready Tray

1	pound dried lima beans, soaked and simmered until tender
2	tablespoons maple syrup
1½	teaspoons dry English mustard
1	cup sour cream
	Salt and pepper
6	strips bacon, friend crisp and crumbled
½	teaspoon thyme and rosemary, mixed

Place the drained beans in a casserole and make a paste of the syrup, mustard, sour cream and season to taste with salt and freshly ground black pepper. Add to the beans and mix gently. Sprinkle top with bacon and herbs. Bake in medium oven, uncovered, for 30 minutes.

LIMA BEANS AND SPARERIBS
Serves 4 to 6

Ready Tray

2	cups large dried lima beans
2	pounds spareribs, cut in serving pieces
1	large onion, quartered
1	bay leaf
3	sprigs fresh parsley
1	teaspoon celery seed
2	teaspoons salt
¼	teaspoon freshly ground black pepper

In a large kettle combine all the ingredients, adding water to just cover. Simmer gently, covered, for 3 or 4 hours, or until desired consistency, adding more liquid if necessary. Before serving remove bay leaf.

Serve with a green salad and brown bread.

FRESH LIMA BEANS AND PORK CHOPS
Serves 6 to 8

Ready Tray
8	pork chops, fat trimmed
2	large onions, finely chopped
2	cups rice
3	tablespoons butter
2	tomatoes, peeled, seeded and chopped
2	cups fresh lima beans
6	cups chicken broth
1	bay leaf
1	pinch rosemary
	Salt and freshly ground black pepper
1	tablespoon fresh parsley, finely chopped

In a heavy skillet sauté the pork chops until golden brown. Remove the chops and cut the meat into bite-size pieces.

Sauté the onions and rice in the butter in a large heavy skillet until the onions are golden and the grains of rice have chalky edges. Add the tomatoes, beans and the reserved pork. Add the chicken broth, bay leaf, rosemary and season to taste with salt and freshly ground black pepper. Cover the pan and reduce the heat, simmer for 30 minutes without stirring. Fluff the rice with a fork.

Arrange the stew on a large platter and sprinkle with the chopped parsley.

TEXAS LIMA BEANS
Serves 4 to 6

Ready Tray
2½	cups large dried lima beans, cooked
1	package (3½ oz.) corn chips
1	can (8-oz.) tomato sauce
1	teaspoon chili powder
½	cup grated sharp American cheese

Drain limas, reserving ⅔ cup liquid. Crush corn chips lightly and arrange in layers with drained limas in 1-quart casserole, reserving some chips for topping.

Blend liquid, tomato sauce and chili powder and pour over all. Top with remaining corn chips and cheese. Bake in moderate 350° oven, uncovered, for 30 minutes.

LIMA BEAN STROGANOFF
Serves 6 to 8

Ready Tray
1	pound large dried lima beans
3	teaspoons salt
¼	cup butter
¾	cup onion, finely chopped
½	pound fresh mushrooms, thinly sliced
1	tablespoon flour
1	tablespoon paprika
2	cups commercial sour cream
2	tablespoons fresh parsley, finely chopped

Cover beans with cold water and refrigerate, covered, overnight. Next day place beans and liquid in a large kettle and add enough cold water, if necessary, to cover. Add 1 teaspoon salt and bring to a boiling point, reduce heat and simmer, uncovered, until beans are tender or approximately for 1½ hours. Stir beans several times while cooking. Drain well.

Place butter in a large skillet and sauté the onion until golden brown. Add mushrooms and cook for 5 minutes, stirring the whole time, then remove from heat. Blend in until smooth the flour and paprika. Return to heat and cook for 3 more minutes or until bubbling.

Add drained beans, remaining salt and sour cream. Heat gently, but do not boil. Sprinkle the top with parsley before serving. Very nice with veal chops.

SPANISH LIMA BEAN AND LAMB STEW
Serves 4 to 6

Ready Tray

1	cup large dried lima beans
1	teaspoon salt
1	quart water
5	slices bacon, cut into small pieces
2	pounds cubed lamb stew meat
9	small onions, peeled
1	green bell pepper, coarsely chopped
4	stalks celery, sliced
2	cups tomato juice
½	teaspoon sage
½	teaspoon thyme
1	tablespoon vinegar
	Salt and pepper

Rinse lima beans and add to boiling salted water; cook for 1 hour covered.

Brown bacon. Rub lamb with salt and pepper and brown in hot bacon fat. Add onions, green pepper and celery to lamb and sauté lightly until vegetables are limp. Stir in remaining ingredients and lima beans with the liquid. Cover and cook slowly for 1 hour.

MUNG BEANS WITH PORK
Serves 6

Ready Tray

1	cup dried mung beans
1½	teaspoons salt
¾	pound lean pork shoulder, cut in thin strips
3	cloves garlic, finely chopped
½	cup onion, finely chopped
2	large tomatoes, coarsely chopped
¼	teaspoon pepper

Cover beans with water and boil for 10 minutes. Drain, cover with cold water and hand-rub the hulls off the beans. Drain, cover the beans with water, add ½ teaspoon salt and boil until tender. Drain beans and reserve liquid.

Trim fat from pork and render. Fry pork strips in fat until brown. Remove meat and brown the garlic and onions. Add tomatoes and simmer slowly for 5 minutes. Add meat and beans and reserved liquid. Add salt and pepper and simmer slowly for 20 minutes. Serve hot.

BAKED NAVY BEANS AND BEER
Serves 10 or 12

Ready Tray

3	cups dried navy beans
¾	pound salt pork, sliced
4	cups beer
¾	cup molasses
2	teaspoons dry mustard
2	teaspoons salt
¼	cup onions, grated

Wash the beans, cover with water and bring to a boil. Remove from heat and let soak for 1 hour. Drain, add fresh water to cover and bring to a boil. Cover and cook over low heat for 1 hour. Drain, reserving the liquid.

Use an earthenware bean pot or heavy casserole. Line the bottom with half the salt pork. Put the beans on top. Mix the beer, molasses, mustard, salt and onions. Pour over the beans and mix once. Add as much of the bean liquid as is needed to barely cover the beans. Place remaining salt pork over the top of the beans. Cover and place in a slow 275° oven and bake for 6 hours, adding the remaining liquid as needed to keep the beans barely covered with liquid. Remove the cover the last 45 minutes of baking, so the top may become nice and brown.

LIMA BEANS AND PORK
Serves 4 to 6

Ready Tray	¼	pound smoked ham, diced
	2	slices bacon, diced
	¼	pound fresh lean pork, diced
	1	tablespoon cornstarch
	2	teaspoons fresh ginger root, finely chopped
	1	clove garlic, finely chopped
	3	tablespoons soy sauce
	3	pounds shelled fresh lima beans
	1	cup beef broth
	¼	teaspoon pepper

Toss the pork with the cornstarch.

Heat a heavy skillet and fry the bacon until crisp. Drain and crumble the bacon, add ginger, garlic and pork. Return to skillet and cook 2 minutes. Add soy sauce and cook for 5 minutes. Remove ingredients and add the beans, broth and pepper. Cover and cook over low flame for 10 minutes. Return the meat and add the ham and cook gently for 5 minutes, until ham is thoroughly heated.

LIMA BEANS AND SHORT RIBS
Serves 4

Ready Tray	1	cup large dried lima beans
	4	onions, medium size, quartered
	4	cups water
	1	teaspoon salt
	1	teaspoon sage
	2	pounds short ribs, cut into 2-inch pieces
	3	tablespoons flour
		Black pepper to taste
	1	teaspoon dry mustard
		Cooking oil

Simmer limas and onions 30 minutes in 4 cups boiling water, covered. Add ½ teaspoon salt and sage and cook 30 minutes longer. Pour into a large casserole, undrained.

Combine 2 tablespoons flour, remaining salt, pepper and mustard, and dredge short ribs. Brown on all sides in hot fat. Cover and cook for 20 minutes. Place ribs in casserole with undrained beans. Thicken drippings remaining in pan with 1 tablespoon flour, blend in ⅔ cup water and cook until thick and smooth, stirring constantly. Pour over ribs and beans and cover. Bake in moderate 350° oven approximately 2 hours.

Serve from casserole.

WESTERN LIMA BEANS
Serves 4 to 6

Ready Tray

½	pound ground beef
1	onion, medium size, finely chopped
3	tablespoons bacon fat
2	cans (8-oz. ea.) tomato sauce
1½	teaspoons salt
1	tablespoon brown sugar
	Dash of poultry seasoning
4	cups large dried lima beans, cooked
½	cup lima bean liquid

Brown the meat and onion lightly in bacon fat, stirring to break the meat into small pieces. Add tomato sauce, bean liquid, salt, sugar and poultry seasoning. Place lima beans in a casserole. Cover with sauce and bake in a moderate 350° oven for 30 minutes, uncovered.

Serve from casserole.

LIMA BEANS, VERMONT STYLE
Serves 6

Ready Tray | 2½ | cups large dried lima beans
| 6 | cups water
| 1 | large onion pierced with
| 8 | whole cloves
| ½ | cup maple syrup
| ½ | cup ketchup
| 2 | teaspoons salt
| 2 | teaspoons Worcestershire sauce
| ¼ | teaspoon freshly ground black pepper
| 1 | bay leaf
| ½ | pound salt pork, thinly sliced

Rinse limas, add water and soak for several hours. Add onion and boil for 5 minutes, uncovered. Turn into buttered casserole without draining. Add remaining ingredients and cover. Bake in a slow 300° oven for 3 hours, adding water if needed to keep moist.

Serve from casserole.

LIMA BEANS AND TOMATOES
Serves 8

Ready Tray | 4 | Spring green onions, finely chopped
| ¼ | cup olive oil
| 1 | pound dried lima beans, soaked and simmered until tender
| ½ | green bell pepper, seeded and finely chopped
| ½ | teaspoon sugar
| | Salt
| | Cayenne pepper
| 1 | can (No. 2) tomatoes
| | Grated Parmesan cheese

Sauté onions in oil until golden brown. Add drained beans and green pepper. Toss lightly to pick up flavor in the pan. Place in deep buttered casserole with sugar, salt and cayenne to taste. Cover with the tomatoes and sprinkle with cheese.

Bake uncovered in a 350° oven for 40 minutes or until the beans are thoroughly heated and the top is crusted over.

BARBECUED LIMA BEANS AND SPARERIBS
Serves 6 to 8

Ready Tray	
1½	cups large dried lima beans
1½	pounds spareribs
1	teaspoon salt
½	cup ketchup
2	tablespoons Worcestershire sauce
½	teaspoon chili powder
1	teaspoon salt
	Dash of Tabasco sauce
1	cup water
1	lemon, sliced
1	large onion, thinly sliced

Simmer beans and spareribs together in 5 cups salted water for 1 hour, covered. Remove from cooking liquid, and when cool, cut spareribs in 3-inch pieces. If desired, bones can be slipped from the ribs for easy eating. Arrange meat in buttered casserole with the lima beans.

Combine ketchup, Worcestershire sauce, chili powder, salt, Tabasco sauce and water. Pour over beans and ribs.

Place lemon and onion over the ribs. Bake, covered, in a moderate 350° oven for 1 hour. Serve from casserole.

BAKED NAVY BEANS AU GRATIN
Serves 8 to 10

Ready Tray	
2	cups dried navy beans
5	cups water
	Salt
10	large Bermuda onions
¼	cup unsulphured molasses
1	teaspoon dry mustard
¼	teaspoon freshly ground black pepper
2	teaspoons Worcestershire sauce
1½	cups grated Cheddar cheese
1	cup soft bread crumbs
2	tablespoons butter, melted

Soak washed beans in water to cover overnight. Next day place beans and liquid in a large kettle, add onions and salt to taste. Cover and simmer gently until onions are tender, but yet retain their shape, approximately 15 minutes. Remove onions from kettle and continue cooking beans until tender. Drain and save the bean liquid to mix with molasses, mustard, pepper and Worcestershire sauce.

Place one half the beans in a 2-quart casserole and sprinkle with ¾ cup grated cheese.

Add remaining beans; arrange onions over top of beans and add liquid mixture. Bake, uncovered, in moderately slow 325° oven for approximately 45 minutes.

Sprinkle remaining grated cheese over onions. Mix bread crumbs and melted butter and sprinkle over onions and beans. Return casserole to oven to melt cheese and brown crumbs for 15 minutes.

Serve the baked beans with generous portions of cole slaw, brown bread and a fresh apple pie for dessert.

NAVY BEANS WITH LENTIL SAUCE
Serves 4 to 6

Ready Tray

1	pound navy beans
1	bay leaf
1	onion pierced with 2 whole cloves
½	pound dried lentils
¼	cup olive oil
½	cup onion, finely chopped
1	clove garlic, finely chopped
1	pinch oregano
¼	cup fresh parsley, finely chopped
1	large can tomato sauce
	Salt and freshly ground black pepper
	Grated Parmesan cheese

Cover beans with water, add bay leaf and onion pierced with cloves and simmer until beans are soft. Separately, simmer lentils in water to cover, without seasonings, until they are tender enough to purée.

Meanwhile, heat oil in skillet and sauté chopped onion and garlic with oregano. Add parsley and tomato sauce and let mixture cook very slowly, uncovered, for about an hour, or until cooked down and well blended. Season to taste with salt and freshly ground black pepper. Add puréed lentils and mix thoroughly.

Drain navy beans, reserving some liquid. In a casserole, alternate layers of the navy beans and sauce, adding a bit of the bean cooking liquid, and top with grated cheese. Bake in a moderate 350° oven until heated thoroughly and the cheese is browned.

NAVY BEAN AND LAMB CASSOULET FRENCH STYLE
Serves 8 to 10

Ready Tray

2	pounds dried navy beans
2	cloves garlic
2	Bermuda onions, medium size, pierced with whole cloves
2	carrots, coarsely chopped
1	bouquet garni (celery leaves, thyme, bay leaf, tied in a cheesecloth bag)
½	pound fresh pork rind
½	pound lean salt pork
1	pound garlic sausage
1	pound boneless lamb, leg or shoulder, cut in bite-size pieces
3	Bermuda onions, medium size, finely chopped
3	cloves garlic, finely chopped
3	tablespoons tomato paste
1	roasted duck, or pieces of goose, (if you are going authentic), removed from bones and cut in bite-size pieces
	Gravy fat and juices from the roasted duck
	Salt and freshly ground black pepper
½	cup finely ground bread crumbs

Place the beans in water to cover with garlic, onions with cloves, carrots, bouquet garni, pork rind and season to taste with salt. Cook over medium heat for 1 hour.

Scald the salt pork and sausage, add to the beans and cook until tender.

Brown the lamb, add onion, garlic, tomato paste and some of the liquid that the beans have been cooked in. Simmer gently for a few minutes. Remove salt pork, pork rind and bouquet garni from the beans. Cut the salt pork in thin slices. Drain the beans.

Use a deep bean pot (or better yet the French pot made of *issel* clay that takes its name from this dish). Into the cassoulet place a layer each of the beans, slices of salt pork, sausage, lamb mixture, duck and repeat until all the ingredients are used. Add the duck gravy and season to taste with salt and freshly ground black pepper. Top with bread crumbs and bake in hot oven for 30 to 40 minutes to mellow the flavor. Serve very hot from the cassoulet.

NAVY BEANS ITALIAN
Serves 4 to 6

Ready Tray

2	cups dried navy beans
1	bay leaf
2	onions, medium size, grated
1	clove garlic, mashed
2	tablespoons fresh parsley, finely chopped
1	teaspoon fresh dill, finely chopped
2	cups whole packed tomatoes
½	cup olive oil or cooking oil
3	small pickles, finely chopped
½	cup green stuffed olives, finely chopped
1	cup celery, finely chopped
	Grated cheese
	Salt and freshly ground black pepper

Use time-saving method or soak beans overnight in water to cover. Pour beans and liquid into saucepan, adding more water if needed, to barely cover. Add bay leaf, onion, garlic, parsley and dill. Boil until beans are tender, but not soft, approximately 1½ hours. Season to taste with salt and freshly ground black pepper.

In separate saucepan, cook tomatoes, pickles, olives and celery in oil until tender. Pour over beans and turn mixture into a casserole or bean pot. Cover and bake in a slow 275° oven about 2 hours. Uncover and sprinkle grated cheese over top and continue baking until cheese is browned. Serve from casserole or bean pot.

SWISS STEAK WITH LIMA BEANS
Serves 4 to 6

Ready Tray	⅓	cup flour
	1	teaspoon dry mustard
	1½	teaspoons salt
	¼	teaspoon black pepper
	¼	teaspoon paprika
	1½	pounds thick round steak, cut into serving pieces
	¼	cup bacon drippings
	1	large onion, thinly sliced
	1	clove garlic, finely chopped
	¾	cup water
	2	cups canned tomatoes
	1	cup large dried lima beans

Blend flour, mustard, salt, pepper and paprika. Pound seasoned flour into the meat. Brown steak in heated bacon drippings and remove to large heavy skillet.

Add onion and garlic to remaining drippings in pan along with water. Bring to boil and pour over meat. Add tomatoes and beans. Cover and simmer slowly until tender, approximately 2 hours.

NAVY BEANS AND CHUTNEY
Serves 4

Ready Tray	2	cups dried navy beans
	6	slices bacon, cut into small pieces
	1	onion, finely chopped
		Salt and pepper
	¼	cup chutney, finely chopped
	1	teaspoon dry mustard
	1	cup water
	½	cup honey

Place beans in large saucepan and add 4 cups cold water. Bring to boiling point, reduce heat and simmer, covered, for 1 hour. Drain off any excess liquid.

Preheat oven to 325°. Add the bacon, onion, salt and pepper to taste, chutney, mustard and water to the beans and stir gently. Pour into a 2-quart shallow baking dish and pour the honey over the top. Cover and bake for 45 minutes. Remove the cover and bake for 30 minutes more.

Serve from baking dish.

NAVY BEANS BOURGUIGNONNE
Serves 4 to 6

Ready Tray

1	pound dried navy beans
1	onion, coarsely chopped
	Salt to taste
2	sprigs of fresh parsley
1	bay leaf
	Milk
1	tablespoon flour
3	ounces butter
1	teaspoon fresh parsley, finely chopped
1	clove garlic, gently crushed
4	ounces fresh cream

Soak washed beans in water to cover overnight. Next day, add more water, if needed, to cover. Add onion, salt to taste, sprigs of parsley and bay leaf and boil until beans are tender. Strain and place the beans in a pan, cover with milk and cook for a few minutes.

Blend the flour with the butter until smooth and add to the beans and stir gently. Add chopped parsley and garlic and keep the preparation on a light fire for a few minutes. Add fresh cream and stir until well blended. When heated through, serve immediately.

NAVY BEANS AND SPARERIBS
Serves 4

Ready Tray

1	pound dried navy beans
2	teaspoons salt
2	pounds spareribs, cut into serving-size pieces
½	teaspoon dry mustard
1	tablespoon sugar
1	tablespoon molasses
1	Bermuda onion, peeled and coarsely chopped
2	tablespoons fat (any kind)

Cover the beans with boiling water, soak 5 minutes and then boil until the skins wrinkle.

Add the salt and spareribs. Stir in the seasonings and onion and add the fat. Cover closely and continue to boil very slowly until the beans are soft and the spareribs tender, at least 2 hours.

NAVY BEAN PURÉE
Serves 6

Ready Tray

2	cups dried navy beans
3	quarts water
1	onion, medium size, finely chopped
½	teaspoon celery salt
2	teaspoons salt
¼	teaspoon freshly ground black pepper
¼	teaspoon dry mustard
4	tablespoons butter
3	hard-cooked eggs, sliced

Soak beans in water overnight or boil briskly until skins break. Add onion and celery salt and cook until beans are very soft. Press beans through a coarse sieve, add salt, freshly ground black pepper and mustard. Cook until mixture thickens to desired consistency. Add butter and stir until melted.

Serve with slices of hard-cooked egg.

BAKED NAVY BEANS EAST COAST
Serves 6 to 8

Ready Tray

3	cups dried navy beans
½	pound sliced bacon, cut into ½-inch pieces
1	teaspoon salt
1	clove garlic, finely chopped
¼	cup light brown sugar, firmly packed
2	teaspoons dry mustard
1	cup dark molasses
1	cup boiling water

Cover beans with cold water, refrigerate covered, overnight. Next day place in large kettle and add to soaking water if necessary to cover with 2 quarts of water. Bring to boiling point, reduce heat and simmer with cover on for 30 minutes. Drain the beans thoroughly.

Preheat oven to 300°. Put beans into a large casserole or bean pot, add bacon and stir until thoroughly combined. Blend the salt, garlic, brown sugar, dry mustard and molasses and pour over the beans. Add the boiling water, enough to cover the beans.

Bake, covered, for 6 hours. Stir the beans occasionally so they will cook evenly. If too dry, add a little more boiling water. Remove cover 30 minutes before end of baking time to brown the top.

DELICIOUS BEAN STEW
Serves 6 to 8

Ready Tray
1 cup dried navy beans
4 quarts water
8 small carrots, diced
4 potatoes, diced
8 stalks celery with leaves, coarsely chopped
¼ head white cabbage, coarsely chopped
2 onions, coarsely chopped
1 large turnip, diced
1 tablespoon fresh parsley, finely chopped
1 clove garlic, finely chopped
2 tablespoons butter
Finely grated sharp American or Parmesan cheese
Salt and freshly ground black pepper

Boil beans until just tender. Add all vegetables and garlic to the beans and allow to simmer gently about 2 hours. Blend in the butter and season to taste with salt and freshly ground black pepper. Sprinkle each portion with the grated cheese.

BEAN RAREBIT
Serves 6

Ready Tray
2 tablespoons butter
2 tablespoons flour
1 teaspoon salt
1 cup milk
1 cup grated American cheese
2 cups boiled navy beans, put through a sieve
Buttered toast
Broiled bacon slices
Slices of ripe tomatoes

Melt butter in chafing dish or saucepan. Blend in flour **and salt**. Add milk slowly until blended and cook until thickened. **Stir in** cheese until melted. Add beans and blend well. Arrange **slices of** buttered toast on platter and pour rarebit over toast. Surround **with** broiled bacon slices and slices of ripe tomato for a well balanced meal.

If rarebit is too thick, dilute with a little cream.

PEA BEAN CASSOULET
Serves 6 to 8

Ready Tray

4	cups dried pea beans
2	quarts water
2	pounds pork, fat goose, mutton and fat bacon, cut into small pieces
2	pounds Cervelat sausages
6	peppercorns
1½	teaspoons salt
1	large Bermuda onion pierced with whole cloves
1	sprig of thyme
1	bay leaf
1	cup thick tomato purée

Soak beans overnight in the water. Next day, simmer the beans in the same water for 3 hours.

Meanwhile, sauté pieces of meat and the sausages lightly in a frying pan. Add peppercorns, salt, onion, thyme, bay leaf and tomato purée. Add enough hot water to cover and simmer for 2 hours, turning the meat occasionally.

Place cooked beans and mixture of meat in large casserole. If there is not enough liquid to cover add more tomato purée or beef stock. Cover and place in 300° oven and bake for 2 hours, uncovering the casserole the last ½ hour to brown surface. Serve from casserole.

NAVY BEAN-CHEESE CROQUETTES
Serves 4

Ready Tray
2	cups sieved, boiled navy beans
1	whole fresh egg, well beaten
2	ounces cheddar cheese, grated
1	cup onions, finely chopped and fried
1	teaspoon salt
¼	teaspoon freshly ground black pepper
2	cups bread crumbs
	Coating crumbs
	Shortening
	Tomato sauce

Thoroughly mix all ingredients, except coating crumbs and shortening.

Shape into small round balls on board sprinkled with fine bread crumbs. Brown in heated shortening and serve with tomato sauce.

BOSTON BAKED PEA BEANS
Serves 12

Ready Tray
4	cups dried pea beans
½	pound salt pork, scored
1	large onion, peeled
¾	cup brown sugar
½	cup molasses
1	tablepoon salt
½	teaspoon pepper
1	teaspoon dry mustard
½	cup vinegar
½	cup ketchup
1	large apple, peeled, cored and finely chopped
1	cup water

Soak beans overnight in water to cover. Next morning simmer approximately 1 hour or until skins crack when beans are blown upon. Drain.

Cut off one slice of salt pork and place in bottom of a 2-quart bean pot. Add the onion and the beans.

Combine the brown sugar, molasses, salt, pepper, mustard, vinegar, ketchup, apple and water and stir into the beans. Imbed, in one piece, the balance of the salt pork and add water to cover the beans. Cover the pot and bake for approximately 7 to 8 hours in 300° preheated oven, adding more water as necessary. Remove the cover during the last hour of baking to allow the beans and salt pork to brown. Do not add any more water.

Serve from bean pot!

FRIDAY STEW
Serves 4 to 6

Ready Tray

1	pound dried navy beans
1	cup potatoes, diced
1	cup carrots, diced
1	cup onions, finely chopped
½	cup fresh parley, finely chopped
2	cups tomatoes, finely chopped
½	cup oil
2	cloves garlic, finely chopped
	Salt and freshly ground black pepper

Soak beans overnight. Next day, using soaking water and enough extra, if necessary, to cover, place beans over medium heat and cook for 1 hour. Add all other ingredients and cook for 1 hour more or until everything is cooked tender.

Serve hot as a main dish in bowls.

CHUCK-WAGON BEANS
Serves 8

Ready Tray
2	pounds dried navy beans
1	large onion, quartered
1	bay leaf
1	teaspoon salt
1	clove garlic, mashed
1	large onion, diced
3	tablespoons honey
	Celery salt
	Cayenne pepper
	Onion rings

Use time-saving method or soak beans overnight in water to cover. Place in kettle with quartered onion, bay leaf, salt and garlic, adding water, if necessary, to cover. Cook until beans are tender.

Mix uncooked diced onion with honey and line bottom of large casserole. Drain beans, reserving liquid, and add beans to casserole. Sprinkle with celery salt and cayenne pepper. Top with onion rings. Cover casserole and bake in 350° oven 30 minutes to 1 hour, adding a little bean liquid, if needed, to keep beans from drying out. Serve from casserole.

THE BEAN DISH
Serves 4 to 6

Ready Tray
1	clove garlic, finely chopped
⅓	cup olive oil
1	pound dried navy beans, soaked and cooked tender
1	pound fresh string beans, cut in 2-inch lengths, cooked tender
1	tablespoon grated lemon peel
	Salt and pepper mill

Sauté garlic in oil until golden brown.

Place the cooked navy and string beans in a casserole and mix lightly.

Add garlic with the oil, grated lemon peel and season to taste with salt and plenty of freshly ground black pepper. Stir gently.
Cover and bake in 350° oven for 30 minutes.

BEER BEANS
Serves 10 or 12

Ready Tray

3	cups dried pea beans
¾	pound salt pork, thinly sliced
4	cups beer, your choice
¾	cup molasses
2	teaspoons dry mustard
2	teaspoons salt
¼	cup onions, grated

Wash the beans, place in a large kettle, cover with water and bring to a boil. Remove from heat and let soak one hour. Add fresh water if necessary to cover and bring to a boil again. Cover, and cook over low heat 1 hour. Drain, reserving the liquid.

Use an earthenware bean pot or heavy casserole. Line the bottom with half the salt pork. Place beans on top. Blend the beer, molasses, mustard, salt and onions and pour over the beans and mix gently once. Add as much of the bean liquid as is needed to barely cover the beans. Place remaining salt pork over the top. Cover the pot and bake in a 275° oven for 7 hours, adding the remaining liquid, as needed, to keep the beans barely covered. Remove cover for last hour of baking time to brown evenly.

PEA BEANS WITH ONION
Serves 12

Ready Tray

4	cups dried, small white pea beans
2½	quarts water
1	ham hock
1	pound ground beef
6	onions, finely chopped
½	teaspoon chili powder
½	teaspoon black pepper
⅛	teaspoon cayenne
3	cans (11-oz. each) tomato soup
1½	cups brown sugar, firmly packed

Wash beans, place in a heavy kettle with water, cover, bring to a boil and simmer gently for 2 minutes. Remove from heat and let soak for 1 hour. Then add ham hock, bring to a boil and simmer slowly for 2 hours, or until the beans are tender.

Brown beef until crumbly. Add onions to meat and cook until onions are transparent. Stir in chili powder, pepper, cayenne and tomato soup and simmer for 10 minutes. Mix with the beans. Stir in the sugar and simmer slowly for 25 minutes until the seasonings are well blended.

PINK BEANS WITH BACON
Serves 4

Ready Tray

1½	cups dried pink beans
2	tablespoons butter or savory drippings
1	cup canned tomatoes
1	teaspoon molasses
1	onion medium size, minced
1½	teaspoons salt
⅛	teaspoon freshly ground black pepper
	Thin slices bacon or salt pork

Cover beans with boiling water and soak 2 hours. Add 1 teaspoon salt, cover and boil until tender, 1½ to 2 hours. Drain and save the liquid for soup.

Combine the beans with butter, tomatoes, molasses, onion, salt and pepper. Cover closely, and bake in a hot 375° oven for 1 hour. Then cover with the salt pork or bacon, which should first be scalded, and continue to bake until bacon or salt pork is brown and crisp.

PEA BEANS BRETONNE
Serves 4 to 6

Ready Tray		
	1	pound navy pea beans
	2	teaspoons salt
	1	whole onion
	1	bay leaf
	3	whole cloves
	1	carrot
	1	ham bone
	2	cloves garlic
	1	onion, finely chopped
	2	ounces bacon fat
	2	cloves garlic, finely chopped
	3	fresh tomatoes, peeled, seeded and diced
	4	ounces tomato purée
		Freshly ground black pepper to taste

Soak beans in cold water overnight. Cook in salted water or stock. Tack bay leaf to whole onion with cloves. Add to beans with carrot, ham bone and 2 cloves garlic. Cook until beans are soft. Simmer chopped onion in bacon fat to golden brown in saucepan. Add chopped garlic, diced tomatoes and purée of tomatoes. Drain off most of liquid from beans and blend beans with tomato liquid. Boil 10 minutes more and season to taste with freshly ground black pepper.

PINK BUCK BEANS
Serves 6

Ready Tray

2	cups dried pink beans
6	cups water
2	teaspoons salt (unless using ham or salt pork)
2	Bermuda onions, medium size, coarsely chopped
2	cloves garlic, thinly sliced
1	bay leaf, left whole
½	pound smoked ham, slab bacon or salt pork
2	cups solid pack tomatoes (1 No. 2 can)
½	cup chopped sweet red or green pepper, if desired
2	teaspoons chili powder
2	tablespoons brown sugar
½	teaspoon dry mustard
¼	teaspoon crushed oregano leaves or
¼	teaspoon cuminseed

Pour the six cups of water over the washed beans in a covered kettle. Let stand 12 to 15 hours overnight. Or, in the morning, put the water in kettle, bring rapidly to boiling point. Gradually add washed beans so boiling continues. Boil two minutes only. Remove from heat, cover and let stand one hour.

Add onion, garlic, bay leaf and salt (omit salt if using ham or salt pork).

Add smoked ham cut in ½-inch cubes, slab bacon or salt pork, sliced through twice each way not quite to the rind.

Bring all to boiling point rapidly; reduce heat to a slow simmer. Cover tightly and let simmer for 1½ hours. Stir in remaining ingredients. Bring again to boil, then reduce heat to slow-simmer.

Season to taste with salt, if necessary. Cover, let simmer at least 2 hours. There should be just enough liquid left to resemble a medium-thick gravy.

Serve in large heated soup dishes.
Buck Beans can be made a day, or even several days in advance and then refrigerated. Reheat just at serving time.

PINK BEANS, WESTERN STYLE
Serves 6 to 8

Ready Tray

1	pound dried pink beans
½	pound salt pork, diced
1	clove garlic, finely chopped
1	large Bermuda onion, thinly sliced
1	can (No. 2) solid pack tomatoes
1	cup Burgundy wine
1	tablespoon sugar
2	teaspoons chili powder
2	teaspoons Worcestershire sauce
	Salt to taste

Wash and pick over beans. Soak and refrigerate overnight in water to cover. Next day, bring to a boil, cover and simmer gently for 3 hours or until tender. Stir occasionally during cooking and add more boiling water, if necessary. (When beans are done, the sauce around them should be medium thick.) Place beans in a large casserole, after draining them.

Place salt pork, garlic, onion, tomatoes, wine, sugar, chili powder, Worcestershire sauce and salt to taste over the beans and stir gently. Place casserole in 350° oven and bake for 45 minutes uncovered. Serve hot from casserole.

BAKED PINTO BEANS AND SPARERIBS
Serves 6

Ready Tray
2	cups dried pinto beans
3	pounds spareribs, cut in serving pieces
2	Bermuda onions, medium size, coarsely chopped
4	tablespoons butter
½	teaspoon thyme
	Salt and freshly ground black pepper

Wash and soak beans in water to cover overnight. Next day place over medium heat and cook until just tender, but not overcooked. Drain and reserve the liquid.

Sprinkle spareribs with salt and freshly ground black pepper. Brown lightly on both sides under brisk flame (or hot broiler) for 20 minutes so that some of the fat is cooked out.

Sauté onions until golden brown in butter.

Place spareribs, beans, onions, thyme, salt and pepper to taste in a large casserole. Cover with bean liquid and place in 350° oven and bake until the spareribs are tender, or approximately 1 hour. Add additional liquid if necessary.

QUICK PINTO BEAN CASSEROLE
Serves 4

Ready Tray
3	cups quick-cooking pinto beans
½	pound smoked ham, cut into ½-inch cubes
1	pound Italian or Spanish hot sausage
1	teaspoon oregano
1	clove garlic, finely chopped
2	green bell peppers, finely chopped
½	cup red wine
	Freshly grated Parmesan cheese

Place beans in kettle with water to cover and cook until just tender. Do not overcook. Drain thoroughly and reserve liquid.

Sauté sausage until nearly cooked. Mix ham, sausages and beans and place in a large casserole. Add oregano, garlic, green pepper. Cover with bean liquid, add wine, place in 350° oven and bake for 1 hour. Sprinkle with freshly grated Parmesan cheese and return to oven for 20 minutes or until the cheese melts into the beans.

WHITE PEA BEANS NORMANDY
Serves 4 to 6

Ready Tray

2	cups dried pea beans
2	tablespoons fresh parsley, finely chopped
½	cup celery, finely chopped
¾	cup onions, diced
2	teaspoons dry mustard
½	teaspoon dried thyme
2	teaspoons salt
¼	cup brown sugar
1	pound lamb stew meat, cut in 1-inch cubes
3	tablespoons olive oil or salad oil
1	clove garlic, quartered
1	cup dry white wine

Soak beans overnight in water to cover. Place in kettle with more water, if necessary, to cover; add remaining ingredients except lamb, oil and garlic. Simmer until just tender, about 1½ hours. Heat oil in skillet with quartered clove of garlic and brown the pieces of lamb.

Place beans in buttered casserole and mix in lamb. Add about 2 tablespoons water to meat juice in skillet, heat until boiling and pour over beans. Cover and cook in slow 325° oven about 4 hours. Moisten with white wine occasionally. Uncover the last ½ hour to let top brown evenly.

PINTO BEAN POT
Serves 8

Ready Tray		
	1	pound Idaho dried pinto beans
	6	cups water
	⅛	teaspoon baking soda
	2	tablespoons bacon drippings or vegetable oil
	½	cup bacon or salt pork bits
	1	cup onion, coarsely chopped
	1	large clove garlic, mashed with
	1	teaspoon salt
	¼	teaspoon coarse ground black pepper
	½	teaspoon crushed oregano
	½	teaspoon ground cumin
	3	teaspoon chili powder
	1	can (8-oz.) tomato sauce
		Thinly sliced onion and green bell pepper rings for garnish
		Shredded Cheddar or Provolone cheese for garnish

Soak beans in water with soda overnight. Cook beans in water in which they soaked. Place beans over high heat. Add drippings or oil, bring to boil. Reduce heat to simmer, cover and cook gently until beans are tender, approximately 2 hours.

Place bacon or salt pork bits in skillet. Add onion and sauté lightly until tender. Add remaining ingredients plus ½ cup bean liquid and heat thoroughly. Add to beans, cover and simmer gently 2 hours until flavors are blended and beans are tender. Or turn into large casserole and bake, covered, in 325° oven for 2 hours. Add salt, if necessary.

When serving, garnish top of bean dish with onion and pepper rings and cheese.

Excellent with barbecued spareribs.

IDAHO'S BUCKAROO BEANS
Serves 6

Ready Tray

1	pound Idaho dried pinto or red beans
6	cups water
2	teaspoons salt (unless using ham or salt pork)
2	medium size onions, coarsely chopped
2	cloves garlic, thinly sliced
1	small bay leaf
½	pound smoked ham, cut in ½-inch cubes, or slab of salt pork, par-boiled, sliced through twice each way not quite to the rind, or ¼ lb. each
2	cups (1 No. 2 can) solid-pack tomatoes
½	cup sweet red or green bell pepper, chopped
2	teaspoons chili powder
2	tablespoons brown sugar
½	teaspoon dry mustard
¼	teaspoon crushed oregano leaves or ground cuminseed

Soak beans overnight in water. Cook beans in water in which they were soaked, using a heavy kettle with cover. Use salt sparingly when using ham or salt pork. Add onion, garlic, bay leaf and ham or salt pork. Bring to boiling point rapidly. Reduce heat to slow simmer, cover tightly and simmer gently for 1 hour.

Add remaining ingredients. Bring to boil rapidly, reduce heat to slow simmer, cover and simmer for 2 hours longer. The covered kettle may be placed in a 325° oven after the first cooking period to finish cooking. There should be just enough liquid left on the beans to resemble a medium-thick gravy.

Serve in large heated soup plates or over-sized coffee cups, with piping-hot buttered corn bread and cool crisp relishes.

PINTO BEAN RAREBIT
Serves 4 or 5

Ready Tray | 1 tablespoon onion, minced
¼ cup butter
¼ cup flour
½ teaspoon salt
½ teaspoon prepared mustard
2 cups milk
¼ teaspoon Worcestershire sauce
1 rounded cup shredded sharp cheese
1½ cups cooked, drained Idaho Pinto beans
Buttered toast

Cook onion slowly in butter, add flour, salt, mustard. Mix thoroughly and cook slowly a few minutes.

Add milk, stirring constantly until thick, then add Worcestershire sauce and cheese. Cook over very low heat or over hot water until cheese is melted.

Add beans, cover and heat thoroughly.

Serve over buttered toast.

RED BEANS AND RICE KOREAN
Serves 6

Ready Tray | 1 cup dried red beans
1 cup rice
7 cups water
2 teaspoons salt
3 cups stock
½ cup flour, sifted
¾ teaspoon baking powder
3 tablespoons cold water

Soak beans in 5 cups of water overnight. Cook in the same water for 2 hours. Force through a sieve.

Wash rice thoroughly and soak for 15 minutes, drain and wash again. Place in a saucepan and add 2 cups of water and the salt. Cover, bring to a boil and cook over low heat for 20 minutes. Add the bean purée to the rice with the stock and cook for 20 minutes longer, stirring occasionally.

Mix the sifted flour and baking powder together. Add the cold water and knead to a soft dough. Roll into balls the size of marbles. Add to the rice and bean mixture and stir well. Cook for 20 minutes more over low heat. Serve very hot.

RED BEANS CHILI CON CARNE
Serves 6

Ready Tray

1	pound dried red beans
3	tablespoons shortening
4	tablespoons chili powder
	Salt
2	onions, finely chopped
	Shortening for frying
1½	pounds round steak, ground

Soak washed beans overnight in water to cover. Next day cook gently until soft. Add shortening and 2 tablespoons of chili powder and season to taste with salt.

Sauté onions in skillet in shortening until soft. Add meat and 2 tablespoons of chili powder and season to taste with salt. Cook gently until meat is seared. Cover with water and cook slowly until done. Add to beans and simmer gently until well blended, adding more water if too thick.

Serve with crackers and sour pickles.

NEW ENGLAND BAKED NAVY BEANS
Serves 6 to 8

Ready Tray	1	quart dried navy beans
	1	8-oz. piece salt pork
	1	teaspoon dry mustard
	2	teaspoons salt
	¼	teaspoon ground ginger
	2	tablespoons sugar
	¼	cup molasses
	2	cups or more boiling water

Cover washed beans with water and soak overnight. Next morning cook slowly until the skins wrinkle when a few in a spoon are blown upon. Rinse the beans with cold water and place in a 4-quart bean pot or casserole.

Pour boiling water over the salt pork, scrape the rind until white and score in ½-in. strips without cutting through the skin. Press the pork gently into the top of the beans.

Mix seasonings well and add 1½ cups boiling water, pour over beans and cover.

Bake about 9 hours in a 250° oven, adding a little boiling water every hour or when needed. The water should never cover the beans, but should appear as tiny bubbles above them.

An onion, if desired, may be placed in the casserole before the beans are added.

CHILI BEANS, SUN VALLEY STYLE
Serves 10

Ready Tray

4	cups dried pinto or red beans
12	cups water
4	teaspoons salt
1	large onion, peeled and whole
1	large bay leaf
1	large garlic clove, thinly sliced
1	tablespoon butter
2	pounds lean ground beef
2	tablespoons fat or finely chopped suet
1	cup water, beef stock, or tomato juice
4	tablespoons chili powder
1½	teaspoons ground cumin
	Salt

Place beans and water in a large kettle. Bring to a boil rapidly and boil for 2 minutes. Remove from heat, cover tightly and let stand for 1 hour. Add salt, onion, bay leaf, garlic and butter. Bring to boil quickly, reduce heat to simmer. Cover and simmer gently for 2 hours or until the beans are just tender.

Brown meat quickly in the fat or suet, breaking into small pieces. Add to beans. Add 1 cup of the liquid to frying pan and heat to boiling point, and add to beans.

Blend the chili powder and ground cumin. Add a little bean liquid and mix to a smooth paste. Add to beans, bring to a boiling point and reduce heat to simmer. Cover and simmer gently for 1½ hours.

Serve the beans in soup plates with corn chips, crisp relishes and long iced drinks. Fruit and cheese make an appropriate dessert.

PASTA E FAGIOLI
Neapolitan or Southern Style
Beans and Paste, Venetian
Serves 4 to 6

Ready Tray
- 1 pound dried pinto beans
- ½ cup olive oil
- 1 onion, finely chopped
- Pinch of cinnamon
- ½ pound fresh pork rind, cleaned and cut in small squares
- 1 prosciutto bone, medium size
- ⅛ pound salt pork, finely chopped
- Salt and freshly ground black pepper
- 6 ounces medium-size noodles, broken in 1-inch pieces

Place beans in a large kettle with plenty of water. Add oil, onion, cinnamon, pork rind, salt pork, prosciutto bone and season to taste with salt and freshly ground black pepper. Be sparing with the salt as the salt pork and prosciutto bone have quite a bit of salt in them.

Cover and boil until extremely well done; then add noodles and enough boiling water to cook the noodles thoroughly.

The consistency of the minestra must be that of a thick purée.

FRIJOLES DE LA OLLA
("cooked in a clay pot for a long time, served in the thick broth")
Serves 6

Ready Tray
- 2 cups Idaho dried red beans
- 6 cups water
- 2 tablespoons salad oil or butter
- 2 teaspoons salt
- 1 whole onion, medium size, peeled

Place washed beans in a heavy saucepot or Dutch oven. Add water, bring to boiling point rapidly and boil 2 minutes. Remove from heat. Cover and let stand for 1 hour.

To cook, add salad oil or butter to beans and soaking water to keep foaming down, and salt and whole onion. Bring to boiling point, reduce heat to simmer; cover and cook until very tender and the liquid is of gravy consistency. Stir occasionally but gently to prevent breaking beans. Remove onion.

Serve very hot in an attractive Mexican clay pottery casserole.

Serve with chili con carne in a side dish.

Excellent for Christmas and all festive occasions and gatherings.

RED BEANS, MEXICAN STYLE
Serves 8

Ready Tray

2½	cups dried red beans
6	cups water
2½	teaspoons salt
1	can (8-oz.) spaghetti sauce
1	onion, finely chopped
½	green bell pepper, seeded and finely chopped
1	clove garlic, finely chopped
1	tablespoon ground chocolate (not cocoa)
½	teaspoon dried rosemary
2	teaspoons chili powder

Wash beans, place in a kettle with water, cover, bring to a boil and cook for 2 minutes. Remove from heat and let soak 1 hour.

Add salt, spaghetti sauce, onion, green pepper, garlic, chocolate, rosemary and chili powder. Cover and simmer gently for 2 hours or until the beans are tender. Turn into a bean pot or casserole and bake in 325° oven for 2 hours.

PINTO BEANS AND CHILI
Serves 6

Ready Tray	2	cups dried pinto beans
	2	pounds round steak, ground
	6	tablespoons butter
	1	large Spanish onion, coarsely chopped
	3	cups consommé
	1	teaspoon salt
	1	tablespoon sweet chili powder
	½	teaspoon fresh oregano, finely chopped
	1	tablespoon fresh parsley, finely chopped

Soak washed beans overnight in water to cover. Next day place over medium heat, cover, and cook beans until tender. Drain thoroughly. Place beans in large casserole.

Meanwhile, roll ground round steak into small balls about 1-inch in diameter. Sauté very quickly until browned on all sides in butter and remove to a hot plate. In the same fat, sauté onions until golden brown, adding consommé, salt, sweet chili powder and oregano and simmer gently for 20 minutes. Pour this sauce over the beans in the casserole, top with the meat balls and sprinkle with parsley. Place in 350° oven and bake uncovered for 20 minutes, or until the flavors have blended. Serve from casserole.

RED BEANS IN WINE
Serves 4

Ready Tray	4	cups cooked red beans, drained
	1	tablespoon butter
	1	large onion, finely sliced
	1	tablespoon flour
	¾	cup red wine
	¼	cup consommé
		Salt and freshly ground black pepper

In a Dutch oven, heat butter, add onion and sauté until golden brown. Add flour and cook until flour is slightly browned. Stir in wine, add beans and consommé; bring to a boil slowly. Cover and simmer for 30 minutes. Season to taste with salt and freshly ground black pepper.

PINTO BEAN CASSEROLE
Serves 8 to 10

Ready Tray

1	cup dried pinto beans
3	cups water
1¾	teaspoons salt
6	tablespoons bacon fat
1	clove garlic, finely chopped
1	Bermuda onion, peeled and finely chopped
1	tablespoon fresh parsley, finely chopped
½	teaspoon freshly ground black pepper
¼	teaspoon ground cloves
1	cup rice

Wash beans, drain. Pour into 3-quart kettle, add 3 cups water; bring to boiling point and boil 5 minutes. Remove from heat, add salt and let soak 1 hour. At end of hour, drain beans, reserving liquid.

Heat fat and sauté garlic, onion and parsley until golden brown. Add pepper and cloves and blend thoroughly. Add beans and sauté lightly.

Measure bean liquid and add sufficient water to make 5½ cups; add sautéed beans and garlic mixture and cook 1 to 1½ hours over low heat, or until beans begin to soften. Add 1 cup washed and drained rice and continue cooking until rice is tender. If mixture becomes dry before rice is done, add a little hot water.

Pour bean-and-rice mixture into well oiled 2-quart casserole and bake in a slow 250° oven for 30 minutes.

PINTO BEANS WITH PIGS' TAILS
Serves 8

Ready Tray
4	cups dried pinto beans
3	pounds loin of pork
6	pigs' tails
3	pounds beef brisket
1½	teaspoons salt
2	cloves garlic
1	teaspoon oregano
2	onions, coarsely chopped
1	bay leaf
1	pound Spanish sausages

Soak washed beans overnight, drain and place beans in large kettle with the pork, pigs' tails, beef, salt, garlic, oregano, onions and bay leaf. Cover with soaking water, add more if necessary, and bring to a boil. Boil for 15 minutes. Skim the scum from the top of the kettle and reduce heat to simmering. Simmer gently 3 to 4 hours or until meat and beans are tender. If liquid cooks down too much, add more boiling water as needed.

Add sausages the last ½ hour of cooking.

Check seasoning, remove meat to a platter or board, and cut beef and pork loin in slices. Remove onion, garlic and bay leaf from the pan and discard. Place beans in the center of a platter and surround with sliced meat, pigs' tails and sausages.

Excellent dish when the weather is chilly outside!

SOY WELSH RABBIT
Serves 4 to 6

Ready Tray

2	tablespoons shortening
2	tablespoons white flour
½	teaspoon salt
2½	cups milk
¼	cup soy flour
1	cup mild cheese, shaved thin
1	egg, well beaten

Melt shortening, blend in flour and salt. Mix some of the milk with soy flour, turning into remainder of milk, add to fat-flour mixture. Cook over hot water, stirring until slightly thickened. Add cheese, stirring gently until it melts. Pour a little sauce into the beaten egg, then pour all back into the sauce and cook 3 minutes longer. Serve on toast or crackers.

SOYBEAN LOAF
Serves 6

Ready Tray

2	cups soybeans, cooked and thoroughly mashed
½	cup fine bread crumbs
2	eggs
½	cup milk
2	tablespoons onion, grated
4	tablespoons butter
½	cup water
1	tablespoon celery salt
	Tomato sauce

Mix all ingredients thoroughly.

Put into a buttered casserole and bake in a 350° oven for 25 minutes uncovered, or until the top is delicately browned.
Serve with tomato sauce.

SOYBEAN CURRY
Serves 6 to 8

Ready Tray

½ cup vegetable or olive oil
1 cup celery, diced
1 clove garlic, finely chopped
1 onion, finely chopped
½ cup carrot, diced
¾ cup green bell pepper, shredded
3 cups cooked soybeans
1½ cups water
1½ teaspoons vegetable broth powder
1½ teaspoons curry powder
½ tablespoon powdered brewer's yeast
Boiled rice
Your favorite chutney

Heat the oil, add celery, garlic, onion, carrot and green bell pepper, sauté lightly until golden brown. Add soybeans, water and vegetable broth powder. Cover and simmer gently for 20 minutes. Add curry powder and simmer for 5 minutes or until all blended. Stir in the brewer's yeast. Add more liquid if necessary to keep moist. Serve with boiled rice and chutney.

SOYBEANS AND SALMON
Serves 4

Ready Tray

1 cup dry soybeans
5 tablespoons oil
4 slices fresh salmon, about 1½ pounds
1 stalk leek, cut into small sections
4 slices fresh ginger
2 tablespoons rice wine or brandy
3 tablespoons soy sauce
1 tablespoon sugar

Soak soybeans in water to cover overnight. Drain.

Heat oil in large skillet and fry salmon to light brown on both sides.

Add leek, ginger, wine or brandy, soy sauce, sugar and soybeans. Cover tightly and simmer gently over medium heat for 25 minutes.

Serve either hot or cold.

PINTO BEANS WITH SAGE
Serves 6

Ready Tray	2	cups dried pinto beans
		Water
	½	pound bacon or salt pork, cut in small pieces
	1	large onion, finely chopped
	1	clove garlic, finely chopped
	1	teaspoon salt
	¾	teaspoon freshly ground black pepper
	½	teaspoon dry mustard
	1½	teaspoons dried sage
	2	teaspoons brown sugar

Cover beans with 6 cups of water and boil for 2 minutes. Remove from heat, cover and let stand for one to two hours to soak.

Sauté the bacon or salt pork until golden brown; then add to the beans. Pour off all but 4 tablespoons fat from the skillet, and sauté the onions and garlic until golden brown. Add to beans.

Blend until smooth the salt, pepper, mustard, sage and sugar with enough water to form a thin mixture, and add to the beans.

Add enough water to cover the beans, cover and boil gently until tender, approximately 2 hours.

SOYBEAN CURD CHOP SUEY
Serves 6 to 8

Ready Tray

5	cups soybean curd, diced
½	cup butter
3	cups onions, shredded
3	cups celery, shredded
2	cups water
2	teaspoons cornstarch
2	tablespoons cold water
3	cups bean sprouts
2	cups sliced Jerusalem artichokes
6	tablespoons soy sauce

Brown the curd lightly in ½ the butter and remove from frying pan. Cook onion and celery in the remainder of the butter for several minutes, until limp. Add the curd and 2 cups water and simmer for 5 minutes. Mix the cornstarch and the 2 tablespoons of cold water until smooth. Stir into mixture and cook for a few minutes longer. Add bean sprouts and artichokes and heat thoroughly. Add soy sauce and serve immediately.

SOYBEAN SPROUT CASSEROLE
Serves 6

Ready Tray

2	tablespoons shortening
2	tablespoons flour
2	cups milk
1	tablespoon Worcestershire sauce
1¼	teaspoons salt
	Paprika
1	cup cheese, diced
¼	cup onion, finely chopped
3	tablespoons celery leaves, finely chopped
2	cups sprouted soybeans
2	cups small noodles, cooked 9 minutes

Heat shortening and stir in flour. Slowly add milk and cook until thick, stirring constantly. Add Worcestershire sauce, salt and cheese, letting cheese melt slightly. Add remaining ingredients except paprika. Mix thoroughly and turn into greased casserole. Dot with butter. Sprinkle with paprika and bake in moderate 350° oven for 30 minutes, uncovered.

BURGUNDY BEANS
Serves 8

Ready Tray

1	pound Idaho dried red beans
5	cups water
⅛	teaspoon soda
1	tablespoon butter
1	can (1 lb.) chili con carne (without beans)
2	cups fresh skinned or solid-pack canned tomatoes
1	cup Burgundy wine
½	cup onion, finely chopped
1	large clove garlic mashed with
2	teaspoons salt
	Monterey Jack or Mozzarella cheese, cut in ½-inch cubes

Place beans in large kettle, add water and soda. Bring to boil. Boil 2 minutes, remove from heat. Cover and let stand 1 hour. Add butter and place over high heat. Bring to boil rapidly. Cover and simmer gently 1½ hours, or until almost tender.

Add chili con carne, tomatoes, wine, onion, garlic with salt to the beans. Cover and simmer gently for 1½ hours, or until beans are tender. Stir occasionally during cooking period.

Add cheese to hot beans just before serving. Let stand, without stirring, for a few minutes to melt cheese. Serve hot! Serve as main course with a green salad and hot, split, garlic-buttered toasted hard rolls.

BEAN SPROUTS-HEKKA
Japanese-Hawaiian
Serves 8 to 10

Ready Tray

1	pound belly fat of pork, cut in small pieces
3	ounces chicken fat, cut in small pieces
1	2½ pound stewing chicken, cut in bite-size pieces
1	can (No. 2) bamboo shoots, drained and sliced, liquid reserved
2	cups canned button mushrooms, drained and chopped, liquid reserved
1	cup rice wine or Sauterne
6	tablespoons sugar
1	pint Japanese soy sauce
1	pound fresh bean sprouts
12	fresh spring green onions, cut in 1-inch lengths
⅔	pound fried bean curd, cut 1-inch long, ¼-inch thick, ½-inch wide
1	pound fresh bean curd, diced
	Boiled hot rice

Braise pork and chicken fat. Strain the fat by removing residue.

Sauté chicken in fat until lightly browned on all sides.

Grease the inside of a 2-gallon size cooking kettle with strained fat. Add chicken and liquid from bamboo shoots and mushrooms and bring to a boil over a high flame. Add wine, 2 tablespoons sugar and 1 cup soy sauce and bring to boil. Add bamboo shoots, mushrooms and bean sprouts. If necessary, add 2 more cups of water. Add root portion of onions, fried bean curd and boil for 5 minutes. Add diced bean curd to pot, stirring cautiously so as not to break up bean curd. Boil slowly for ½ hour.

Add green portion of onions and simmer for 45 minutes. Remove from fire and let stand for ½ hour. Add remaining sugar and soy sauce and blend gently. Heat thoroughly and serve with rice in individual side dishes. Provide additional soy sauce on table.

FRESH ROMAN BEANS WITH VEAL LUNGS
Serves 4

Ready Tray	2	pounds green beans (semi-mature), fresh Roman or cranberry
	1	pound veal lung, cut in 1-inch cubes
	2	tablespoons olive oil
	4	ounces prosciutto (lean and fat), minced
	1	onion, small, finely chopped
	1	clove of garlic, minced
	1	celery branch, minced
	1	small bunch fresh parsley, minced
	2	ounces white wine
	4	fresh tomatoes, peeled, seeded and chopped
		Salt and freshly ground black pepper

Shell the beans and cook in salted water till almost done, then place aside.

Place lung in warm water to cover and let stand for 30 minutes, then drain.

In a separate pot, over medium heat, sauté in oil the prosciutto, onion, garlic, celery and parsley, stirring until almost a thick paste. Add a spoonful of water if too dry. When light brown, add the well-drained lungs and stir well until lightly browned on all sides. Add wine and stir gently. When wine has evaporated, add tomatoes and cook together for at least 45 minutes.

Drain the beans, reserving some of the liquid in which they were cooked, and add to the lungs. Add enough of the bean water to make a medium consistency. Cover the pot and let cook on very low fire for 1 hour.

SHRIMP, CHICKEN, AND BEAN SPROUTS
Serves 6 to 8

Ready Tray		
	4	tablespoons peanut oil
	2	cloves garlic, finely chopped
	2	pounds raw shrimp, shelled and deveined
	1	pound fresh mushrooms, sliced
	1	cup bamboo shoots, sliced
	1	cup cooked chicken, thinly sliced
	4	cups chicken broth
	1	teaspoon salt
	½	teaspoon Accent
	2	cups fresh bean sprouts
	1	teaspoon sugar
	2	tablespoons cornstarch

Heat oil in a heavy skillet and sauté garlic, shrimp, mushrooms, bamboo shoots and chicken for 5 minutes, stirring constantly, over high flame. Place in a large kettle. Add 3½ cups broth, salt and Accent. Cover and cook 5 minutes over high flame. Add bean sprouts and cook 2 minutes more.

Mix together the sugar, cornstarch and remaining broth. Stir into kettle and cook gently until the sauce thickens.

GREEN ROMAN BEANS WITH SAUSAGES
Serves 4

Ready Tray		
	2	pounds fresh green Roman beans, semi-mature, shelled
	8	Italian sausages, fresh or cured
	1	tablespoon olive oil
	2	tablespoons tomato sauce
		Salt and freshly ground black pepper

Cook the shelled beans in salted water to cover until tender. Drain and set aside. Reserve some of the liquid.

Puncture the sausages with a fork, place them in a pan large enough to hold them in one layer, barely cover with cold water and cook them slowly. Do not turn them. When the water is almost completely evaporated, pick the sausages out and keep warm. Add oil and tomato sauce to juices in pan and simmer for 5 minutes. Add 2 ounces of the bean liquid and boil for 10 minutes more.

Add drained beans to sauce, season to taste with salt and freshly ground black pepper, stir gently, cover and simmer for 15 minutes; the beans will acquire the flavor of the sauce. Add the sausages and heat thoroughly.

Serve 2 sausages per serving with a mound of beans in the center.

SOY CHEESE SOUFFLÉ
Serves 4 to 6

Ready Tray

2	tablespoons shortening
2	tablespoons flour
1	cup milk
½	cup grated cheese, your choice
⅓	cup soy grits or flour
¾	teaspoon salt
4	eggs, separated

Melt the shortening, blend in the flour, then the milk. (If soy flour is used, reserve ¼ cup milk.) Stir and cook over heat until sauce thickens. Add cheese and stir until it melts. Add the dry soy grits or soy flour mixed with ¼ cup milk. Season. Beat the egg yolks and whites separately. Mix sauce with egg yolks, and fold in the stiffly-beaten whites. Pour into a greased dish and bake in a very moderate 300° oven for 1 hour or until it sets. Serve hot.

STRING BEAN CASSEROLE
Serves 4

Ready Tray	1	pound tender string beans, cut in 2-inch lengths
	6	ounces fresh veal and pork, ground together fine
	1	clove garlic, minced
	1	tablespoon grated Parmesan cheese
	2	tablespoons parsley, finely chopped
		Bread crumbs
	2	tablespoons olive oil
	4	young chicken livers
	2	ounces dry mushrooms, soaked in a little water to soften
	1	ounce butter
	1	tablespoon flour
	6	ounces milk
		Salt and pepper
	2	tablespoons grated Parmesan cheese

Boil the beans in salt water until tender, drain, replace in pot with 2 ounces butter; stir well, cover and keep warm.

Mix the ground meat with the garlic, cheese, parsley, bread crumbs, season to taste with salt and freshly ground black pepper. Shape into meat balls, ½-inch in diameter. Fry in olive oil; when almost done, add chicken livers, mushrooms and a little hot water. Simmer until tender.

Blend the butter and flour to a smooth paste, add milk and place over medium heat and cook until thick. Add to meat and mix well.

Place half of the beans in a low casserole, cover with sauce, then pour in the balance of the beans. Sprinkle with bread crumbs and Parmesan cheese, dot with small pieces of butter and place in hot 450° oven and bake 15 minutes, uncovered.

FRIED BEAN SPROUTS WITH PORK
Serves 4

Ready Tray
½	pound pork, shredded
4	tablespoons soy sauce
1	teaspoon rice wine or brandy
1	teaspoon cornstarch
8	tablespoons oil
½	stalk leek, shredded
½	pound bean sprouts
1	teaspoon sugar

Dredge shredded pork with 2 tablespoons soy sauce, wine or brandy and cornstarch.

Heat oil and fry pork with leek. When meat changes color, add bean sprouts.

Add remaining 2 tablespoons soy sauce and sugar, mix well, and cook gently for 8 minutes. Serve hot.

BAKED STRING BEANS
Serves 8

Ready Tray
2	packages frozen French-cut green beans
2	cans cream of mushroom soup
4	tablespoons milk
1	teaspoon monosodium glutamate
	Salt and pepper to taste
1	small can French fried onion rings

Cook beans in ½ cup of water for 10 minutes. Drain and add the soup, milk, monosodium glutamate, season to taste with salt and pepper. Stirring gently, turn into a well-buttered casserole and top with onion rings. Place in a moderate 350° oven and bake 45 minutes, or until thoroughly heated and top gently browned.

STRING BEANS CHINESE
Serves 6

Ready Tray
3	tablespoons peanut oil
1	clove garlic, finely chopped
½	teaspoon powdered ginger
½	pound beef, ground
3	onions, thinly sliced
1	pound fresh string beans, cut in 2-inch lengths
1	cup stock
2	tablespoons soy sauce
2	sprigs fresh parsley
1	bay leaf
1	teaspoon salt
½	teaspoon freshly ground black pepper

Heat oil in a heavy skillet. Add garlic, ginger, meat and onions. Cook over high heat for 3 minutes, stirring constantly. Reduce heat and add string beans, stock, soy sauce, parsley, bay leaf, salt and pepper. Cook over low heat for 30 minutes, stirring occasionally. Discard the bay leaf and add more salt and pepper if necessary.

Serve with boiled rice.

PRESSURE-COOKED STRING BEANS WITH NOODLES
Serves 4 to 6

Ready Tray
2	tablespoons butter
1	onion, thinly sliced
1	pound string beans, cut lengthwise
3	cups peeled tomatoes, diced
1	teaspoon sugar
1	teaspoon salt
¼	teaspoon pepper
½	pound broad noodles
¾	cup fried croutons

Melt butter in the pressure cooker; sauté onion until soft and light golden.

Add beans, tomatoes, sugar, salt and pepper. Close the cooker, bring to 15 pounds pressure and process 4 minutes. Cool under cold running water until pressure subsides.

Cook the noodles until tender in salted water. Drain thoroughly. Add a little butter and toss until mixed well. Place in a deep serving dish and cover with the beans and tomatoes. Sprinkle with croutons and serve with cottage cheese.

STRING BEANS AND CHICKEN BREASTS
Serves 4

Ready Tray		
	⅓	cup flour
	½	teaspoon thyme
	¼	teaspoon sage
	2	pounds chicken breasts, split in two
	3	tablespoons butter
	1	onion, thinly sliced
	3	potatoes, medium size, peeled and diced
	1	pound fresh string beans, cut lengthwise
	1	small piece green ginger root, shaved

Mix the flour, thyme and sage together. Dip the chicken breasts in this, and sauté in butter in a skillet until brown on both sides. Place chicken in a buttered casserole.

Brown onion and potatoes in skillet and turn into casserole.

Thicken juices in skillet with rest of seasoned flour and thin with 1½ cups water. Add green beans to casserole, sprinkle with ginger and pour gravy over all. Bake, uncovered, in a medium 350° oven for 25 minutes, or until chicken is tender and beans are cooked.

STRING BEANS AND CHICKEN
WITH MUSTARD SAUCE
Serves 4

Ready Tray
1	cup plus 2 tablespoons milk
½	cup sugar
1	tablespoon dry English mustard
	Pinch of salt
1	tablespoon cornstarch
1	egg yolk, beaten light
¼	cup diluted tarragon vinegar (2 tablespoons vinegar, 2 tablespoons water)
3	tablespoons bacon fat
1	2½ pound chicken, cut in serving pieces
1	pound green string beans, sliced lengthwise

Put 1 cup milk in a double boiler and let come to a boil. Mix dry ingredients together and blend with the 2 tablespoons cold milk. Add gradually to the boiled milk, stirring constantly. Reduce heat and add egg yolk. Add vinegar and cook 3 minutes, until slightly thickened.

Sauté chicken in bacon fat until delicately browned and place in a casserole. Arrange the beans over the top, pour mustard sauce over all, cover and bake in 350° oven until chicken and beans are tender, approximately 45 minutes.

BEAN SPROUT EGG FOO YUNG
Serves 4 to 6

Ready Tray
6	eggs
1	teaspoon salt
2	tablespoons green pepper, finely chopped
½	cup onion, finely shredded
2	cups cooked bean sprouts, well drained
1	tablespoon fat to fry each cake

Beat the eggs until light. Add the remaining ingredients except the fat and mix well. Melt 1 tablespoon fat in a 6-inch skillet. Pour ½ cup of the mixture into the skillet and brown both sides, turning only once (5 minutes). Repeat until the mixture is used. Serve with rice and soy sauce.

CHILI CON CARNE
Serves 6
Serve with Frijoles de la Olla

Ready Tray		
	½	cup beef fat, chopped
	1½	pounds beef shoulder or round, cut in 1-inch cubes
	1¼	cups onion, finely chopped
	2½	tablespoons chili powder
	½	teaspoon oregano
	½	teaspoon cumin
	1	small bay leaf
	2	medium cloves garlic, crushed
	1	teaspoon salt
	½	teaspoon sugar
	2	cups tomato purée (#303 can)
	1½	cups beef bouillon

Sauté beef fat until crisp. Add cubed meat and brown lightly.

Add onion, reduce heat and cook onion until tender.

Add chili powder, oregano, cumin, bay leaf, garlic, salt, sugar, purée and beef bouillon. Stir gently. Cover and let simmer approximately 1 hour or until meat is tender and sauce is thickened. Add more chili powder if desired.

Serve hot over the frijoles.

STRING BEANS AND PORK
Serves 4

Ready Tray | ½ pound fresh lean pork, cut in strips 1-inch long by
              | ½-inch wide
              | 1 tablespoon soy sauce
              | 1 teaspoon cornstarch
              | 1 teaspoon sugar
              | 1 teaspoon salt
              | ½ teaspoon pepper
              | 2 tablespoons peanut oil
              | 1 pound fresh string beans, cut in 2-inch lengths
              | ½ cup boiling water

Mix the pork with the soy sauce, cornstarch, sugar, salt and pepper and let stand 15 minutes.

Heat oil in a saucepan, cook the pork quickly over a high flame for 5 minutes, stirring constantly.

Add beans and cook for 2 minutes, stirring constantly.

Pour in the water, cover, reduce heat and cook gently for 15 minutes.

Serve with boiled rice.

EASTMAN FAMILY BAKED BEANS
(A Genuine New England Recipe)
Serves 10 to 12

Ready Tray | 4 cups dried beans, preferably soldier beans or white
              | marrow fat beans
              | ½ pound salt pork, cut in cubes
              | 3 teaspoons salt
              | ½ teaspoon mustard
              | 1 teaspoon ginger
              | 1 cup brown sugar (or maple syrup or molasses)

Soak beans overnight in cold water. In the morning parboil beans until their skins break when blown upon and they do not rattle when stirred. Drain. Put them in an earthen pot in layers with salt pork, salt, mustard, ginger and brown sugar. Fill with fresh water to top of pot and add water as needed.

Bake in 350° oven for 6 to 8 hours.

BRAISED SHARK'S FINS AND BEAN SPROUTS
Serves 4 to 6

Ready Tray

¼	pound refined shark's fins
1	stalk leek, cut in 1-inch lengths
5	slices ginger
5	cups chicken broth
1	cup crab meat, flaked
¼	pound fresh bean sprouts
6	dried mushrooms, soaked in water and finely shredded
2	tablespoons rice wine or brandy
3	tablespoons soy sauce
1	teaspoon sugar
½	teaspoon monosodium glutamate (Accent)
1	tablespoon cornstarch, mixed with
½	cup water

Soak shark's fins overnight in water to cover. Boil fins with leek and ginger in plenty of water for 1 hour. Drain and rinse. Boil fins again in chicken broth for 30 minutes.

Add crab meat, bean sprouts, mushrooms, wine or brandy, soy sauce, sugar and monosodium glutamate. Stir thoroughly. Simmer 10 minutes.

Add cornstarch mixture and thicken. Serve hot.

HOME BAKED BEANS, IDAHO STYLE
Serves 12 to 14

Ready Tray		
	4	cups dried Great Northern large white beans
	3	quarts cold water
	1	onion, medium size, pierced with 2 whole cloves
	1	bay leaf
	1	clove garlic, peeled
	2	tablespoons butter
	½	pound salt pork
	1	onion, medium size, peeled, but whole
	¼	cup brown sugar, firmly packed, light or dark
	1	teaspoon dry mustard
	1	teaspoon salt
	½	cup molasses, light or dark
	½	cup ketchup
	½	teaspoon Worcestershire sauce
	3	cups bean liquid

Soak beans in water overnight. Cook beans in water in which they soaked. Add clove-pierced onion, bay leaf, garlic and butter. Cover and place over high heat. Bring to boil, reduce heat to simmer and cook until skins wrinkle and start to crack, approximately 45 minutes. Remove from heat. Discard onion, bay leaf and garlic. Drain and reserve the liquid.

Scrape and wash salt off salt pork. Cut through to skin in 1-inch squares. Place whole onion in a 4-quart heavy bean pot and cover with beans. Bury salt pork in center, cut side up.

Mix together all ingredients, except bean liquid. If not quite enough to make 3 cups, add water. Bring to boil, mix with seasonings and pour over beans. Cover and place on shallow baking pan or large square of foil with turned-up sides to catch any spillovers, in a 250° oven and bake slowly 7 to 8 hours. At end of baking time, remove from oven and check for salt, adding more if necessary. Add a little boiling water if you don't see the sauce peeking through. With a wooden spoon, gently bring salt pork to surface and replace pot in oven, uncovered, to bake for ½ hour longer to brown surface. Serve piping hot from the bean pot!

GRANDMOTHER'S BROWN SUGAR BEANS
Serves 8

Ready Tray

1	pound dried Idaho Great Northern large white beans
5	cups water
⅛	teaspoon soda
2	teaspoons salt
1	or 2 tablespoons butter
1	onion, medium size, peeled, but whole
¾	cup dark brown sugar, firmly packed
1	teaspoon dry mustard
6	slices lean bacon, cut in 3 pieces each
	Salt and pepper mill

Soak beans in water overnight. Cook beans in same water. Add baking soda, salt, butter and whole onion. Cover and bring to boil. Reduce heat to simmering and allow to cook with little or no stirring, approximately 1½ hours, or until beans are almost tender. Drain and reserve liquid.

Remove onion. Place half of beans in casserole. Sprinkle with half of brown sugar and mustard. Add balance of beans, brown sugar, mustard and season to taste with salt and freshly ground black pepper. Add remaining bean liquid and enough hot water, if needed, so that liquid can be seen at edges of casserole. Top beans with bacon. Bake uncovered in 350° oven, approximately 1 hour.

Just before serving, sprinkle bacon lightly with brown sugar. Allow to brown under broiler for crusty-sweet bacon.

Serve hot from casserole.

Goes well with any meat, especially those from the barbecue grill. Perfect partners are coleslaw or sliced tomatoes.

PAPA ROSSI'S PASTA E FAGIOLI
(South Italy Style)
(From a 2000 year-old-recipe)
Serves 6 to 8

Ready Tray

1 pound white dried beans
1 cup good olive oil
Salt to taste
1 clove garlic, unshelled
1 large leaf Italian bay leaf
1 level teaspoon coarse ground red hot pepper
Few branches fresh parsley
½ pound salad macaroni

Soak the washed beans overnight in cold water with a ratio of three times the volume of beans to which salt to taste has been added.

Next day, do not drain, but place them on the fire and start cooking slowly. Bring to boil, remove foam and add the oil, garlic and bay leaf. The importance of these last 3 ingredients is not discovered except by a true food connoisseur as the oil becomes incorporated into the beans as they cook, changing their flavor, as does the delicate flavor of the whole clove of garlic and of the Italian bay leaf. (This leaf is much wider than the American bay leaf and not as bitter.) Cook the beans gently for 2 hours or until just tender.

Begin cooking the pasta in boiling water seasoned with salt. Let it boil for 6 to 7 minutes. Drain and reserve 1 cup of the macaroni liquid. Add the pasta to the beans, after having removed the bay leaf and garlic clove.

Add the hot ground pepper and stir everything together gently. Place on fire to simmer and add some of the hot pasta liquid as needed, until the pasta is cooked and blended with the beans, about 6 or 7 minutes more.

Serve on hot dish, garnish with red ground pepper and parsley.

STRING BEANS ORIENTAL
Serves 8 to 10

Ready Tray

3	packages (9-oz. ea.) frozen French-style green beans
1	onion, medium size, thinly sliced
½	cup butter or margarine
⅓	cup flour
2	cups milk
¾	cup sharp Cheddar cheese, shredded
⅛	teaspoon Tabasco sauce
2	teaspoons soy sauce
1	teaspoon salt
½	teaspoon black pepper
1	teaspoon monosodium glutamate
1	can (8-oz.) sliced mushrooms, drained
1	can (5-oz.) water chestnuts, drained and sliced
⅓	cup sliced almonds

Cook beans in salted water until just barely tender. Drain and set aside.

Sauté onion in butter until soft. Add flour and blend. Slowly add milk and cheese. Cook until smooth and thick, stirring constantly. Add seasonings. Stir in cooked beans, mushrooms and water chestnuts. Turn into 2-quart casserole. Sprinkle almonds over top. Bake, uncovered, at 375° for 30 minutes, or until bubbly.

Prepare sauce and combine ingredients in advance, if you prefer. Then leave it in the refrigerator until baking time.

STRING BEANS AND FRANKFURTERS
Serves 4

Ready Tray	2	slices bacon, finely chopped
	1	onion, finely chopped
	1	clove garlic, finely chopped
	1	pound green string beans, slivered
	1	cup beef bouillon
	¼	pound salt pork, finely chopped
	8	small new potatoes, peeled and cut in quarters
	4	garlic-flavored frankfurters, skinned and cut in half
		Salt and freshly ground black pepper

Sauté bacon in heavy skillet, pour off most of the fat, leaving a thin film in the skillet. Add onion, garlic, beans, bouillon and salt pork and stir gently. Place potatoes and frankfurters over the top of the beans and season to taste with salt and freshly ground black pepper. Cover and place over low heat and cook until tender, approximately 1 hour.

STRING BEANS WITH DRIED SHRIMP
Serves 6

Ready Tray	½	cup dried shrimp
	1	onion, thinly sliced
	3	tablespoons sesame oil
	5	cups string beans, diagonally sliced
	1¼	teaspoons sugar
	¼	cup soy sauce
	2	teaspoons white sesame seeds, browned and pulverized

Wash shrimp and soak in water to cover for 30 minutes. Drain and cut in very small pieces. Fry with onions in hot oil until onions are tender. Add beans, sugar, soy sauce and pulverized sesame seeds. Cover and simmer gently until the beans and shrimp are tender. Serve hot.

RED BEANS, COUNTRY-STYLE
Serves 10 to 12

Ready Tray	1	pound Idaho dried red beans
	6	cups water
	⅛	teaspoon soda
	2	tablespoons butter or vegetable oil
	½	pound bulk pork sausage
	1	cup onions, coarsely chopped
	2	cups tart cooking apples, peeled, thinly sliced
	2	medium cloves garlic, peeled and mashed into
	2	teaspoons salt
	¼	teaspoon freshly ground black pepper
	1	teaspoon chili powder
	1	teaspoon dry mustard
	¼	cup brown sugar, firmly packed
	1½	cups tomato juice
	¼	cup Jamaica rum
		Sour cream for garnish

Soak washed beans in water overnight. Cook beans in water in which they were soaked in a heavy kettle. Add soda and butter or oil. Bring to boiling point, uncovered, reduce heat to low. Cover and simmer gently for 2 hours, or until beans are tender.

Flatten out sausage in heavy skillet, brown one side. Turn, breaking up in fairly good-sized pieces. When browned, add to beans with 2 tablespoons of sausage fat and other ingredients, except the rum and sour cream. Mix gently, bring quickly to boiling point, reduce heat, cover and simmer slowly for 2 hours, or until tender and the liquid is thick. Or bring to boiling point, turn into a casserole, cover and bake in 325° oven, approximately 2 hours.

5 minutes before serving, stir in the rum. Garnish each serving with a dollop of sour cream.

STRING BEAN SUPREME
Serves 8

Ready Tray

2	tablespoons butter
1	onion, medium size, finely chopped
3	tablespoons fresh parsley, finely chopped
2	tablespoons flour
2	tablespoons water
1	teaspoon salt
¼	teaspoon black pepper
½	teaspoon lemon peel, grated
2	cans (16-oz. ea.) French-style green beans, drained
1	cup commercial sour cream
½	cup natural Cheddar cheese, shredded
½	cup dry bread crumbs

Melt butter in skillet or saucepan. Add onion and parsley and sauté until onion is transparent. Gradually stir in flour, then water, salt, pepper and lemon peel. Simmer for about 3 minutes. Add beans and sour cream. Mix well. Spoon into 2-quart casserole. Sprinkle top with cheese, then crumbs. Bake, uncovered, at 350° for 30 minutes or until golden brown.

WHITE BEANS, COUNTRY STYLE
Serves 4 to 6

Ready Tray

1	pound dried white beans
	Salt and freshly ground black pepper
1	clove garlic, finely chopped
1	bay leaf
6	tablespoons butter
2	onions, medium size, finely chopped
1	green bell pepper, finely chopped
3	fresh tomatoes, peeled and coarsely chopped
½	teaspoon dried oregano leaves, fresh, if available
¼	cup fresh parsley, finely chopped

Cover washed beans with 5 cups cold water and soak overnight, covered, in the refrigerator. Next day, season to taste with salt and freshly ground black pepper, and add garlic and bay leaf. Bring to boiling point, reduce heat and simmer, covered, until the beans are tender, or approximately 2 hours. Stir occasionally while beans are cooking. Drain thoroughly.

Place 4 tablespoons butter in a large skillet and sauté onions until golden brown. Add green pepper and tomato and cook for 5 minutes. Add the oregano leaves and parsley and blend well. Add to beans with the remainder of the butter and stir gently before serving.

STRING BEANS AND HAM
Serves 4

Ready Tray
2	pounds fresh string beans, cut lengthwise
3	tablespoons butter
3	tablespoons flour
1	cup milk
½	teaspoon nutmeg
	Salt and pepper
1	cup Cheddar cheese, grated
⅔	cup ham, coarsely chopped

Cook the beans in water to cover until tender. Drain.

Melt butter and blend in flour until smooth, add milk gradually, stirring constantly until thickened. Reduce heat.

Add nutmeg and season to taste with salt and pepper.

Add cheese and stir until melted. Add beans and turn into buttered casserole. Sprinkle ham over the top and bake in a 350° oven until thoroughly heated and the top is delicately browned, approximately 30 minutes. Serve from casserole.

YANKEE BEANS WITH SPAGHETTI
Serves 4

Ready Tray
1	pound dried Yankee beans
2	teaspoons salt
½	teaspoon freshly ground black pepper
½	pound spaghetti
	Chopped, cooked crisp bacon
	Plenty of croutons
	Chopped parsley
	Sweet pickles or pickle relish

Cover beans with boiling water and soak for 2 hours. Then bring to a boil and cook until the beans are tender and the liquid is about half evaporated. Drain off the liquid in a separate pan and in it, boil the spaghetti until tender. Serve in bowls, placing the hot beans in the bottom, covered with a little of the spaghetti. Then sprinkle some of the cooked, chopped bacon and repeat, finishing with the bacon and croutons. Pour some of the soup around and garnish with the pickles and parsley.

This is a whole meal dish and should be served with a green salad or cole slaw, or tart fruit salad.

PRESSURE-COOKED STRING BEANS AND PORK CHOPS
Serves 4

Ready Tray
4	thick, smoked loin pork chops, fat trimmed
1	can (8-oz.) tomatoes
1	large onion, diced
1	teaspoon dried Italian seasoning
½	teaspoon freshly ground pepper
2	teaspoons salt
1½	pounds fresh string beans, cut in 2-inch lengths

Place smoked loin pork chops in the bottom of a pressure cooker. Add tomatoes, onion, seasonings and string beans. Cover tightly and bring pressure to 15 pounds. Process 10 minutes only after steam starts to eject.

Cool cooker immediately under cold running water.

STRING BEAN CURRY AND FISH
Serves 8

Ready Tray		
	2	cups onions, finely chopped
	1	clove garlic, finely chopped
	2	teaspoons powdered ginger
	½	teaspoon dried ground chili peppers
	1	teaspoon turmeric
	2	teaspoons salt
	½	cup cooked shrimp, finely chopped
	4	tablespoons peanut oil
	1	pound fresh string beans, cut in 2-inch lengths
	2	cups water
	3	tablespoons lemon juice, blended with
	2	tablespoons plum jam
	4	fillets of mackerel or shad

Pound to a thick paste, the onions, garlic, ginger, chili peppers, turmeric, salt and shrimp.

Heat oil in a heavy skillet and sauté the paste for 5 minutes over a high flame. Add beans and sauté lightly for 3 minutes. Add water, lemon juice blended with plum jam and cook gently over low heat for 5 minutes.

Place fish in the sauce, cover and cook over low heat for 20 minutes, or until fish flakes easily.

Serve with boiled rice.

HERBED BEANS, IDAHO STYLE
Serves 6

Ready Tray		
	2	cups dried Idaho Great Northern large white beans
	5	cups water
	1	large meaty ham bone
	1½	teaspoons salt
	1	large whole onion, pierced with 2 whole cloves
	1	bay leaf
	2	large cloves garlic, whole
	2	tablespoons fresh parsley, finely chopped
	1	teaspoon fresh, winter savory, finely chopped
	1	teaspoon fresh marjoram, finely chopped
	1	teaspoon fresh thyme, finely chopped
		Pan juices from roast or
	3	tablespoons butter

Cover beans with water, add hambone and bring to boil quickly. Boil 2 minutes. Remove from heat, cover and allow to stand 1 hour.

Cook beans in water in which they were soaked. Place over high heat. Add 1 teaspoon butter to keep down the foam. Add remaining ingredients, except herbs and meat drippings. Bring to boil, cover and reduce heat to simmer. Simmer gently for 2 hours, or until beans are tender but not mushy. Remove hambone, cut meat in small pieces and return to beans. Stir in fresh parsley and herbs and pan juices or butter and serve piping hot!

Serve a crisp green salad, cornbread sticks, relishes, beverage of your choice and a deep dish fruit pie for a complete meal.

These beans may be prepared in advance, refrigerated and reheated for immediate use.

ITALIAN-MADE BEAN CASSEROLE
Serves 6

Ready Tray		
	2	cups dried Great Northern large white beans
	6	cups cold water
	2	teaspoons salt
	½	cup olive oil
	1	cup onion, coarsely chopped
	2	cloves garlic, finely chopped
	1	cup celery, coarsely chopped
	2	tablespoons snipped fresh parsley
	½	teaspoon dried crushed thyme
	¼	teaspoon dried crushed sweet basil
	¼	teaspoon coarse ground black pepper
	1	cup fresh skinned or solid-pack canned tomatoes
	⅔	cup bean liquid and tomato juice combined
		Grated Parmesan or Romano cheese

Soak beans in water overnight. Cook beans in water in which they were soaked. Place over high heat. Add 1 teaspoon butter to keep down the foam. Bring to boil, cover and reduce heat to simmer. Stir occasionally. Add salt and simmer gently until tender. Drain, reserve liquid.

Heat oil over low heat, add onions, garlic and celery. Cook until tender, but not browned. Add parsley, thyme, sweet basil, pepper, tomatoes and bean-tomato liquid. Bring to boil, add to beans and mix lightly. Turn into a 1½ quart casserole. Cover and bake in 350° oven 1 hour. Remove from oven, dust top of beans generously with grated cheese and return to oven, uncovered, for 10 minutes to brown cheese lightly.

Serve piping hot with additional cheese to sprinkle over each serving. Excellent with roast leg of lamb.

TWELFTH-NIGHT WELSH RABBIT
Serves 5 or 6

Ready Tray		
	1	pound sharp natural Cheddar cheese, thinly sliced
	1	tablespoon butter
	½	cup ale, beer or cream
	1½	teaspoons dry mustard
	2	teaspoons Worcestershire sauce
	3	dashes Tabasco sauce
	⅛	teaspoon paprika
	1	well-beaten egg
	2	cups cooked, Idaho large white Great Northern beans, drained
		Triangles of buttered toast

In top of double boiler or in blazer pan in hot water jacket of your chafing dish mix dry seasonings. Pour in ale, beer or cream. Let stand until hot. Add cheese and sauces. Stir all, always in the same direction until cheese is melted.

Add a tablespoon cheese mixture to beaten egg, combine and stir into cheese mixture. Stir in cooked beans gently. (The egg is not ordinarily added but it is a precaution against mixture separating as it stands, which may happen with buffet parties.)

To serve: When thoroughly hot, serve over hot buttered toast triangles in individual shallow heated dishes, garnishing with a strip of crisp bacon, if desired.

WHITE BEANS WITH PROSCIUTTO
Serves 4

Ready Tray		
	1	pound dried white beans
	½	pound prosciutto rind
	2	ounces prosciutto fat, finely chopped
	1	clove garlic, finely chopped
	2	tablespoons fresh parsley, finely chopped
	1	tablespoon lard
	1	onion, thinly sliced
	3	tablespoons tomato sauce
		Salt and freshly ground black pepper

Soak the washed beans overnight in water to cover. Next day, place over medium heat and cook until tender.

In a separate pot, cover the prosciutto rinds with water and boil for 5 minutes. Drain and wash well. Cut in 1-inch squares and re-place in pot with plenty of water, cover and simmer gently until thoroughly tender.

By the time the beans and prosciutto rinds are done, you must have prepared the prosciutto fat, the garlic and parsley and minced them together to almost a paste. Place this in a pan with the lard and onion and sauté until rich brown in color. Add the tomato sauce with a little juice from the beans or the rinds. Simmer for several minutes, then combine with the beans and the rinds. Season to taste with salt and freshly ground black pepper and simmer slowly for 30 minutes. Easy on the juice: when cooked, should be eaten with a fork.

WHITE BEAN CURRY
Serves 6

Ready Tray		
	1½	cups dried white beans
	2	tablespoons butter
	4	pounds lamb, cut into 2-inch cubes
	3	onions, finely chopped
	8	tomatoes, medium size, peeled and finely chopped
	2	teaspoons salt
	¼	teaspoon dried ground chili peppers
	2	tablespoons curry powder
	1	tablespoon sugar
	¼	cup water
	2	tablespoons vinegar
	1	cup sour apples, chopped
	½	cup seedless raisins

Soak washed beans in water to cover overnight. Next day boil gently for 1 hour.

Heat butter in heavy kettle that has a tight-fitting cover. Add the onions and sauté for 5 minutes. Add the meat and brown well on all sides. Add tomatoes, salt and chili peppers, cover and cook over low heat for 30 minutes. Mix the curry powder, sugar, water and vinegar together until smooth. Add to meat and stir well.

Drain the beans and add together with the apples and raisins. Cover and cook very slowly for 2½ hours, or until meat is very tender. If necessary, add small amounts of water. Serve with boiled rice.

BAKED WHITE BEANS
Serves 6

Ready Tray
3	cups quick-cooking white beans
1	teaspoon salt
1	Bermuda onion, medium size
1	pound salt pork, sliced and cut in ½-inch pieces
⅔	cup molasses
2	teaspoons dry mustard
1	teaspoon freshly ground black pepper

Place beans in kettle, add salt and cover with water. Place over medium heat and simmer until beans are just tender. Drain.

Place onion in the bottom of a bean pot or large casserole. Place a layer of beans over the onion, a layer of salt pork, repeating layers until the ingredients are used.

Combine the molasses, mustard and freshly ground black pepper until smooth. Pour over beans in casserole. Pour enough hot water over the beans to cover. Place, covered, in a slow 250° oven and bake 4 to 5 hours, adding boiling water when necessary to keep the beans covered.

Remove cover and bake beans 1 hour longer, without adding any more hot water. Allow the liquid to bake down and the top of the beans to brown nicely.

VI

Bean Breads, Pastries and Desserts

Soybean grits, soy flour and soy milk are obtainable in **Health Food Stores.**

The soybean pulp is prepared by pressing cooked soybeans through a coarse sieve or by putting them through a food grinder.

Soy Flour imparts to baked goods a rich yellow color resembling that obtained when liberal quantities of eggs are used. It browns more quickly than when wheat flour alone is used and in addition, it gives a richer brown to baked products.

Soy Milk can be used in making wholesome beverages and in various recipes to increase the nutritive value of the food being prepared, especially for individuals who are allergic to cow's milk. Soy milk is a complete substitute for cow's milk (Medizinische Klinik, 42 15:1 August, 1947).

Canned soy milk is available, manufactured by Madison Foods, or it can be freshly prepared at home from dry soy milk powder which is obtainable under the trade names of "Soyalac" (Loma Linda Food Company) and "Soyamel" (Worthing Foods).

ST. JOHN'S BREAD CAKE

What is St. John's Bread? In the first place, it isn't bread, and although it is often called locust bean, it isn't the locust that John the Baptist ate in the wilderness. (Those were real locusts, roasted.) It is the pod of the carob tree and is properly known as the carob bean. It grows now, as it did in biblical times, in the Holy Land, and can flourish wherever oranges grow; in California, along the Mediterranean coast and in Florida. The pod is ground to make ingredients for a bread cake. Both pod and flesh are sweet and juicy; only the hard seeds should be discarded. Agriculturists say that it yields a considerable amount of food per acre and it is predicted that more and more carob trees will rear their tall evergreen heads in our land.

Ready Tray

8	egg yolks
½	cup sugar
½	cup St. John's bread (carob bean), well-dried and grated
½	cup fine dry bread crumbs
8	egg whites, beaten stiff
2	cups confectioners' sugar
2½	tablespoons rum
	Water
	Walnut halves
	Silver shot

Beat yolks with sugar until thick and light in color. Beat in St. John's bread and bread crumbs. Fold in egg whites and pour into 2 buttered and floured 8-inch layer pans. Bake in a moderate slow 275° oven for 10 minutes, increase heat to 375° and bake for 30 minutes longer. Invert on cake rack to cool and remove from pans.

Blend until smooth the confectioners' sugar, rum and just a little water to make a spreadable paste. Spread over layers and put cake together, cover top and garnish with walnut halves and sprinkle with silver shot. Cool thoroughly before slicing.

This is really something different and tasty!

PRESSURE-COOKED BOSTON BROWN BREAD

Ready Tray
2	cups buttermilk
¾	cup dark molasses
1	teaspoon salt
1	teaspoon baking soda
1	cup coarse entire wheat flour
1	cup rye meal
2	cups granulated cornmeal
¾	cup seedless raisins

Mix together thoroughly the buttermilk and molasses. Add salt and the soda dissolved in 1 tablespoon water.

Add wheat flour, rye meal, cornmeal and raisins. Blend until smooth.

Pour into pint-sized cans or molds. Tie 2 thicknesses of waxed paper over the top.

Place cans or molds on rack in the pressure cooker. Pour hot water halfway the depth of the molds. Close the cooker.

Pre-steam 30 minutes without pressure, then bring pressure to 15 pounds and process 40 minutes.

Remove from molds and cool thoroughly.

BISCUITS
Makes 16

Ready Tray
1	cup soy flour
1	cup all-purpose flour
3	teaspoons baking powder
½	teaspoon salt
6	tablespoons shortening
¾	cup milk

Sift soy flour and white flour separately. Measure and sift together with remaining dry ingredients. Cut in shortening and blend in milk. Toss out on a lightly floured board and knead lightly. Roll dough to about ½-inch thickness. Cut with a 2-inch biscuit cutter. Place on greased baking sheet and bake in hot 450° oven for 15 minutes.

HIGH SOY YEAST BREAD
2 Loaves

Ready Tray

1	cup milk, scalded and cooled to lukewarm
2	tablespoons sugar
2	teaspoons salt
2	tablespoons shortening
1	cup water
1	cake fresh yeast
¼	cup lukewarm water
1½	cups soy flour, sifted
4½	cups all-purpose flour, sifted

Place lukewarm milk in a bowl, add sugar, salt, shortening and water. Let stand for 5 minutes. Add yeast which has been softened in ¼ cup lukewarm water.

Add both flours gradually to yeast mixture, mixing thoroughly until a stiff dough is formed. Turn out on a lightly floured board and knead until smooth and satiny and the dough no longer clings to the hands. Shape into a smooth ball. Place in a large greased bowl, grease top lightly, cover and let rise in a warm place (80°) until double in bulk, approximately 1¾ hours. Punch down. Let rise again, about 1 hour, until double in bulk. Divide into 2 equal parts and round each into a smooth ball. Cover and let rise 15 minutes. Shape into loaves and place in greased bread loaf pans and let rise until doubled in bulk, about 1 hour. Bake in a moderately hot 375° oven for 20 minutes, reduce heat to 350° and bake 25 minutes longer. Brush with melted butter, remove from pans and cool on cake rack.

YEAST BREAD
2 Loaves

Ready Tray		
	2	cups milk, scalded and cooled
	2	cakes compressed yeast
	1	tablespoon salt
	2½	tablespoons sugar
	6	cups sifted all-purpose flour
	1⅓	tablespoons melted shortening
	½	cup plus 1 tablespoon stirred full-fat soy flour

Pour the lukewarm milk into a mixing bowl. Add yeast, salt and sugar and stir until dissolved. Add 3 cups of the white flour and beat thoroughly. Add shortening, soy flour and the balance of white flour gradually, forming a dough that will not cling to the bowl. Turn dough out on a floured board and knead until it no longer sticks to the board. Return to a greased bowl and brush the surface with melted shortening. Cover and let rise in a warm place (80°) until the dough is double in bulk. Fold dough under and let rise again. Turn out again on floured board, fold dough under and let stand 10 minutes before shaping. Form dough into 2 smooth rolls. Place the rolls in greased bread pans, brush with melted shortening and let rise until double in bulk. Bake in moderate 350° oven for 50 to 60 minutes. Remove from pans at once and cool.

COFFEE BREAD

Ready Tray		
	⅓	cup sugar
	⅓	cup shortening
	½	teaspoon salt
	1	cup milk, scalded
	1	yeast cake, dissolved in ¼ cup water
	2	eggs
	3½	cups all-purpose flour
	½	cup low-fat soy flour

Add sugar, shortening and salt to scalded milk, cool to lukewarm, add dissolved yeast cake and eggs. Add enough of combined flours to make a stiff batter. Cover and let rise until double in bulk. Beat thoroughly and spread evenly in 2 greased round layer cake tins. Sprinkle with nut mixture . . . let rise. Bake 40 minutes, beginning with hot 450° oven and decreasing after 10 minutes to 350°. To make topping adhere, brush surface of dough with honey or corn syrup, spread the topping and pat down.

CURRANT NUT BREAD

Ready Tray
- ⅔ cup soy flour
- 1½ cups all-purpose flour
- 2 teaspoons baking powder
- ½ teaspoon ground nutmeg
- ½ teaspoon salt
- ½ cup sugar
- 2 tablespoons shortening
- ¾ cup currants
- ½ cup nut meats
- 1 egg, well beaten
- ¾ cup milk
- 1 teaspoon orange rind, grated
- 1 teaspoon orange juice

Sift soy flour and all-purpose flour separately. Measure and sift together with remaining dry ingredients. Cut in shortening. Add currants and nut meats. Combine well-beaten egg and milk and add to first mixture. Add orange rind and juice and mix well. Place in a well-greased loaf pan. Bake for 50 minutes in 350° oven.

SOUTHERN CORN BREAD

Ready Tray
½	cup soy flour
½	cup all-purpose flour
1	teaspoon salt
3	teaspoons baking powder
2	tablespoons sugar
¾	cup white corn. meal
2	eggs, beaten
1	cup milk
4	tablespoons melted butter

Sift soy flour and all-purpose flour separately. Measure, combine, and sift again with salt, baking powder, sugar and corn meal.

Combine beaten eggs, milk and melted butter. Add to dry ingredients and beat until smooth. Pour into a well-greased 8 x 8 inch pan and bake in hot 400° oven for 30 minutes.

WHOLE WHEAT BREAD
2 Loaves

Ready Tray
2	cups milk, scalded and cooled
¼	cup molasses
1	tablespoon salt
1	cake yeast
½	cup stirred soy flour
2½	cups sifted all-purpose flour
2½	cups stirred whole wheat flour
2	tablespoons melted shortening

Combine the lukewarm milk, molasses and salt in a mixing bowl. Crumble the yeast into the mixture and blend thoroughly.

Sift the flours together, add to the liquid mixture and beat thoroughly. Add shortening and knead to form a dough that will not cling to the sides of the bowl. Turn out on a lightly floured board and knead until smooth and elastic, about 10 minutes. Place dough in greased bowl, brush surface with melted shortening, cover and let rise in warm place (80°) until double in bulk. Fold dough under, let rise again until doubled. Turn out again on board, fold under and let stand 15 minutes before shaping. Shape into 2 loaves and place in greased bread loaf pans, brush with melted shortening and let rise until double in bulk. Bake in 350° oven for 1 hour. Remove bread from pans immediately and place on cake rack to cool.

DOUGHNUTS

Ready Tray

¼	cup butter
1	cup sugar
2	eggs
1⅓	cups soy flour
2⅔	cups white flour
4	teaspoons baking powder
1	teaspoon salt
1¼	teaspoons nutmeg
¾	teaspoon cinnamon
1	cup milk
1	teaspoon vanilla

Cream butter, add sugar gradually and continue creaming until light and fluffy. Beat in whole eggs. Sift soy flour and white flour separately and measure. Combine and add baking powder, salt, nutmeg, cinnamon and sift together. Add dry ingredients, alternately with milk. Stir in vanilla. Roll dough ¼-inch thick on a lightly floured board. Cut with doughnut cutter. Fry in deep fat 350° until doughnuts are brown on one side, then turn and fry on second side. Drain on absorbent paper. Sugar lightly, if desired.

BRONZE CAKE

Ready Tray		
	¾	cup butter
	1½	cups brown sugar
	¾	cup soy flour
	1½	cups cake flour
	3	teaspoons baking powder
	½	teaspoon salt
	1	cup milk
	1	teaspoon vanilla extract
	4	egg whites

Cream the butter until soft, add sugar gradually and cream thoroughly.

Sift soy flour and cake flour separately and measure. Add baking powder and salt and sift together twice. Add dry ingredients alternately with the milk, beating after each addition. Stir in vanilla. Beat egg whites until stiff and fold lightly into the batter. Pour batter into 2 nine-inch layer cake pans which have been lined on the bottom with wax paper and then greased.

Bake in moderate 325° oven for 30 minutes. Frost and fill with a fluffy white icing and sprinkle with nuts, if desired.

GRIDDLE CAKES

Ready Tray		
	½	cup soy flour
	1	cup white flour
	3	teaspoons baking powder
	¾	teaspoon salt
	3	tablespoons sugar
	1	egg
	1⅓	cups milk
	3	tablespoons shortening, melted

Sift soy flour and white flour separately and measure. Combine, add baking powder, salt and sugar and sift again. Beat egg, add milk and melted shortening. Add dry ingredients and stir just until well combined. Drop batter from tablespoon onto a hot griddle which has been lightly greased. Spread cakes out lightly with back of spoon. Cook on one side until puffed, full of bubbles and cooked on edges. Turn and brown other side.

Serve with your favorite syrup or preserves.

BEAN PASTE CAKES JAPANESE
Makes 22 cakes

Ready Tray

1	cup dried red kidney beans
⅞	cup sugar
2¼	cups flour
3	teaspoons baking powder
½	teaspoon salt
1½	tablespoons sesame oil
¼	cup water
⅜	cup sugar

Soak beans overnight in water to cover. Cook in same water until a thick paste is obtained. Cool thoroughly. Add ⅜ cup sugar, cook for 15 minutes over low heat, stirring often, until a thick paste is obtained. Cool thoroughly.

Sift the flour, baking powder, salt, ⅜ cup sugar. Cut in oil until well blended. Add water gradually, making a dough the consistency of biscuit dough. Place on a lightly floured board, knead a few minutes and form into balls 1½ inches in diameter. Flatten each piece of dough, fill the center with ¾ tablespoon of the bean paste and fold the dough around the filling. Place upside down on wax paper.

Steam in a covered streamer for 15 minutes. Serve cold with tea or at the end of a dinner.

SOUTHERN SPOON BREAD
Serves 5 to 6

Ready Tray

2	cups milk
1	teaspoon salt
⅓	cup sifted soy flour
⅓	cup white corn meal
1	tablespoon sugar
2	tablespoons melted butter
3	eggs, unbeaten
2	teaspoons baking powder

Scald milk. Combine salt, soy flour and corn meal. Add slowly to scalded milk, stirring constantly. Cook and continue stirring until thick and smooth. Add sugar and butter. Remove from heat and add eggs, one at a time, beating vigorously after each addition. Add baking powder and beat well. Pour batter into a well-greased shallow casserole or deep pie pan and bake in hot 400° oven for 35 minutes. Serve at once with butter.

NUT BREAD

Ready Tray

1	cup sifted soy flour
1½	cups sifted white flour
2	tablespoons sugar
3	teaspoons baking powder
1	teaspoon salt
½	teaspoon cinnamon
1	cup chopped nuts
2	eggs
1	cup milk
4	tablespoons melted fat

Sift together the dry ingedients and add the nuts. Beat the eggs, add milk and fat, then add to the first mixture. Let the dough stand in a well-greased bread pan for 20 minutes. Bake for one hour in a 350° oven.

NUT MIXTURE

Ready Tray
4	tablespoons sugar
1½	teaspoons cinnamon
4	tablespoons soy grits
1	cup stale bread crumbs
4	tablespoons melted butter

The soy grits may be soaked first, but they can be used without soaking. Mix all ingredients together and brush over top of coffee bread.

DUMPLINGS

Ready Tray
½	cup sifted flour
2	teaspoons baking powder
½	teaspoon salt
¼	cup soy grits
1	egg
⅓	cup milk

Sift together the flour, baking powder, salt and soy grits. Beat the egg and pour in the milk. Mix all ingredients just enough to blend. Drop the batter by spoonfuls over boiling stew, kraut, soup or gravy. Cover the pan tightly to hold in steam and boil gently for 15 minutes without lifting the cover. Serve at once.

CHERRY PIE
One 9-inch pie

Ready Tray │ 3   cups canned cherries
│ 2   tablespoons corn starch
│ ⅓   cup soy flour
│ 1   cup sugar
│ ⅛   teaspoon salt
│ ¼   teaspoon cinnamon
│ 2   tablespoons butter
│ ¼   teaspoon almond flavoring
│ Pastry for double crust pie

Measure fruit. Drain juice from fruit and measure into pan. There should be one and one-fourth cups of juice. If less than this amount, add water. Combine cornstarch, soy flour, sugar, salt and cinnamon and stir into juice. Cook until thickened. Remove from heat and stir in butter and almond flavoring. Add the drained fruit and pour into pastry-lined 9-inch pie pan. Cut balance of pastry into ½-inch strips. Arrange in lattice design across top of pie filling. Trim and crimp edges of pastry. Bake in a hot 425° oven for 10 minutes, then reduce heat to 350° for 25 minutes.

YEAST ROLLS
30 to 36 rolls

Ready Tray │ 1   cake yeast
│ ¼   cup lukewarm water
│ 1   cup milk
│ 4   tablespoons shortening
│ 2   tablespoons sugar
│ 1½ teaspoons salt
│ 1   egg
│ ½   cup soy flour
│ 3½ cups sifted white flour

Soften yeast in lukewarm water. Scald the milk and add shortening, sugar and salt. Cool to lukewarm. Add soy flour and white flour to make a batter. Add yeast and egg. Beat well. Add enough extra flour to make a soft dough. Turn out on a lightly floured board and knead until satiny. Place in a greased bowl, cover and let rise until double in bulk, 1½ to 2 hours. When light, punch down and shape into rolls. Let rise until double in bulk. Bake in a moderate 375° oven for 15 minutes.

SPICE CAKE

Ready Tray

½	cup soy flour
1¼	cups all-purpose flour
2	teaspoons baking powder
½	teaspoon salt
¾	teaspoon cloves
½	teaspoon allspice
¾	teaspoon nutmeg
¼	teaspoon mace
½	cup shortening
½	cup brown sugar, firmly packed
¾	cup dark corn syrup
2	eggs, well beaten
¾	cup milk

Sift soy flour and all-purpose flour separately. Measure and add baking powder, salt and spices and sift together twice. Cream shortening until soft, add sugar gradually, creaming well. Slowly stir in corn syrup. Add well-beaten eggs in four portions and blend each portion thoroughly with the creamed mixture. Add sifted dry ingredients alternately with milk, beating well after each addition. Pour into 2 well-greased eight-inch layer cake pans which have been lined on the bottom with wax paper. Bake in 375° oven for 25 minutes. Turn out and cool on rack. Put together with any desired filling, or fill with jam and dust with powdered sugar.

CHINESE ALMOND COOKIES
3 Dozen

Ready Tray	
1	cup stirred soy flour
1	cup sifted all-purpose flour
½	teaspoon salt
½	teaspoon baking powder
½	cup shortening
1	cup powdered sugar
2	eggs
2	tablespoons milk
1	teaspoon vanilla
½	teaspoon almond extract
	Almonds, blanched and halved

Sift the dry ingredients together. Cream the shortening and beat in the sugar. Beat one egg and one egg yolk, saving one egg white for glazing. Add to the sugar mixture and mix well. Add the flavoring to the milk. Add the flour and the milk alternately with the dry ingredients to the shortening and sugar, beating thoroughly. Roll the mixture on a floured board to ¼-inch thickness, and cut it with a cookie cutter. Put a half almond on each cookie. Brush the cookies with the egg white and sprinkle them with granulated sugar. Bake in 375° oven for 12 to 15 minutes, until pale straw color.

BUTTER CRUNCH
16 pieces

Ready Tray	
½	cup stirred soy flour
1	teaspoon baking powder
1	cup brown sugar
⅓	cup shortening
1	egg, beaten
1	cup nuts, chopped

Sift flour and baking powder together. Cream together sugar and shortening. Add other ingredients and mix thoroughly. Place in a greased and floured pan, 9 x 9 x 1-inches. Bake in 325° oven for 30 minutes. Cool, and cut in rectangles or diamonds.

ORANGE CAKE

Ready Tray

¾	cup soy flour
1	cup cake flour
2	teaspoons baking powder
½	teaspoon salt
½	cup shortening
¾	cup sugar
2	eggs, well beaten
⅓	cup milk
⅓	cup orange juice
1	teaspoon orange rind, grated
½	teaspoon orange extract

Sift soy flour and cake flour separately and measure. Combine and add baking powder and salt and sift together twice. Cream shortening until soft, add sugar gradually. Separate eggs. Beat yolks and add, blending well. Add dry ingredients alternately with liquid, adding milk first and then orange juice. Beat egg whites until stiff and fold lightly into batter. Stir in orange rind with extract. Pour batter in 2 eight-inch round layer cake pans which have been lined on the bottom with wax paper and then greased. Bake in a moderately slow 350° oven for 30 minutes. Use orange filling between layers and cover with orange icing.

MUFFINS
Makes 16

Ready Tray		
	1	cup soy flour
	1	cup white flour
	¾	teaspoon salt
	2	teaspoons baking powder
	2	tablespoons granulated sugar
	1	egg
	⅞	cup milk
	5	tablespoons shortening

Sift soy flour and white flour separately. Measure and sift together with rest of dry ingredients. Combine lightly beaten egg, milk and melted shortening and add to dry ingredients. Blend lightly. Pour into well greased muffin pans and bake in hot 400° oven for 20 minutes.

COCOA
Serves 2

Ready Tray		
	1½	tablespoons cocoa
	2	tablespoons sugar
	⅛	teaspoon salt
	2	cups soybean milk

Mix cocoa, sugar and salt; add small amount of milk and boil mixture for 2 minutes.

Add rest of milk and heat to desired temperature.

ORANGE ROLLS
2 dozen rolls

Ready Tray

1	cake compressed yeast
¼	cup lukewarm water
1	cup orange juice
	Grated rind of 1 orange
½	cup honey
2	eggs, beaten
2	teaspoons salt
2	tablespoons butter
1⅔	cups soy flour
4	cups white flour
3	tablespoons wheat germ

Dissolve yeast cake in the lukewarm water. Add other ingredients, stirring in the flours last. Knead until smooth. Set to rise in a warm place until double in bulk. Knead well and shape into rolls, let rise until double. Bake at 400° for 25 minutes.

CREAMY RICE WITH RAISINS
Serves 4

Ready Tray

½	cup rice
2	cups soybean milk
½	teaspoon salt
1½	tablespoons sugar
¼	cup raisins

Wash rice and soak overnight.

Add milk, salt, sugar and raisins and mix well. Put in a buttered baking dish and bake slowly uncovered for 2 to 3 hours, stirring occasionally.

WAFFLES
Makes 6

Ready Tray	1	cup soy flour
	1	cup white flour
	2	teaspoons baking powder
	½	teaspoon salt
	½	cup sugar
	6	tablespoons melted butter
	2	eggs, beaten light
	1½	cups milk

Sift dry ingredients together. Add butter and milk to form a batter, then add eggs and blend until smooth.

Bake in a hot waffle-iron.

EGG NOG
Serves 4

Ready Tray	2	eggs, separated
	4	teaspoons soy flour
	2	cups milk
	½	teaspoon vanilla
	8	teaspoons sugar
		Nutmeg

Beat egg yolks until light. Beat in soy flour, a teaspoonful at a time. Add milk slowly, beating after each addition. Add vanilla. Beat egg whites until they hold a peak, add sugar slowly, beating constantly. Fold egg whites and sugar into the milk mixture and pour into glasses containing ice cubes. Top with a sprinkling of nutmeg and serve at once. A nourishing beverage for an after-school snack for the children.

MOLASSES PUFFS
Serves 4 to 6

Ready Tray
- ¼ recipe whole wheat bread
- 3 tablespoons shortening
- ¼ cup molasses
- ⅓ cup soy grits

Melt the shortening in an 8 by 8-inch baking pan. Add the molasses and soy grits and mix. When the bread dough is light, shape into small rolls. Place rolls on top of the molasses mixture, brush with melted shortening and let rise until double in bulk.

Bake in 375° oven for 30 to 40 minutes. Serve hot.

APPLE CRISP

Ready Tray
- 4 cups sliced apples
- ¾ cup sugar
- ¼ teaspoon cinnamon
- ½ cup brown sugar
- ⅔ cup soy flour
- ¼ cup butter

Combine the sliced apples, sugar and cinnamon and place in a shallow greased pan.

Mix brown sugar and flour and work in butter until a crumbly mixture is formed. Sprinkle this mixture over the apples and bake uncovered in hot 400° oven for 25 minutes.

PIE CRUST
For one 9-inch pie

Ready Tray
¼	cup soy flour
1¼	cups enriched flour
¾	teaspoon salt
½	cup shortening
3	tablespoons ice water

Sift soy flour and enriched flour separately. Measure and sift together with salt. Cut in shortening and blend in water. Toss on a lightly floured board and knead gently to bind together. Roll out and fit carefully into 9-inch pie plate. Tuck under edges of crust and crimp edges with fingers. Prick well with fork. Bake in hot 400° oven for 15 to 20 minutes. Cool on a rack. Pour in filling of your choice and top with whipped cream, if desired.

PUMPKIN PIE
One 9-inch pie

Ready Tray
¼	cup soy flour
1¼	cups milk
1½	cups cooked pumpkin
½	cup sugar
½	teaspoon salt
1	teaspoon cinnamon
¼	teaspoon ginger or allspice
½	teaspoon nutmeg or mace
2	tablespoons shortening
2	eggs, slightly beaten

Blend the soy flour with ¼ cup of the milk. Mix with the pumpkin and remaining milk, sugar, salt and sp:es. Heat over hot water. Add the shortening and beaten eggs, and mix well. Pour the hot filling into a deep prebaked soy pastry shell. Bake in 350° oven about 30 minutes, or until the filling sets.

PEANUT BUTTER COOKIES
Makes about 72

Ready Tray		
	1½	cups sifted all-purpose flour
	½	cup sifted soy flour
	3¼	teaspoons baking powder
	½	teaspoon salt
	1½	cups all-bran
	½	cup shortening
	½	cup peanut butter
	½	cup brown sugar, firmly packed
	1½	cups granulated sugar
	2	eggs
	5	tablespoons milk

Sift flour, baking powder and salt; stir in the bran.

Cream shortening thoroughly. Add peanut butter and cream until smooth.

Add sugar gradually, cream well. Add eggs and beat thoroughly.

Add flour mixture alternately with milk. Shape into 1½ inch rolls; wrap in waxed paper and chill thoroughly. Cut in ¼-inch slices. Bake on ungreased cookie sheet in hot 400° oven.

BROWNIES
2 Dozen

Ready Tray
⅓	cup shortening
2	squares chocolate
1	cup sugar
2	eggs, slightly beaten
1	teaspoon vanilla
¾	cup nuts, chopped
½	cup soyflour, stirred
1	teaspoon salt

Melt together the shortening and the chocolate over hot water. **Add** remaining ingredients in the order given and mix well.

Spread the batter evenly in a pan, 9 x 9 x 2-inches and bake in 325° oven for 35 minutes.

Cool before cutting.

OATMEAL PUDDING
Serves 2

Ready Tray
1	cup soybean milk
¼	cup oatmeal
½	teaspoon salt
⅓	cup brown sugar, firmly packed
½	teaspoon cinnamon
¾	cup chopped apple

Heat milk to boiling and add oatmeal slowly with constant stirring. Add sugar mixed with cinnamon and the chopped apple. Boil until thick. Serve with boiled custard.

PEANUT CANDY
3 Dozen pieces

Ready Tray
- ½ cup stirred soy flour
- 2 cups brown sugar
- ¼ cup peanut butter
- ½ cup milk
- ¼ teaspoon salt
- ½ cup chopped peanuts

Combine first 4 ingredients. Boil 5 minutes over low heat, stirring constantly. Remove from heat, add salt and beat until thick. Add nuts, and pour into a greased pan, 8 x 9 x 1-inches. When cold, cut into small pieces.

BOILED CUSTARD
Serves 4

Ready Tray
- 2 cups soybean milk
- ¼ cup sugar
- ⅛ teaspoon salt
- 2 eggs, beaten
- ½ teaspoon vanilla

Heat milk, sugar and salt in double boiler. Stir in beaten eggs and heat until mixture coats a spoon. Cool, add vanilla before serving.

CHOCOLATE SOUFFLÉ
Serves 4 to 6

Ready Tray		
	1	tablespoon shortening
	1	tablespoon flour
	½	cup milk
	1	square chocolate
	¼	cup sugar
	2	tablespoons soy grits
	2	eggs, separated
	¼	teaspoon salt
	½	teaspoon vanilla

Melt the shortening, blend with flour, add milk and cook until thick, stirring constantly.

Melt the chocolate over hot water, add to the white sauce with the sugar and soy grits. Mix well. Add this hot mixture to the well-beaten egg yolks. Fold in stiffly-beaten egg whites to which salt and vanilla have been added. Bake in a greased dish in a very moderate 300° oven until set, about 45 minutes.

APPLE BETTY
Serves 6 to 8

Ready Tray		
	2	cups soft bread crumbs
	½	cup soy grits mixed with
	½	cup water
	½	cup sugar
	1	teaspoon cinnamon
	1	teaspoon salt
	1	quart diced apples
	2	tablespoons melted butter
		Lemon juice, if desired

Mix bread crumbs and moistened soy grits. Mix sugar, cinnamon and salt. In a greased baking dish, put a layer of the crumb mixture, then a layer of apples. If apples are mild-flavored, you may add a little lemon juice to them. Sprinkle the dry seasonings over apples. Repeat layers until all ingredients are used, saving enough crumb mixture to put over the top. Pour melted butter over top layer. Cover and bake for 45 minutes, or until apples are soft. The last 15 minutes of baking, remove cover so the top will brown delicately. Serve hot with cream or vanilla sauce.

APPLE COBBLER

Ready Tray		
4	cups sliced apples
½	cup sugar
¼	teaspoon salt
¼	teaspoon nutmeg
½	teaspoon cinnamon
¼	cup light molasses
1	tablespoon butter
½	cup soy flour
1	cup white flour
½	teaspoon salt
3	teaspoons baking powder
2	tablespoons sugar
¼	cup shortening
¾	cup milk

Pare, core, slice and measure apples. Place in a 10 x 6½ x 2-inch baking dish. Combine sugar, salt, nutmeg and cinnamon and sprinkle over apples. Add molasses and dot with butter. Place in hot 375° oven for 25 minutes.

Meanwhile, sift soy flour and white flour separately. Measure and sift together with the salt, baking powder and sugar. Cut in shortening. Blend in milk to make a soft dough. Spoon dough evenly over partially cooked apples. Return to oven and bake for 25 minutes at 375°.

FRUIT BALLS
24 Balls

Ready Tray

¼	cup raisins
¼	cup pitted prunes
¼	cup dried bananas
¼	cup chopped nuts
¼	teaspoon salt
⅓	cup soy flour, stirred
1	teaspoon orange peel, grated
2	tablespoons orange juice
	Coconut or
	Powdered or granulated sugar

Grind fruit in food chopper. Add next 5 ingredients and mix thoroughly. Form into small balls, and roll in coconut or sugar.

SUGAR COOKIES
6 Dozen

Ready Tray

1¾	cups soy flour, stirred
1¾	cups sifted all-purpose flour
1	teaspoon baking powder
1	teaspoon salt
1	cup shortening
1½	cups sugar
2	eggs, well beaten
2	teaspoons vanilla

Sift the first four ingredients together. Cream the shortening; add the sugar gradually and beat until light. Add eggs and vanilla, blend thoroughly. Combine with the dry ingredients, mix thoroughly and chill. Roll the mixture to ¼-inch thickness on a lightly floured board and cut into the desired shapes. Sprinkle the cakes with sugar and bake in 350° oven for 12 minutes.

Index